The Psychobiology of Mind-Body Healing

New Concepts of Therapeutic Hypnosis

Other Books by the Same Author

Dreams and the Growth of Personality

Mind-Body Communication in Hypnosis (edited with Margaret O. Ryan)

Life Reframing in Hypnosis (edited with Margaret O. Ryan)

Healing in Hypnosis (edited with Margaret O. Ryan
and Florence A. Sharp)

The Collected Papers of Milton H. Erickson (editor)

Experiencing Hypnosis: Indirect Approaches to Altered States
(with Milton H. Erickson)

Hypnotherapy: An Exploratory Casebook (with Milton H. Erickson)

Hypnotic Realities (with Milton H. Erickson and S. I. Rossi)

A NORTON PROFESSIONAL BOOK

The Psychobiology of Mind-Body Healing

New Concepts of

Therapeutic Hypnosis

ERNEST LAWRENCE ROSSI

W · W · NORTON & COMPANY, INC. · *NEW YORK* · *LONDON*

Published simultaneously in Canada by Penguin Books Canada Ltd., 2801 John Street, Markham, Ontario L3R 1B4.
Printed in the United States of America

Library of Congress Cataloging-in-Publication Data

Rossi, Ernest Lawrence.
  The psychobiology of mind-body healing.

  Bibliography: p.
  Includes index.
  1. Hypnotism—Therapeutic use. 2. Mind and body.
3. Healing. 4. Psychobiology. I. Title.
RC495.R65 1986   615.8'512   86-12513

ISBN 0-393-70034-8

W. W. Norton & Company, Inc., 500 Fifth Avenue, New York, N.Y. 10110
W. W. Norton & Company, Ltd., 37 Great Russell Street, London WC1B 3NU

    4 5 6 7 8 9 0

Dedicated to the pioneers of psychobiology, whose long, unsung research is now facilitating the dawn of a new age in which we stand on the threshold of the mind-gene-molecule connection; and to Margaret Ryan, whose editorial assistance and sensitive consciousness have helped bring this volume to its current stage of development.

Foreword

THE *Psychobiology of Mind-Body Healing* supplies the missing link between the theory that the mind can make a significant difference in dealing with disease and the clinical observations of physicians that the theory works in enough cases to be taken seriously. This book identifies what the medical profession calls "pathways," that is, the way attitudes or emotions are processed by the body in creating physiological or biochemical change. The past ten years have seen extraordinary advances in the knowledge of such pathways—so much so, that the concept of a patient-physician partnership is rapidly becoming a dominant feature in contemporary medicine. In such a partnership the physician brings the best that medical science has to offer and the patient brings his or her resources in the form of a healing system and the confidence and determination to get the best out of what the physician has to offer.

This book provides state-of-the-art information on the interaction of the nervous system, the endocrine system and the immune system. The facts assembled and summarized in this work make it impossible any longer to say that "hard" evidence is lacking to support the belief that what we think and believe can sometimes have a profound effect on our ability to deal with major challenges, whether with respect to disease or the way we function in our daily lives.

Norman Cousins
August 1986

Contents

List of Boxes

List of Tables

List of Figures

Preface

THIS VOLUME BEGAN as a personal quest a few years ago. I wanted to learn something of what everyone was speculating about but no one really seemed to understand: Is it really possible to use mind and mental methods to heal body illness? The quest was intensely personal because, having reached a certain age, I was beginning to experience cardiac symptoms that might have a psychosomatic basis. The quest was also professional because, as a clinical psychologist trained in hypnotherapy by the late Milton H. Erickson, I was getting more and more requests with ever increasing expectations that I should be able to ameliorate all sorts of pain, cancer, arthritis, and a host of other body ills I had hardly ever heard of. Clearly, the trend of the times—the *zeitgeist*—was to explore more about the whole area of mind-body relationships.

By now there are thousands of correlational studies that report statistically significant relationships between attitudes of mind, mood, and "sociocultural" factors with the ills of the body. These studies tend to leave many of us vaguely unsatisfied, however: We all know that correlation is not causation. We really do not understand how something as insubstantial as "mind" can effect something as solid as our own flesh and blood. Where is the connection between mind and body? Can you see it under a microscope? Can you measure it in a test tube?

It was really a struggle that required a lot of dogged determination to plough through the new medical and psychophysiological texts that were buzzing about mind-body relationships, stress, psychoneuroimmunology, neuroendocrinology, molecular genetics, and the neurobiology of memory and learning. These fields all deal with concepts and data that most of us have not even heard of if we have been out of school for more than ten years.

What was most irritating in my investigations was the realization that none of the specialists who seemed to know something ever shared their knowledge with those outside their narrow area of expertise. As I put the facts and implications of the different specialty areas together, I kept coming up with what seemed to be bizarre notions that apparently were based on solid research but no one seemed willing to acknowledge.

For example: Is there really a mind-gene connection? Does mind move not only our emotions and blood pressure, but also the very genes and molecules that are generated within the microscopic cells of our body? Is there any real evidence for this? Well, if you push any endocrinologist hard enough, he/she will admit that, "Yes, it is really true!" Under "mental" stress, the limbic-hypothalamic system in the brain converts the neural messages of mind into the neurohormonal "messenger molecules" of the body. These, in turn, can direct the endocrine system to produce steroid hormones that can reach into the nucleus of different cells of the body to modulate the expression of genes. These genes then direct the cells to produce the various molecules that will regulate metabolism, growth, activity level, sexuality, and the immune response in sickness and health. There really is a mind-gene connection! Mind ultimately does modulate the creation and expression of the molecules of life!

Knowing that mind-body communication and healing involve a real process that can be seen and measured, the next question becomes, "How do we learn to utilize these natural processes of mind-body communication to facilitate our emotional and physical well-being? These processes of mind-body communication usually function autonomously on an unconscious level. When things are going well for us, mind-body healing takes place all by itself, without our having to give it a thought. When things are going badly for us, however, problems in the natural flow of mind-body communication—illness and symptoms—also happen all by themselves!

Can we learn to correct these malfunctioning mind-body patterns to facilitate our own healing and health when things are going badly for us? I'd like to believe that the explorations and approaches developed in this book are a significant step in learning to utilize our natural processes of mind-body communication for self-healing, just when we need it.

While much of the material of this book comes from historical and modern methods of therapeutic hypnosis, it should be recognized that the new approaches to mind-body healing developed herein are not limited to the formal induction of hypnosis or trance. Since the inception of hypnosis more than 200 years ago, it has been impossible to find general agreement among professionals on just exactly what hypnosis is. No definition or empirical test has ever been devised to accurately assess whether or not a hypnotic state even exists! It may be that our understanding of the healing inherent in what has been called "hypnosis" or "thera-peutic trance" will continue to change as long as our conceptions of con-sciousness and the nature of mind continue to evolve. These processes of healing are a natural function of whatever mind, imagination, and life are.

This means that the psychobiological perspective and approaches to mind-body healing developed in this book can be used by therapists of any school or theoretical persuasion. These approaches are designed to supplement the therapeutic methodology of all health workers, whatever their fields of expertise. What this book offers is a broader frame of refer-ence, a more effective language for accessing and facilitating the natural processes of healing that are an inherent characteristic of life itself. There is thus nothing fixed or final about these approaches; they are but step-pingstones on a path of greater health and self-facilitation that will con-tinue for as long as we are here to pursue it.

Ernest Lawrence Rossi
Malibu, 1986

Acknowledgments

I EXTEND THANKFUL appreciation to my colleagues for the support and feedback they have provided during the development of this volume:

Jeanne Achterberg	Patrick Jichaku
Kenneth Bowers	Camillo Loriedo
Kristina Erickson	Karl Pribram
Stephen Gilligan	Joyce Mills
Melvin Gravitz	Lewis Wolberg
James Hall	Michael Yapko
Ernest Hilgard	Jeffrey Zeig

A special note of thanks to Aline Lapierre for her clear and accurate medical artwork; and to Susan Barrows, whose enthusiasm, support, and skill have made possible the rapid publication of this volume.

SECTION I

The Psychobiology of Mind-Body Communication

1

The Placebo Response:
A Rejected Cornerstone of
Mind-Body Healing

SOME INTERESTING STORIES have been told over and over again because they express truths that our thinking minds can understand in no other way. This certainly is the case with the many folktales, both ancient and modern, of how unexpected illness and "miracle cures" have taken place. Modern science tends to reject these anecdotal accounts as unreliable or, at best, as mere examples of the "placebo response": The person gets better only because of a cultural belief or suggestion that deludes everyone into thinking healing took place. The placebo response is rejected as a "nuisance factor" that no one understands; it is unreliable and therefore unreal. Let us begin this chapter by retelling a few of these healing tales—the ones reported by highly regarded medical experts—to learn if we can discern a common denominator in them. Perhaps it will turn out that the placebo response has been, in fact, the rejected cornerstone of what could become a practical approach to building a new understanding of mind-body communication and healing.

THE LIKABLE MR. WRIGHT:
CANCER AND THE IMMUNE SYSTEM

One of my earliest teachers in these mysteries of mind and body was old Bruno Klopfer, a short, powerfully built gnome of a man who was so short-sighted he had to hold a book right up to his nose in order to read the print. His eyeglasses magnified his eyes to such a degree that I was usually too stupified to say anything to him. Bruno was reputed to have been a sort of minor genius with the Rorschach Inkblot test, and he had written a standard three-volume work in the field. Yet his humble manner gave no hint of his interpretive wizardry, which went well beyond what he was able to write and teach.

Bruno's civility and perfect manners were a natural endowment from his European background; he was always poised to listen fully when anyone, particularly a student, was speaking. I would sometimes steal a long, sideward glance at him during the fireside seminars he organized for Jungian analysts in training on the California coast at Asilomar during the early 1960s. Yet always, it seemed, behind his outward attention, there was another part of him far, far away, communing with who-knows-what levels of imagination and wisdom. If he caught you looking at him, he would immediately ''come back'' with only the slightest eyeblink and a wan, collegial smile.

One of Bruno's well-documented feats was his ability to distinguish between the Rorschach records of patients who had rapid versus slowly progressing cancers. In his Presidential Address to the Society of Projective Techniques in 1957, he tried to impart something of his skills in this area by presenting his views on the psychological variables in human cancer. As I said, he was a humble man, so instead of talking about his successes, he chose to present a detailed case history of one of his failures. This was the case of the likable Mr. Wright, who so intrigued Bruno that he spoke of him often. I believe this case meant something important to that wise part of Bruno that was so often far away. I will therefore present it here, exactly as he published it. The original report on Mr. Wright was written by one of his personal physicians, Dr. Philip West, a reliable observer who played an important part in the story (Klopfer, 1957, pp. 337–339).

> Mr. Wright had a generalized far advanced malignancy involving the lymph nodes, lymphosarcoma. Eventually the day came when he developed resistance to all known palliative treatments. Also, his increasing anemia precluded any intensive efforts with X-rays or nitrogen mustard, which might otherwise have been attempted. Huge tumor masses the size of oranges were in the neck, axillas, groin, chest and abdomen. The spleen and liver were enormous. The thoracic duct was obstructed, and between 1 and 2 liters of milky fluid had to be drawn from his chest every other day. He was taking oxygen by mask frequently, and our impression was that he was in a terminal state, untreatable, other than to give sedatives to ease him on his way.
>
> In spite of all this, Mr. Wright was not without hope, even though his doctors most certainly were. The reason for this was that the new

drug that he had expected to come along and save the day had already been reported in the newspapers! Its name was "Krebiozen" (subsequently shown to be a useless, inert preparation).

Then he heard in some way that our clinic was to be one of a hundred places chosen by the Medical Association for evaluation of this treatment. We were allotted supplies of the drug sufficient for treating 12 selected cases. Mr. Wright was not considered eligible, since one stipulation was that the patient must not only be beyond the point where standard therapies could benefit, but *also* must have a life expectancy of at least three, and preferably six, months. He certainly didn't qualify on the latter point, and to give him a prognosis of more than two weeks seemed to be stretching things.

However, a few days later, the drug arrived, and we began setting up our testing program which, of course, did *not* include Mr. Wright. When he heard we were going to begin treatment with Krebiozen, his enthusiasm knew no bounds, and as much as I tried to dissuade him, he begged so hard for this "golden opportunity," that against my better judgment, and against the rules of the Krebiozen committee, I decided I would have to include him.

Injections were to be given three times weekly, and I remember he received his first one on a Friday. I didn't see him again until Monday and thought as I came to the hospital he might be moribund or dead by that time, and his supply of the drug could then be transferred to another case.

What a surprise was in store for me! I had left him febrile, gasping for air, completely bedridden. Now, here he was, walking around the ward, chatting happily with the nurses, and spreading his message of good cheer to any who would listen. Immediately I hastened to see the others who had received their first injection at the same time. No change, or change for the worse, was noted. Only in Mr. Wright was there brilliant improvement. The tumor masses had melted like snowballs on a hot stove, and in only these few days, they were half their original size! This is, of course, far more rapid regression than the most radio-sensitive tumor could display under heavy X-ray given every day. And we already knew his tumor was no longer sensitive to irradiation. Also, he had had no other treatment outside of the single useless "shot."

This phenomenon demanded an explanation, but not only that, it almost insisted that we open our minds to learn, rather than try to explain. So, the injections were given three times weekly as planned, much to the joy of the patient, but much to our bewilderment. Within 10 days [Mr. Wright] was able to be discharged from his "death-bed," practically all signs of his disease having vanished in this short time. Incredible as it sounds, this "terminal" patient, gasping his last breath through an oxygen mask, was now not only breathing normally, and fully active, he took off in his plane and flew at 12,000 feet with no discomfort!

This unbelievable situation occurred at the beginning of the "Krebiozen" evaluation, but within two months, conflicting reports began to appear in the news, all of the testing clinics reporting no results. At the same time, the originators of the treatment were still blindly contradicting the discouraging facts that were beginning to emerge.

This disturbed our Mr. Wright considerably as the weeks wore on. Although he had no special training, he was, at times, reasonably logical and scientific in his thinking. He began to lose faith in his last hope which so far had been life-saving and left nothing to be desired. As the reported results became increasingly dismal, his faith waned, and after two months of practically perfect health, he relapsed to his original state, and became very gloomy and miserable.

But here I saw the opportunity to *double-check* the drug and maybe, too, find out how the quacks can accomplish the results that they claim (and many of their claims are well substantiated). Knowing something of my patient's innate optimism by this time, I deliberately took advantage of him. This was for purely scientific reasons, in order to perform the perfect control experiment which could answer all the perplexing questions he had brought up. Furthermore, this scheme could not harm him in any way, I felt sure, and there was nothing I knew anyway that could help him.

When Mr. Wright had all but given up in despair with the recrudescence of his disease, in spite of the "wonder-drug" which had worked so well at first, I decided to take the chance and play the quack. So deliberately lying, I told him not to believe what he read in the papers, the drug was really most promising after all. "What then," he asked, "was the reason for his relapse?" "Just because the substance deteriorated on standing," I replied, "a new super-refined, double-strength product is due to arrive tomorrow which can more than reproduce the great benefits derived from the original injections."

This news came as a great revelation to him, and Mr. Wright, as ill as he was, became his optimistic self again, eager to start over. By delaying a couple of days before the "shipment" arrived, his anticipation of salvation had reached a tremendous pitch. When I announced that the new series of injections was about to begin, he was almost ecstatic and his faith was very strong.

With much fanfare, and putting on quite an act (which I deemed permissible under the circumstances), I administered the first injection of the doubly potent, *fresh* preparation—consisting of *fresh water* and nothing more. The results of this experiment were quite unbelievable to us at the time, although we must have had some suspicion of the remotely possible outcome to have even attempted it at all.

Recovery from his second near-terminal state was even more dramatic than the first. Tumor masses melted, chest fluid vanished, he became ambulatory, and even went back to flying again. At this time he was certainly the picture of health. The water injections were continued, since they worked such wonders. He then remained symptom-free for over two months. At this time the final AMA announcement appeared in the press—"nationwide tests show Krebiozen to be a worthless drug in treatment of cancer."

Within a few days of this report, Mr. Wright was readmitted to the hospital *in extremis*. His faith was now gone, his last hope vanished, and he succumbed in less than two days.

Bruno Klopfer's summary of Mr. Wright's personality as revealed in his Rorschach record is as follows (Klopfer, 1957, p. 339):

Mr. Wright's Rorschach record was obtained before his transformation from optimism to pessimism took place. It reflects the picture of a personality with what I called previously a "floating ego organization." This is reflected in his actual behavior and the great ease with which he followed first the suggestion of the drug advertisement and later on the deliberate experimentally motivated suggestion of his doctor without any sign of defensiveness or even criticalness. His ego was simply floating along and therefore left all available vital energy free to produce a response to the cancer treatment which seemed nothing short of miraculous.

Unfortunately this situation could not last since it was not reinforced by any deep-rooted personality center with a long-range point of view which could have counteracted the catastrophic effect of his disappointment about the drug. To use a symbolic analogy, while he was floating along on the surface of the water under the influence

of his optimistic auto-suggestion or suggestion, he was transformed
into a heavy stone and sank to the bottom without any resistance
at the moment when the powers of this suggestion expired.

The case of Mr. Wright all too vividly illustrates the hope and failure
of our attempts at mind-body communication and healing as they currently exist. We don't understand yet all the important factors in any
individual situation, and we have only the vaguest ideas about how to
facilitate mind-body healing in a *reliable* manner. Yet, we do know considerably more about it today than 30 years ago when Mr. Wright showed
his doctors the power of optimism.

We know today, for example, that cancer growth can be controlled by
the person's immune system; if you can improve the immune system, it
can destroy the cancer. Obviously, Mr. Wright's immune system must
have been activated by his belief in a cure. The incredible rapidity of his
healing also suggests that his autonomic and endocrine systems must have
been responsive to suggestion, enabling him to mobilize his blood system
with such amazing efficiency to remove the toxic fluids and waste products
of the fast diminishing cancer. As we shall learn later in this book, we now
know a lot more about the "limbic-hypothalamic system" of the brain as
the major mind-body connector modulating the biological activity of the
autonomic, endocrine, and immune systems in response to mental suggestion and beliefs. In summary, Mr. Wright's experience tells us that it
was his *total belief in the efficacy* of the worthless drug, Krebiozen, that
mobilized a healing placebo response by activating *all* these major systems
of mind-body communication and healing. But we are getting ahead of
ourselves. First, let me tell you a story about another one of my teachers.

FRANZ ALEXANDER'S POSITIVE INTERPRETATIONS:
CONSCIOUSNESS, THE HYPOTHALAMUS, AND THE ENDOCRINE SYSTEM

Franz Alexander, who was a world leader in psychosomatic medicine,
made pioneering efforts to relate psychoanalysis to the physiology of the
body (Alexander 1939/1984). He taught those of us who were lucky enough
to be his students that it wasn't enough to simply understand and analyze
patients. He had an inspired way of phrasing Freudian interpretations in
a positive manner in order to evoke confidence, belief, and the placebo
response as a natural form of mind-body healing.

Alexander was truly a master in his understanding of the relations between personality, emotional conflict, and the endocrine system. Like
Klopfer, he was a gift to America, trained in the classical European intel-

lectual tradition. Alexander was a patrician type, with beautifully tailored suits and well manicured fingernails. Those fingernails—they would occasionally drum silently on the conference table while a colleague droned on somewhere in the room. It didn't matter to Alexander; he also had the gift of quietly slipping into his own inner vision quest while apparently remaining with the rest of us who were stumbling about on the outside.

Alexander's recognition of the positive aspects of mind-body adaptations to even the most difficult environmental stressors is indicated by the following clinical examples of thyrotoxicosis (hyperthyroidism, or overactivity of the thyroid gland). The thyroid is a part of the endocrine system that produces hormones that regulate metabolism and growth. The brief case histories he cites are suggestive of how early life stresses can overstimulate the growth functions regulated by the thyroid, resulting in a precocious though precarious sort of psychological maturity (Alexander, 1950, pp. 178–181):

> Threat to security in childhood is a very common finding, both in neurotics and in healthy individuals. Characteristic of patients with thyrotoxicosis is their manner of handling this insecurity. Because of the external circumstances described above, these patients cannot overcome their anxiety by turning to their parents for help. Their dependent needs are constantly frustrated by fate or by parental attitudes, by loss of one or both parents, or by parental rejection, as well as by conflicts of more complex nature which involve guilt. Since they are frustrated in their dependent needs, they make a desperate attempt to identify themselves prematurely with one of the parents, usually the mother. ("If I cannot have her, I must become like her, so that I can dispense with her.") This precocious identification is beyond their physiological and psychological capacity and results in a persistent struggle to master the anxiety and insecurity by a pseudo self-reliance.
>
> . . . Examples of premature need for self-sufficiency, manifested in active participation in the support of the family or in taking care of younger siblings, follow:
>
> B.R., a 13-year-old white girl, is described by the mother as a "little old lady" because she is so prematurely grownup, obedient, and reliable. She learned to cook when she was six and has cooked and helped with the housework ever since. Whenever her mother became ill, she swept and cleaned the house and took care of the whole family. She acted as second mother to her younger brother.
>
> H.D., a 35-year-old single man, the last of eight children, is the

only surviving male. Two older brothers died at ages ten and three respectively, and one brother died at home one week after birth when the patient was two. His father was a puritanical man who was harsh and impersonal to hide his own weakness and insecurity. He was apparently demonstrative of affection and fondled his children as long as they were helpless infants but demanded adult behavior as soon as they were able to walk and talk. The mother was depreciated by the father because she had had an illegitimate child in her adolescence (patient's oldest sister) and was married "out of pity" by the patient's father. She was unable to stand up to the father and during the patient's infancy worked in the family store for several years. The father prevented the mother as well as the older sisters from giving the patient much attention. After the patient entered the first grade, his father insisted that no one read him the funny papers any more because he should learn to read for himself. Constant pressure was brought to bear on him to behave like an adult and yet he was constantly restricted in the active pursuit of his interests.

E.B., a 24-year-old single colored woman, was a prodigy and progressed rapidly in her school years. She was extremely conscientious, never truant. Her mother was a teacher and "a very intelligent and beautiful woman." The patient was obviously competing with her but never expressed her hostility openly. When her mother became ill, the patient took over the responsibility for her two younger sisters and assumed the function of mother toward them. She supported them financially even during her college years. She has always been self-sufficient and extremely ambitious and has controlled or repressed most of her feminine desires in order to reach her intellectual goals.

Alexander recognized that mental stress somehow interacted with the hypothalamus, which in turn stimulated the entire endocrine system via the pituitary and thyroid. The hypothalamus was the bridge between *psyche* and *soma*, and perhaps even the locus of consciousness itself. In Alexander and French's edited volume, Grinker quotes with approval Ingham's (1938) view of the situation (1948, p. 70):

The neurologic concept of consciousness is that it is a state of activity of the entire nervous system, and in particular of the brain, which varies quantitatively from the maximum degree of mental action to complete inactivity, as in coma or general surgical anesthesia. Although all parts of the brain may contribute to the mental processes during consciousness, mental activity of all kinds appears to depend on the normal functioning of groups of neurons in the primitive diencephalon [i.e., the hypothalamus]. The normal cycles of sleeping and waking are evidences of the physiologic activity of this mechanism. As it would appear that energy liberated in the diencephalon is essential for the activation of all the rest of the nervous system so far as psychologic phenomena are concerned, it may be postulated that the "center" of consciousness is located in this region, and much clinical and experimental evidence supports this view. It is surely not accidental that other primitive functions of the nervous system related to the vegetative processes, instincts, and emotions have been found to be dependent on structures in the basal region of the brain in close proximity to those postulated as the center of consciousness. The application of this concept of consciousness to psychiatry seems obvious, since quantitative variations of consciousness are manifested in disturbances of behavior in terms of intelligence, emotions, and instinctive action.

Although this view may sound a bit quaint to our modern ear, it can be regarded as an early, psychobiological approach to the concept of mind-body communication and consciousness. I will update this view in the next chapter, in which I speak of consciousness as "a process of self-reflective information transduction." Alexander had a high regard for the work of the physiologist Walter Cannon, who did a great deal of pioneering research in the area of psychosomatic medicine and, in particular, the psychobiological basis of seemingly strange and bizarre occurrences, such as voodoo death.

VOODOO DEATH AND LIFE!
THE "GIVING-UP" COMPLEX AND THE AUTONOMIC NERVOUS SYSTEM

Walter Cannon, who was regarded as one of the most creative and authoritative medical physiologists of his day, tells the following stories of voodoo death and recovery (1957, pp. 183–184):

Dr. S. M. Lambert of the Western Pacific Health Service of the Rockefeller Foundation wrote to me that on several occasions he had seen evidence of death from fear. In one case there was a startling recovery. At a Mission at Mona Mona in North Queensland were many native converts, but on the outskirts of the Mission was a group of non-converts including one Nebo, a famous witch doctor. The chief helper of the missionary was Rob, a native who had been converted. When Dr. Lambert arrived at the Mission he learned that Rob was in distress and that the missionary wanted him examined. Dr. Lambert made the examination, and found no fever, no complaint of pain, no symptoms or signs of disease. He was impressed, however, by the obvious indications that Rob was seriously ill and extremely weak. From the missionary he learned that Rob had had a bone pointed at him by Nebo and was convinced that in consequence he must die. Thereupon Dr. Lambert and the missionary went for Nebo, threatened him sharply that his supply of food would be shut off if anything happened to Rob and that he and his people would be driven away from the Mission. At once Nebo agreed to go with them to see Rob. He leaned over Rob's bed and told the sick man that it was all a mistake, a mere joke—indeed, that he had not pointed a bone at all. The relief, Dr. Lambert testifies, was almost instantaneous; that evening Rob was back at work, quite happy again and in full possession of his physical strength.

And a less fortunate outcome:

> Dr. Lambert . . . wrote to me concerning the experience of Dr. P. S. Clarke with Kanakas working on the sugar plantations of North Queensland. One day a Kanaka came to his hospital and told him he would die in a few days because a spell had been put upon him and nothing could be done to counteract it. The man had been known by Dr. Clarke for some time. He was given a very thorough examination, including an examination of the stool and the urine. All was found normal, but as he lay in bed he gradually grew weaker. Dr. Clarke called upon the foreman of the Kanakas to come to the hospital to give the man assurance, but on reaching the foot of the bed, the foreman leaned over, looked at the patient, and then turned to Dr. Clarke saying, "Yes, doctor, close up him he die" (i.e., he is nearly dead). The next day, at 11 o'clock in the morning, he ceased to live.

Cannon (1942, 1963) concluded that voodoo death was due to a heightened and prolonged exposure to the emotional stress of believing one was under the witch doctor's spell. The actual physiological cause was an over-activated sympathetic nervous system. Cannon believed that voodoo death was possible only because of the "profound ignorance and insecurity" of native populations who lived "in a haunted world." In a more recent study in our own society of the problem of "sudden and rapid death during psychological stress," Engel (1971) came to a similar conclusion in ascribing death to "rapid shifts between sympathetic and parasympathetic cardiovascular effects." Engel believed this "biological emergency pattern" (1968) becomes fatal when the person feels unable to cope and has lost all expectation that there will be any change or help from any other source. The person dies because of an acute "giving-up-given-in" complex. In a recent review of this area, Hahn (1985) describes the relation between voodoo death, the autonomic nervous system, and the selection of native healers as follows (p. 182):

> Lex (1974) similarly explains the pathogenesis of voodoo death and the therapy of curing rituals in terms of three stages of "tuning" of the sympathetic and parasympathetic processes of the autonomic nervous system. "Suggestion" passes a lowered threshold of analytic judgment to effect what is suggested. Lex also explains the common requirement of traditional medical systems that healers have suffered the conditions that they come to treat: Their prior illness gives these healers first-hand acquaintance with and sensitivity to the vagaries of the autonomic nervous system.

As we shall see in the successive chapters of this volume, the autonomic nervous system with its two branches, the sympathetic (which activates heart rate, respiration, blood pressure, tension, etc.) and the parasympathetic (with generally relaxing effects opposite to the sympathetic system), is, indeed, one of the major systems of mind-body communication and the placebo response in illness or healing.

The Healing Heart and Mind: Norman Cousins' Positive Emotions

Thus far in this chapter we have illustrated how negative life circumstances and attitudes can lead to illness and death via the mind's modulation of the autonomic, endocrine, and immune systems. Sensitive physicians have always known that the reverse is true as well, and wise observers in most cultures have recognized that a positive frame of mind can have a salutary effect in healing the gravest illness.

No one has done more in current American culture to illustrate this truth with well-documented and poignant examples from his own life than Norman Cousins in his two books, *Anatomy of an Illness* and *The Healing Heart*.

Cousins' personal experience with mind-body healing began at the age of ten when he was misdiagnosed and sent to a tuberculosis sanitarium for six months. Left to their own devices, he and some of his fellow patients found a way to a positive attitude and healing, which Cousins describes as follows (1979, pp. 155-156):

> What was most interesting to me about that early experience was that patients divided themselves into two groups: those who were confident they would beat back the disease and be able to resume normal lives, and those who resigned themselves to a prolonged and even fatal illness. Those of us who held to the optimistic view became good friends, involved ourselves in creative activities, and had little to do with the patients who had resigned themselves to the worst. When newcomers arrived at the hospital, we did our best to recruit them before the bleak brigade went to work.
>
> I couldn't help being impressed with the fact that the boys in my group had a far higher percentage of "discharged as cured" outcomes than the kids in the other group. Even at the age of ten, I was being philosophically conditioned; I became aware of the power of the mind in overcoming disease. The lessons I learned about hope at that time played an important part in my complete recovery [as an adult] and in the feelings I have had since about the preciousness of life.

This early life experience with the therapeutic value of optimistic views and creative activities led to a lifetime of accomplishment as the editor of one of America's leading periodicals, *The Saturday Review*, and more recently as Adjunct Professor at UCLA's School of Medicine. Cousins' carefully documented recovery (1979) from a serious arthritic and rheumatoid-like collagen disease of the connective tissues (diagnosed as *ankylosing spondylitis*) by treating himself with generous, positive doses of good humor (primarily in the form of old *Marx Brothers* movies and reruns of Allen Funt's *Candid Camera*) is becoming part of a new folklore of healing. His more recent recovery from a heart attack involving both myocardial infarction and congestive heart failure (Cousins, 1983) has been discussed by the four heart specialists and physicians most closely associated with the case. Among the factors they described as significant in Cousins' self-therapeutic attitude are:

1) The absence of panic in the face of the obviously grave symptoms of his heart attack. (Such panic is part of the emotional syndrome that kills victims of voodoo death.)

2) His unshakable confidence in his body's ability to utilize its own wisdom in facilitating healing.
3) An irrepressible good humor and cheerfulness that created an auspicious, healing environment for himself, as well as for the entire hospital staff.
4) Taking a full share of responsibility for his recovery by establishing a close "partner relationship" with his physicians.
5) His focus on creativity and meaningful goals, which made recovery worth fighting for and life worth living.

Cousins summarized his experiences of personal healing by emphasizing that positive attitudes and emotions can affect the biochemistry of the body to facilitate rejuvenation and health. Positive attitudes and emotions are the essence of well-being and the placebo response. As he aptly stated, "The placebo is the doctor who resides within" (Cousins, 1979, p. 69). This statement reflects a profound change from the traditional view of the placebo as a "nuisance factor."

Let us now take a closer look at what recent research on the placebo response can tell us about mind-body healing.

THE 55% PLACEBO CONNECTION

During the same time period when the anecdotal accounts of mind-body healing described previously were being assembled by early leaders in the field of psychosomatic medicine, more scientifically objective double-blind studies of clinical pain were being conducted. (In double-blind studies, neither doctors nor patients know who is getting real medication and who is getting inert placebos.) Beecher's analysis and review (1959) of 15 double-blind studies concluded that 35% of the patients with a wide variety of postoperative pain found significant relief with placebos (inert medication or "sugar pills"). In a more recent review (Evans, 1985), these conclusions were confirmed with 11 more double-blind studies in which it was found that 36% of the patients received at least 50% of pain relief from placebos. The most carefully controlled clinical studies of placebos with humans thus consistently find that about one-third of the patients receive more than 50% relief. Under the right circumstances, the medically inert placebo is somehow able to facilitate belief and expectation on the psychological level. This accesses and activates very real mind-body healing mechanisms that some now call the "placebo response."

The placebo response is not limited to pain relief. It has been found to be a mind-body healing factor in all of the following illnesses (items 1 through 3), therapeutic procedures (items 4 through 6), and even in the expectation of getting help (item 7).

1) Hypertension, stress, cardiac pain, blood cell counts, headaches, pupillary dilation (*implicating the autonomic nervous system*);
2) Adrenal gland secretion, diabetes, ulcers, gastric secretion and motility, colitis, oral contraceptives, menstrual pain, thyrotoxicosis (*implicating the endocrine system*);
3) The common cold, fever, vaccines, asthma, multiple sclerosis, rheumatoid arthritis, warts, cancer (*implicating the immune system*);
4) Surgical treatments (e.g., for angina pectoris or "heart pain");
5) Biofeedback instrumentation and medical devices of all sorts;
6) Psychological treatments such as conditioning (systematic desensitization) and perhaps all forms of psychotherapy;
7) Making an appointment to see a doctor.

In a review of these studies, most investigators (White, Tursky, & Schwartz, 1985) conclude that the placebo response, which has been demonstrated across such a wide range of problems and treatment modalities, must be a "true *general* ingredient in *all clinical* situations" (Wickramasekera, 1985). One of the most informative of these recent studies has been written by Fredrick Evans, a psychologist who has done a great deal of original experimental work in this area. Evans has brought together a mass of data to answer two basic questions about how the placebo response functions in a variety of medical situations (1985, p. 215):

1) How powerful is the placebo response in terms of its clinical efficacy?
2) To what extent is the placebo response mediated by verbal and nonverbal expectational factors?

To deal with the first question about the clinical efficacy of the placebo response, Evans studied the data on double-blind studies of drug analgesia, since these were the most numerous and carefully controlled examples of experimental research. As is indicated in the accompanying box, the efficacy of an unknown analgesic is determined by calculating an index of drug efficiency. *There is a remarkably consistent degree of placebo response, averaging about 55% of the therapeutic effect for all the analgesic drugs studied.*

That is, while morphine obviously has more potent analgesic effects than aspirin, about 55% of the potency of *each* is a placebo response. As Evans describes it (1985, p. 223):

In other words, the effectiveness of a placebo compared to standard doses of different analgesic drugs under double-blind circumstances seems to be relatively constant. This is indeed a rather remarkable

BOX 1 Comparing Efficiency of Placebo and Analgesics

Illustration of Calculation of Index of Drug Efficiency for Evaluating Placebo Efficiency Compared to Analgesic Drugs

Index of analgesic drug efficiency:

$$\frac{\text{Reduction in pain with unknown drug}}{\text{Reduction in pain with known analgesic (typically morphine)}}$$

Pain criterion:

Reduction in pain by 50% of initial level over drug level.
or
change in pain of 50% on rating scale (typically 10- or 5-point)

Index of placebo efficiency for morphine:
(averaged across six double-blind non-crossover-design studies)

$$\frac{\text{Reduction in pain with placebo}}{\text{Reduction in pain with morphine}} = 56\%$$

Index of Placebo Efficiency Comparing Placebo with Morphine, Aspirin, Darvon, and Zomax (Derived from Available Single-Trial Double-Blind Published Studies)

Number of double-blind studies	Placebo efficiency for	%
6	Morphine	56
9	Aspirin	54
2	Darvon	54
2	Codeine	56
3	Zomax	55

Used by permission from Evans (1985).

and unique characteristic for any therapeutic agent! The effectiveness of the placebo is proportional to the apparent effectiveness of the active analgesic agent.

It is worth noting that this 56% effectiveness ratio is not limited to comparing placebo with analgesic drugs. It is also found in double-blind studies of nonpharmacological insomnia treatment techniques (58% from 13 studies) and psychotropic drugs for the treatment of depression such as tricyclics (59% from 93 studies reviewed by Morris & Beck, 1974) and lithium (62% from 13 studies reviewed in Marini, Sheard, Bridges & Wagner, 1976). Thus, it appears that placebo is about 55–60% as effective as active medications, irrespective of the potency of these active medications.

The implication of these findings is that *there may be a 55% placebo response in many, if not all, healing procedures*. Such a consistent degree of placebo response also suggests *there is a common, underlying mechanism or process that accounts for mind-body communication and healing, regardless of the problem, symptom, or disease*.

This brings us to Evans' second question about the extent to which the placebo response is mediated by verbal and nonverbal expectational factors. He discusses three factors that have been found by investigators to mediate the placebo response: (1) suggestion (or hypnosis); (2) anxiety reduction; and (3) the expectancy aroused by cultural or medical belief systems. It has been assumed in the past that *placebo* and *suggestion* were essentially the same sort of phenomenon. The surprising conclusion from a variety of well-controlled experimental studies comparing the placebo response with hypnotic suggestion, however, is that there is no correlation or relationship between them (Evans, 1977, 1981; McGlashan, Evans, & Orne, 1969; Orne, 1974). During experimental conditions in the laboratory, hypnotic suggestion and the placebo response appeared to operate by different mechanisms or levels of response. One way of understanding the difference is to say that hypnotic responsiveness is a specific, innate ability and skill that involves the capacity to access or change one's own patterns of mind-body communication by the use of psychological suggestion alone. The placebo response, in contrast, is a more general, automatic mind-body communication that utilizes physical treatment methods to reduce anxiety and facilitate healing by marshalling powerful cultural expectations and beliefs in the treatment method. Other researchers, to be discussed in the next chapter, believe that while hypnotic and placebo responses appear to be different in the way they are facilitated on a social-cultural level, they are essentially similar modes of creative mentation on the psychobiological level, where they are mediated by the patient's right cerebral hemisphere.

The issues raised in this section are complex. However, we will assimilate their implications for a general theory of mind-body communication and healing gradually, as more understanding unfolds in each successive chapter of this book. For now, it is enough to note that for at least one-third of the population, a "55% placebo connection" is a consistent healing factor operative with many different drugs, therapeutic procedures, and psychophysiological symptoms and problems. The consistency of this healing response across so many different conditions suggests that it is mediated by a common mechanism or communication link between mind and body. In the next two chapters, we will learn that the "limbic-hypothalamic system" of the brain is the most obvious anatomical candidate for the role of connecting mind and body. Indeed, it is a unique psychophysiological communication channel between the expectations and creative processes of mind and the emotional physiology of the body. It is the common denominator mediating the placebo response in such apparently diverse circumstances as the naive belief of the likable Mr. Wright, the negative expectations of voodoo victims, and the very real healing possible via positive interpretations by Franz Alexander and positive emotions by Norman Cousins.

2

Information Transduction
in Mind-Body Healing and Hypnosis

TRANSDUCTION REFERS TO the conversion or transformation of energy or information from one form to another. A windmill transduces wind energy into the mechanical energy of the turning blades. If the mechanical energy of the turning blades is attached to a generator, it is transduced into electrical energy, which can in turn be transduced into light energy by an electric bulb. In the typical clinical application of biofeedback techniques, the biological "energy" of the body's muscle tension can be transduced into the visible "information" of a measuring device that enables the subject to alter his muscle tone. These examples, together with the basic concepts of information, communication and cybernetic theories, have led to a view of all biological life as a system of information transduction.

A history of the evolution of the concept of information transduction as the basic problem of psychobiology and hypnosis is summarized in Table 1. For the purposes of this book, it is convenient to begin our survey with the views of Bernheim, who is generally recognized as being one of the "fathers" of therapeutic hypnosis. In the following quotation, Bernheim described his understanding of the essence of hypnotic suggestion as a process of "transforming the idea received into an act" (Bernheim, 1886, pp. 137–138):

> The one thing certain is, that a *peculiar aptitude for transforming the idea received into an act* exists in hypnotized subjects who are susceptible to suggestion. In the normal condition, every formulated idea is questioned by the mind. After being perceived by the cortical centres, the impression extends to the cells of the adjacent convolutions; their peculiar activity is excited; the diverse faculties generated by the gray substance of the brain come into play; the impression is

TABLE 1 Evolution of the concept of information transduction as the basic problem of psychobiology and mind-body healing

RESEARCHERS	CONCEPT
Bernheim (1886)	Ideosensory and ideomotor reflex converts hypnotic suggestion into body processes.
Selye (1936, 1982)	Transduction of information via the "stress" hormones of the *hypothalamic-pituitary-adrenal axis* is the essential mechanism of psychosomatic problems.
Papez (1937)	Mental experience is transduced into the psychophysiology of emotions by the *limbic-hypothalamic system* and related structures.
Scharrer & Scharrer (1940) Harris (1948)	Central nervous system controls endocrine's hormonal messengers via *hypothalamus*.
Moruzzi & Magoun (1949)	The ascending reticular activating system (ARAS) of the brain stem projects to the *limbic-hypothalamic system* to stimulate wakefulness.
Shannon & Weaver (1949)	Mathematical theory of communication.
Wiener (1948)	Cybernetic view of life as systems of information transduction.
Meyers & Sperry (1953) Sperry (1964)	Consciousness associated with left and right hemispheres which function independently when neural connections are severed between them.
Olds & Milner (1954) Delgado, Roberts & Miller (1954)	Discovery of reward and punishment centers in the *limbic-hypothalamic system*.
Jouvet (1973, 1975)	"Paradoxical sleep" or dreaming as a process of integrating behavior via cortical and *limbic-hypothalamic system*.
Black (1963, 1969)	Hypnosis can modulate psychophysiological mechanisms of the immune system.
Nauta (1964)	"Fronto-limbic" system integrates "planning" functions of anterior frontal cortex with *limbic-hypothalamic system*.
Delbruck (1970)	Information transduction is the basic problem of psychobiology.
Weiner (1972, 1977)	Psychosomatic problems are a function of mind-body information transduction involving *limbic-hypothalamic*-pituitary system.

(*continued*)

TABLE 1 *Continued*

RESEARCHERS	CONCEPT
Bowers (1977)	An informational approach to hypnosis involves "the transduction of semantic information into a form that is somatically encodable."
Ader (1981)	Psychoneuroimmunological research demonstrates how the *hypothalamus* mediates mind-body communication with immune system.
Mishkin (1982)	Sensory information is stored and integrated with "cross-modal association" areas in the *limbic-hypothalamic system*.

elaborated, registered, and analyzed, by means of a complex mental process, which ends in its acceptation or neutralization; if there is cause, the mind vetoes it. In the hypnotized subject, on the contrary, the transformation of thought into action, sensation, movement, or vision is so quickly and so actively accomplished, that the intellectual inhibition has not time to act. When the mind interposes, it is already an accomplished fact, which is often registered with surprise, and which is confirmed by the fact that it proves to be real, and no intervention can hamper it further. If I say to the hypnotized subject, "Your hand remains closed," the brain carries out the idea as soon as it is formulated. A reflex is immediately transmitted from the cortical centre, where this idea induced by the auditory nerve is perceived, to the motor centre, corresponding to the central origin of the nerves subserving flexion of the hand;—contracture occurs in flexion. There is, then, *exaltation of the ideo-motor reflex excitability, which effects the unconscious transformation of the thought into movement, unknown to the will.*

The same thing occurs when I say to the hypnotized subject, "You have a tickling sensation in your nose." The thought induced through hearing is reflected upon the centre of olfactory sensibility, where it awakens the sensitive memory-image of the nasal itching, as former impressions have created it and left it imprinted and latent. This memory sensation thus resuscitated, may be intense enough to cause the reflex act of sneezing. There is also, then, *exaltation of the ideo-sensorial reflex excitability, which effects the unconscious transformation of the thought into sensation, or into a sensory image.*

In the same way, the visual, acoustic, and gustatory images succeed the suggested idea.

The mechanism of suggestion in general, may then be summed up in the following formula: *increase of the reflex ideo-motor, ideo-sensitive, and ideo-excitability.*

Although Bernheim's words now sound a bit antiquated, he aptly described information transduction as the basic process of therapeutic hypnosis. Indeed, virtually all modern approaches to mind-body communication attempt to facilitate the process of converting words, images, sensations, ideas, beliefs, and expectations into the healing, physiological processes in the body.

After a period of abeyance, modern research in hypnosis was initiated by Hull (1933), Erickson,* and Hilgard (1977), who stimulated a new generation of researchers (Fromm & Shor, 1979; Sheehan & Perry, 1976). These researchers developed methodologies for objective studies that led to an informational approach to understanding hypnotherapeutic phenomena. For example, in his pioneering volume, *Mind and Body* (1969), Stephen Black used a very broad philosophical and experimental approach, guided by information theory, in his investigations of how hypnosis could modulate psychophysiological mechanisms of the immune system. Bowers has summarized the informational view of hypnosis as follows (1977, p. 231);

> . . . The tendency to split etiological factors of disease into either psychic or somatic components, though heuristic for many purposes, nevertheless perpetuates, at least implicitly, a mind-body dualism that has defied rational solution for centuries. Perhaps what we need is a new formulation of this ancient problem, one that does not presuppose a formidable gap between the separate "realities" of mind and body.
>
> One way of reformulating the question involves the concept of information. The entire human body can be viewed as an interlocking network of informational systems—genetic, immunological, hormonal, and so on. These systems each have their own codes, and the transmission of information between systems requires some sort of transducer that allows the code of one system, genetic, say, to be translated into the code of another system—for example, immunological.
>
> Now, the mind, with its capacity for symbolizing in linguistic and

---

* See all four volumes of *The Collected Papers of Milton H. Erickson on Hypnosis* for a comprehensive presentation of Erickson's hypnosis research spanning five decades (Erickson, 1980).

extra-linguistic forms, can also be regarded as a means for coding, processing and transmitting information both intra- and inter-personality. If information processing and transmission is common to both psyche and soma, the mind-body problem might be reformulated as follows: How is information, received and processed at a semantic level, transduced into information that can be received and processed at a somatic level, and vice versa? That sounds like a question that can be more sensibly addressed than the one it is meant to replace. And some knowledgeable people are beginning to ask it. For example, in a discussion section of the New York Academy of Science's Second Conference on Psychophysiological Aspects of Cancer, Jonas Salk commented on a stimulating paper by Shands (1969) as follows: ''Human language is a specialized form of communication. You then jumped to the molecular level, and I was glad you did that, because there are parallels in that both express forms of communication. The code needs to be translated . . . ''

Unfortunately, we are a long way from being able to understand the complex mechanisms that help to transduce information from a semantic to a somatic level, but some such mechanisms surely exist, since, as we have seen, the selective and specific impact of suggestion on body structure and functioning seems very well supported indeed. And I would like to suggest that the capacity for deep hypnosis is an important variable in this transduction process. We have already shown that the healing potential of suggestions seems to be maximized in persons capable of deep hypnosis.

A great deal of progress has been made in the ten years since these words were written. An approach to answering questions about how hypnosis can facilitate the process of mind-body information transduction will be surveyed in the following sections of this chapter. First we will review evidence for the view that the limbic-hypothalamic system is the major mind-body transducer. Then we will outline how many of the major pathways of brain activity involved with memory, learning, and behavior support the limbic-hypothalamic system in this process of mind-body information transduction.

THE LIMBIC-HYPOTHALAMIC SYSTEM:
THE MAJOR MIND-BODY INFORMATION TRANSDUCER

The most significant development in mind-body research began when the young Hans Selye broke through the prejudices of the medical establishment of his day to introduce the psychological idea of *stress* as a factor worthy of study (Selye, 1936, 1976). Selye's lifetime of ground-breaking research culminated in a theory of how mental and/or physical stress is transduced into "psychosomatic problems" by the hormones of the "hypothalamic-pituitary-adrenal axis" of the endocrine system. Selye called this transduction process the "General Adaptation Syndrome." An overview of Selye's General Adaptation Syndrome, updated to emphasize the mind-modulating role of the limbic-hypothalamic system on the autonomic, endocrine, and immune systems, is illustrated in Figure 1. (In addition, Figure 1 provides an overview of the entire process of mind-body information transduction that is presented in greater detail throughout this volume.)

Selye's work was in agreement with the anatomical research of Papez (1937), who demonstrated that mental experience was transduced into the physiological responses characteristic of emotions in a circuit of brain structures that constituted much of what is now called the *limbic-hypothalamic system*. The Scharrers (1940) and Harris (1948) then initiated the exquisitely detailed work which led to the discovery that "secretory cells within the hypothalamus," could function as molecular information transducers by converting the neural impulses that encoded "mind" into the hormonal messenger molecules of the endocrine system that regulated "body." The conversion of these neuronal signals of mind into the messenger molecules of body was called "neuroendocrinal transduction" by Wurtman and Anton-Tay (1969).

The next major breakthrough in understanding the role of the limbic-hypothalamic system in mediating and modulating mind-body communication and behavior came with the discovery of *pleasure (reward) centers* and *pain (punishment) centers*. When miniature electrodes are carefully inserted into certain areas of the hypothalamus (particularly, the medial forebrain bundle and the lateral and ventromedial nuclei*), experimental animals will press a lever up to 15,000 times per hour to give themselves a sense of reward (Olds, 1977; Olds & Milner, 1954). Indeed, the animals would rather press the lever giving them the good feeling than eat! On the other hand, placing the electrodes in closely adjacent areas such as the periventricular structures of the hypothalamus and the thalamus, among others, touches off the centers for pain and punishment (Delgado, 1969; Delgado, Roberts, & Miller, 1954). To demonstrate the potency of the punishing and inhibiting centers of pain-controlling behavior, Delgado—with an inimitable élan not seen previously in neurophysiologists—actually stood alone in a bull ring with an aggressive fighting bull. At the moment the bull was about to charge him, Delgado pushed the button

---

* See Figure 2 in Chapter 6.

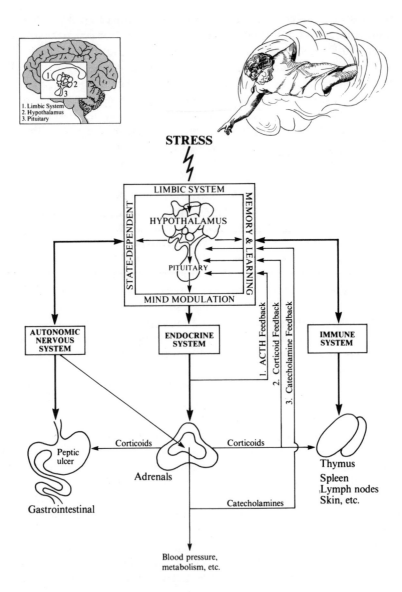

FIGURE 1 Selye's General Adaptation Syndrome updated to emphasize the mind-modulating role of the limbic-hypothalamic system on the autonomic, endocrine, and immune systems. The state-dependent memory and learning theory of therapeutic hypnosis is illustrated by the limbic system ''filter'' (square box) surrounding the hypothalamus.

that fired an electrode implanted in the pain centers of the bull's brain. The bull instantaneously stopped in his tracks, as the crowd roared its approval of a most dramatic, public demonstration of mind-body science. These demonstrations of the reward and punishment centers in the limbic-hypothalamic system again suggest why it is the major center of mind-body information transduction: Pleasure and pain are the great reinforcers of learning, behavior, and how we experience and express ourselves.

Since it was known that the corticoid hormones from the adrenals could suppress the immune system, it was supposed that this was the psycho-biological route by which the mental mechanisms of hypnosis could affect the body's immune system. In a series of incisive studies, however, Black (1963, 1969; Black & Friedman, 1965) was able to demonstrate that this was not the case. Hypnosis was effective in modulating the immune system, particularly by inhibiting allergic skin reactions, but this therapeutic response was mediated by an as yet unknown mind-body process. This mystery is only now in the process of being resolved by psychoneuro-immunological research (Ader, 1981), which is demonstrating how the immune system can communicate directly with the hypothalamus via its own "messenger molecules," called "immunotransmitters."

By 1970 the physicist Delbruck was able to state that an understanding of the mechanisms of information transduction was the central problem of neurobiology. In his monumental survey of psychobiology and human disease, Weiner (1972, 1977) took his inspiration from Delbruck and explored a number of models of information transduction to determine which were most appropriate for an understanding of psychosomatic problems. Weiner recognized the value of therapeutic hypnosis in a variety of the psychosomatic problems he studied, but concluded that we still do not know enough about the specific biology of each disease to determine the exact psychobiological routes of healing. In order to explore what these routes might be, we will review those areas of the brain that funnel their stimuli and information-processing activities into the limbic-hypothalamic system in the next four sections.

THE RETICULAR ACTIVATING SYSTEM: THE AWAKENED, NOVELTY-SEEKING, AND DREAMING MIND

Another line of significant research for understanding mind-body information transduction began with the research of Moruzzi and Magoun (1949). They discovered the ascending reticular activating system (ARAS) in the brain stem, which projects its nerve connections to the limbic-hypothalamic system, thalamus, and widely throughout the cortex to stimulate the brain into wakefulness. The reticular formation has been described as "a state-level structure within the pons and brain stem" (Bloom, Lazerson, & Hofstadter, 1985) that plays an important role in body-mind information transduction: It receives sensory information from all of the body's neural pathways and acts as a "filter," passing on to the brain only the information that is novel or persistent.

It is the brain's ability to wake up, to become alert and attentive to novel patterns of sensory stimuli and information, that enables it to focus its activity on new learning and creativity. The mind's ability to attend to the new has its psychobiological basis in the activity of a cluster of norepinephrine-containing neurons in the locus coeruleus of the pons area of the brain stem. When novel stimuli are received by the locus coeruleus, its neural connections stimulate the onset of brief states of heightened responsiveness in the higher cortical areas of the brain, and in the limbic-hypothalamic center that integrates memory and houses the reward or pleasure mechanisms. In other words, the locus coeruleus transduces novel stimuli into a heightened psychobiological state. Dull, repetitive situations, on the other hand, decrease the activity of the locus coeruleus and lead to relaxation, drowsiness, and sleep. The fact that what is novel and fascinating actually heightens brain activity is a very important, though still generally unappreciated, precondition for all forms of creatively-oriented psychotherapy and mind-body healing experiences. It is one of the fundamental principles used in the language of human facilitation that we will explore in Chapter 5.

The relation between activity in the locus coeruleus and dreaming was discovered by Jouvet (1975). When he destroyed the part of the nucleus locus coeruleus that normally inhibits motor activity during dreaming, he found that cats would act out their dreams in the form of what he called "pseudohallucinatory" behavior. From these observations, he developed an interesting theory of dreaming as a process of integrating genetic or innate behavior (Jouvet, 1973, 1975) that has become the psychobiological basis for more recent theories of dreaming as an experimental theater wherein many patterns of mind-body communication and healing can be explored (Dement, 1965, 1972; LaBerge, 1985; Mindell, 1985a, b; Rossi, 1972/1985).

What is the difference between the activity of the dreaming and the awake mind? One answer to this question is in the voluntary, overall organization of mental activity. There may be creative, very revealing bursts of metaphorical imagery in the dream, but they are not usually under voluntary control. LaBerge (1985) has recently described experiments in which specially trained (and talented) subjects apparently could control the content of some of their dream states, as well as their access to some of their own psychophysiological functions (e.g., sexual arousal, respiration). This relatively rare ability, called *lucid dreaming*, however, may be the exception that proves the rule. The successful lucid dreamer is the individual who can use a certain degree of conscious planning and voluntary control to transduce mind into physiological responses. Let us now turn our attention to the major areas of the brain that are involved in this planning and voluntary control process.

THE FRONTAL CEREBRAL CORTEX: THE ORGANIZING AND PLANNING MIND

The frontal (or prefrontal) cerebral cortex, with its specialized planning functions, has been described as the most recently developed area of the human brain. Proportionately larger than that of any other animal, it occupies one-quarter of the total mass of the cerebral hemisphere and does not attain maturity until the child is about seven years old. The frontal cortex has rich connections with both the reticular formation (ARAS) and the limbic-hypothalamic systems, which we reviewed in the two previous sections. The integration of information transduced in these two areas by the organizing activity of the frontal cortex is the main subject of this section.

The awakening and attention-getting novel stimuli transduced into the brain by the reticular formation and its specialized nuclei (e.g., the locus coeruleus) are organized and expressed as normal human responsiveness by the planning and sequencing functions of the frontal cortex. The frontal cortex also has such rich connections with the limbic-hypothalamic system that some investigators have considered it as a single "fronto-limbic system" (Nauta, 1964, 1972; Nauta & Domesick, 1980; Nauta & Feirtag, 1979). Luria has summarized the overall planning and organizing function of the frontal cortex as follows (1966, p. 233):

> . . . The fact that the frontal region is closely connected with the underlying structures of the limbic lobe, and through them with other nervous apparatuses concerned with interoception, gives reason to suppose that it receives signals of the various changes taking place in the organism and that it is intimately involved in *the regulation of body states*. Evidently, changes in body state occur not merely because of the appearance of new stimuli, evoking arousal reactions, but also because of the body's response activity. It may be postulated that these changing states may lead to corresponding further changes in the activity of the body. There are, therefore, important grounds

for believing that *the frontal lobes synthesize the information about the outside world received through the exteroceptors and the information about the internal states of the body* and that *they are the means whereby the behavior of the organism is regulated in conformity with the effect produced by its actions.*

The organization and synthesis of external and internal information for the *"regulation of body states"* are important for our developing understanding of mind-body communication and healing. This regulation of body states takes place when the organized stimuli of the external and internal worlds are funneled through the limbic-hypothalamic system. Psychophysiologists such as Achterberg (1985; Achterberg & Lawlis, 1980, 1984) have assembled evidence for the view that mind-body communication and healing are mediated by the "body image." The body image is an organization of visual imagery that apparently is constructed in the fronto-limbic system, particularly with the help of the right cerebral hemisphere. To approach an understanding of this idea, we will now overview the process of information transduction by the right and left cerebral hemispheres and their contributions to the facilitation of mind-body communication.

THE CEREBRAL HEMISPHERES: THE LOGICAL AND METAPHORICAL MINDS

A great area of discovery about information transduction in the brain during the 1950s and 1960s was initiated by Meyers and Sperry (1953), who discovered that when the nerve connections (the corpus callosum) between the left and right cerebral hemispheres in the cat were severed, each hemisphere apparently functioned in part independently. Since this operation did not seem to impair mental faculties, Sperry (1964) and his colleagues resorted to this surgical procedure with carefully selected human subjects who had very severe and uncontrollable *grand mal* epileptic seizures. If the source of the epilepsy was located in one cerebral hemisphere, they reasoned, the operation would at least prevent the seizure activity from spreading to the other half of the brain. The operation was remarkably successful in relieving the epilepsy. When psychologists carefully examined these "split-brain" patients, however, they encountered a series of fascinating discoveries about the intrinsic differences in the way information was transduced or processed in left and right hemispheres (Gazzaniga, 1967, 1985). For the purposes of our study of mind-body communication and healing, it is most important to note that the left hemisphere is specialized in the verbal-linguistic transduction of speech and analytical thinking, while the right plays a more predominant role in the holistic, analogical-metaphorical information transduction characteristic of emotions, imagery, and particularly, the body image (Achterberg, 1985). The basic hypothesis that has emerged is that the right hemisphere's modes of information transduction are more closely associated with the limbic-hypothalamic system and mind-body communication in the placebo response and therapeutic hypnosis. Ian Wickramasekera has recently summarized this idea as follows (1985, pp. 274–275):

> . . . Good placebo responders, like good hypnotic subjects, inhibit the critical, analytic mode of information processing that is characteristic of the dominant verbal hemisphere. Good placebo responders will tend to be individuals who are prone to see conceptual or other relationships between events that seem randomly distributed to others. They will inhibit the interfering signals of doubt and skepticism, which are consequences of the more analytic mode of information processing typical of the dominant (left) hemisphere. Like good hypnotic subjects, good placebo responders are likely to embroider or elaborate on the given stimulus properties of a drug potentiating it, out of their own rich subjective repertoires. Alternatively, they may negate or attenuate the effects of a . . . drug through negative attributions.
>
> Shapiro (1971) describes placebo nonresponders as "rigid and stereotypic and not psychologically minded" (p. 445). There is a striking similarity between this description and that of a poorly hypnotizable subject. There is increasing evidence (Bakan, 1969; Graham & Pernicano, 1976; Gur & Gur, 1974; Lachman & Goode, 1976) that hypnotizability or suggestibility is predominantly a right-hemisphere (nondominant or minor-hemisphere) function for right-handed people. Minor-hemisphere functions include holistic and imaginative mentation with diffuse, relational, and simultaneous processing of information (Ornstein, 1973; Sperry, 1964); the tendency to "see" some relationship or "meaning" in data, however randomly generated (e.g., a Rorschach inkblot), would appear to be an aspect of creative mentation that is posited to be a property of the nondominant hemisphere. This explanation can account for the common features of good placebo responders and good hypnotic subjects.

The intense interest of psychotherapists of all persuasions in learning to facilitate the creative mind-body healing potentials of the right hemisphere has led to many controversial efforts to find observable facial or body language cues about the process. Eye movements associated with characteristic styles of thought or reflection were independently described by Teitlebaum (1954) and Day (1964). Bakan first suggested that right or left cerebral hemispheric dominance or activity could be the basis of the tendency for eyes to move to the right or left, respectively, when involved with the transduction of logical versus analogical information.

In more recent reviews of the many research studies in this area, Bakan (1980) concluded that the right hemisphere does, in fact, have a primary role in the production of *raw imagery*. This raw imagery tends to be facilitated during sleep, dreaming, muscular relaxation, free association, mind wandering, and under the effects of certain drugs that block interhemispheric communication. When the cerebral hemispheres are in good communication, however, the raw imagery of the right hemisphere is ''cooked'' or transduced by the left hemisphere. This has led to the ''paradoxical'' finding that subjects who do well in structured tests of imagery and spatial relations tend to move their eyes to the right, indicating a heightened left-hemispheric involvement. Observations of eye movements as a clue to which hemisphere is most activated must therefore take into account the degree to which the imagery is transduced by a primary process (raw) or secondary process (cooked).

This difference between the cerebral transduction of raw and cooked imagery may be characteristic of all the other sensory modalities. It is found, for example, that the right cerebral hemisphere is activated by music in the untrained listener who is simply enjoying it, while the professional musician's left hemisphere is activated while he is analyzing the same music (Mazziotta, Phelps, Carson, & Kuhl, 1982). These differences in information transduction by the left and right cerebral hemispheres (Rossi, 1977) is the basis of many of the approaches to the facilitation of mind-body communication that we will explore in later chapters.

MEMORY AND LEARNING, MIND AND CONSCIOUSNESS

The direction of recent psychobiological research in memory and learning is confirming the importance of mind-body information transduction in the limbic-hypothalamic area of the brain for understanding how sensation and perception are integrated with thought and behavior. In this section we will cover only the two areas that are of greatest significance for our theme. These concern (1) the role of hormones in memory and learning; and (2) the manner in which sensation and perception are integrated with memory and learning in the limbic-hypothalamic system.

McGaugh, a physiological psychologist, has summarized the role of hormones in memory and learning as follows (1983, pp. 163–164):

> It is well known that sensory stimulation activates nonspecific brain systems [via the ARAS system, as we have seen above]. Sensory stimulation also results in the release of hormones, including ACTH, epinephrine, vasopressin, and the opioid peptides, enkephalin and endorphin. A great deal of recent research has shown that learning and memory are affected by these hormones. . . . These findings raise two important questions. First, is the release of these stress-related hormones part of the normal . . . processes involved in the endogenous modulation of memory storage? Second, do the effects of treatments known to produce retrograde amnesia and retrograde enhancement of memory involve influences of hormones? If the answer to these questions is yes, as much recent research suggests, then the major question to be addressed is the basis of the effects of endogenous hormones on brain activity underlying memory storage. . . . Our findings, as well as those of other laboratories, suggest that retention is influenced by epinephrine released from the adrenal medulla (McGaugh et al., 1982). We have for several years also studied the effects on memory of post-training electrical stimulation of the brain. Our recent findings . . . indicate that the effects of amygdala [a part of the limbic system] stimulation on memory may involve the release of peripheral epinephrine. The convergence of these two lines of research has provided evidence strongly supporting the view that *hormones released by experience act to modulate the strength of the memory of the experience and suggest that central modulating influences on memory [in the limbic-hypothalamic system] interact with influences of peripheral hormones.* (Italics added)

McGaugh's research provides us with what may become the basis of many therapeutically useful methods of facilitating mind-body communication and healing. Although our understanding of the incredible intricacies of these processes is still at an elementary level, it is nonetheless sufficient to suggest an important integration of the work of Hans Selye and Milton Erickson in the field of psychosomatic medicine, as we shall see in Chapter 4.

The work of Mortimer Mishkin and his colleagues at the National Institute of Mental Health is tracing the route by which the sensory information in the visual area of the cortex is transmitted to the limbic system where it is stored and integrated with processes of memory and learning. The limbic system (particularly its component structures, the amgydala and hippocampus) is the area where information stored by many different sensory systems can be combined and integrated. This type of ''cross-modal association'' makes sensory-perceptual information available to the hypothalamus for flexible patterns of information transduction into the body's psychophysiological responses (Murry & Mishkin, 1985).

We may regard this research on cross-modal association as the latest formulation of Bernheim's original concept of the *ideodynamic* as the psychophysiological basis of therapeutic hypnosis. Mishkin's work is thus a new research base for the investigation of mind-body communication and healing in hypnotherapy. His research into the relation between the visual modality and the limbic system must be extended to all other sensory modalities.

In an earlier work (Rossi, 1972/1985), I concluded from a study of the phenomenological content and processes of dreams that inter-modal shifts between sensations, perceptions, emotion, imagery, cognition, identity, and behavior were characteristic of the process of psychological growth and change. Mishkin's work is providing the experimental foundation for such psychological studies of creative development and for the renaissance of new methodologies that are currently being developed in psychotherapy to facilitate these processes (Mills & Crowley, 1986). We will continue the study of these processes of information transduction in the ''language of human facilitation'' presented in Chapter 5.

Mishkin's work is clarifying the great debate between the *behaviorist* and *cognitive* approaches to understanding how memory and learning take place and the role of thinking, awareness, and consciousness in the process. Mishkin (Mishkin, Malamut, & Bachevalier, 1984; Mishkin & Petri, 1984) has developed a two-level psychobiological theory that has a place for both behaviorist and cognitive frameworks. *Habits*, which have been described by behaviorists as automatic stimulus-response connections that take place whenever there is an adequate reward, are designated by Mishkin as the more basic process that operates at all levels of life, from the most primitive one-celled organisms to man. A cognitive process of self-reflection and thinking is not required for the formation of such habits. The acquisition of information, knowledge, and a self-conscious and self-driven memory system, as described by the cognitive learning theorists, requires the evolution of a ''cortico-limbic-thalamic'' pathway that is characteristic of all the more advanced life forms, such as mammals and man.

From the broad perspective developed in this chapter, *we could define consciousness or mind as a process of self-reflective information transduction*. This definition may not be satisfying for philosophers, but it is sufficient as a practical guide for our thinking about mind-body communication and how we may go about creating new approaches to mind-body healing. The major processes and pathways of self-reflective information transduction described in this chapter are beginning to emerge as the psychobiological basis of self-driven consciousness and mind-body communication. All of these pathways focus on the limbic-hypothalamic system* as the major center of mind-body information transduction.

If we were more advanced in our understanding of psychobiology, we would know which specific mind methods would facilitate each of these major pathways to mind-body communication. What type of procedure, for example, would most effectively stimulate the ARAS to create a heightened state of cortical activity to facilitate new learning in a particular individual? How shall we help a patient access memory and habit systems with visual imagery via the occipital, temporal, limbic-hypothalamic route? What questions about planning what aspects of life experience would most usefully engage the fronto-limbic system of a teenager in quandary about life goals? What combination of logical-verbal and analogical-metaphorical modes of information transduction would optimize left and right cerebral hemispheric integration for creative problem-solving in any specific situation?

Although we are far, indeed, from being able to answer these questions, the very act of posing them is a step in the direction of resolving them. Current experimental techniques, such as the PET Scan (Positron Emission Transaxial Tomography) and Magnetic Resonance Imaging, moreover, are making available means for testing whatever ideas and hypotheses we develop in this area. In the later chapters of this book we will explore a number of ways and means of accessing and facilitating each of these major pathways of mind-body communication and healing.

---

* For the reader sophisticated in anatomical studies, it may be well to point out that we are using the term "limbic-hypothalamic system" in this book in the broadest sense to include the following: amygdala, hippocampus, cingulate gyrus, fornix, septum, and certain nuclei of the thalamus and the Papez circuit.

3

State-Dependent Learning in Mind-Body Healing and Hypnosis

IN ORDER TO FULLY appreciate the scope of the state-dependent theory of mind-body healing and hypnosis, it is necessary to review its evolution over 200 years (outlined in Table 2). In Chapter 1 we saw how Bernheim originated the concept of information transduction in mind-body healing and hypnosis. In this chapter, we begin with the words of James Braid (1795–1860), who originated the concept of the altered state or state-dependent theory of mind-body healing and hypnosis. Braid recommended that hypnosis be defined as follows (quoted in Tinterow, 1970, pp. 370–372):

> Let the term *hypnotism* be restricted to those cases alone in which . . . the subject has no remembrance on awakening of what occurred during his sleep, but of which he shall have the most perfect recollection on passing into a similar stage of hypnotism thereafter. In this mode, *hypnotism will comprise those cases only in which what has hitherto been called the double-conscious state occurs.*
>
> And, finally, as a generic term, comprising the whole of these phenomena which result from the reciprocal actions of mind and matter upon each other, I think no term could be more appropriate than *psychophysiology*.

In the first part of this quotation, Braid defines hypnotism as a process of dissociation or reversible amnesia giving rise to the "double-conscious state." Modern researchers would call this a process of "state-dependent memory and learning": What is learned and remembered is dependent on one's psychophysiological state at the time of the experience. Memories acquired during the state of hypnosis are forgotten in the awake state but are available once more when hypnosis is reinduced. Since memory is

TABLE 2 Evolution of the state-dependent memory, learning, and behavior therapy of mind-body healing and therapeutic hypnosis

RESEARCHERS	CONCEPT
Braid (1855)	Double-conscious state manifest as "reversible amnesia" is the "psychophysiological" basis of hypnosis.
Janet (1889, 1907)	Dissociation manifest as a block or reversible amnesia between the conscious and unconscious is the source of psychopathology that can be accessed and healed by hypnosis.
Freud (1896) Jung (1910) Rank (1924)	The root of psychoanalysis: Emotional trauma leads to dissociation, repression, complexes, and amnesia as the basis of neurosis and functional psychosis.
Erickson (1932, 1943a, b, c, d, 1948)	Demonstrated how traumatic amnesias and psychosomatic symptoms are psycho-neuro-physiological dissociations that can be resolved with "inner resynthesis" in hypnotherapy.
Cheek (publications from 1957 to 1981)	Hypnosis occurs spontaneously at times of stress, suggesting that this phenomenon is a state-dependent condition.
Overton (1968, 1972, 1973)	Reviewed 40-year literature establishing state-dependent memory and learning as a valid experimental basis of dissociation in many paradigms of drug and psychophysiological research.
Fischer (1971a, b, c)	State-bound information and behavior are conceptualized as the psychophysiological basis of "altered states," dissociations, mood, multiple personality, dreams, trance, religious, psychotic, creative, artistic, and narcoanalytic phenomena.
Rossi (1972, 1973)	Psychological shocks and creative moments occur when habitual patterns of state-dependent memories and associations are interrupted.
Erickson & Rossi (1974)	Research in state-dependent learning lends experimental support to the general view of all amnesias and psychological experiences as state-bound.
Hilgard & Hilgard (1975) Hilgard (1977)	Formulated the *neodissociation theory of hypnosis*, which implies that state-dependent memory and learning are the same class of psychophysiological phenomena as hypnotic dissociation.

(*continued*)

TABLE 2 *Continued*

RESEARCHERS	CONCEPT
Rossi (1981, 1982)	Formulated *ultradian theory of hypnotherapeutic healing*: (1) The source of psychosomatic problems is stress-induced distortions of state-dependent ultradian psychobiological rhythms in the suprachiasmatic nucleus of the hypothalamus; (2) Erickson's "utilization" hypnotherapy normalizes these ultradian rhythms with autonomic system balance.
Werntz (1981) Werntz et al. (1981)	Correlation of ultradian rhythms in nasal and cerebral hemispheric dominance is centrally controlled by hypothalamus mediating autonomic system balance.
Benson (1983a, b)	The "relaxation response" in yoga and meditation has its psychosomatic healing source in "an integrated hypothalamic response resulting in generalized decreased sympathetic nervous system activity."
Zornetzer (1978) McGaugh (1983) Izquierdo (1984)	The endogenous state dependency hypothesis of memory formation; "peripheral hormones" of the adrenals modulate memory and learning in the limbic-hypothalamic system.

dependent upon and limited to the state in which it was acquired, we say it is "state-bound information."

In the second part of the quotation, Braid invented the generic term *psychophysiological* to denote all the phenomena of "the reciprocal actions of mind and matter upon each other." This early use of the term psychophysiological was his way of conceptualizing the process of information transduction between mind and body in healing and hypnosis.

Pierre Janet (1859–1947) was the next major figure in the history of hypnosis to use the phenomenon of reversible amnesia as the basis for building a "dissociation theory" of mind-body problems. A dissociation or "block" between the conscious and unconscious minds was conceptualized as the source of psychopathology that could be accessed and healed by hypnosis. Freud adopted this view and used "free association" rather than the formal induction of hypnosis to access the dissociated or repressed memories that had become the basis of psychological and psychosomatic problems.

The earliest roots of psychoanalysis were concerned with investigating the necessary and sufficient conditions for such reversible amnesias and dissociations. In his pioneering paper on "The Aetiology of Hysteria," Freud (1896) discussed the role of trauma as follows (cited in Freud, 1956, p. 186):

> For let us be quite clear that tracing an hysterical symptom back to a traumatic scene assists our understanding only if the scene in question fulfills two conditions—if it possesses the required *determining quality* and if we can credit it with the necessary *traumatic power*.

Life circumstances that had the requisite "determining quality" and "traumatic power" led to the formation of complexes. The effects of such complexes on memory and behavior were investigated experimentally by C. G. Jung in his association experiments and described as follows (Jung, 1910, p. 363):

> At the end of the [association] experiment, the subject is questioned as to whether he correctly recalls the reaction he gave previously to each single stimulus word; it then becomes apparent that forgetting normally takes place at or immediately after disturbances caused by a complex. We are in fact dealing with a kind of "Freudian forgetting" [that is, repression]. This procedure provides us with complex indicators which have proven to be of practical value.

Otto Rank (1924/1952) later pushed the possible source of complexes and neurosis back to the original trauma of birth. Thus the entire edifice of psychoanalysis could be said to rest upon this effort to explain how trauma gave rise to emotional complexes by initiating dissociation, repressions, and amnesias.

Milton H. Erickson (1902–1980) then demonstrated how amnesias caused by psychological shocks and traumatic events are psycho-neuro-physiological dissociations that can be resolved by "inner resynthesis" in hypnotherapy (Erickson, 1948/1980). One of Erickson's early students, David Cheek, M.D., systematized an ideomotor signaling approach for investigating emotional trauma, stress, and psychosomatic symptoms. Over a 25-year period, Cheek's clinical case studies led him to formulate the theory that severe stress invariably causes an altered state, identifiable as a form of spontaneous hypnosis which encodes state-bound problems and symptoms. He recently expressed his view as follows (Cheek, 1981, p. 88):

> Hypnosis occurs spontaneously at times of stress (Cheek, 1960), suggesting that this phenomenon is a state-dependent condition

mobilizing information previously conditioned by earlier similar stress (Cheek, 1962b).

At such times, the individual tends to revert in memory and physiological behavior to an earlier moment of great stress. The formal induction of hypnosis may suddenly release disturbing memories of experiences associated with spontaneous hypnoidal states. This can be helpful in the search for factors responsible for maladaptive behavior but can embarrass an inexperienced hypnotist who may find his subject identifying him with some evil person in past experience. This flashback phenomenon is nonspecific. The trigger mechanism may evoke a totally inappropriate response, as I have frequently found in evaluating anesthesia experiences.

Cheek's many clinical publications comprise the most extensive documentation of the psychobiological approach to mind-body communication and healing currently available in the literature on therapeutic hypnosis. His approach will be described and illustrated in more detail in Chapter 5.

When Erickson and I updated the history of therapeutic hypnosis with basic theory and research in modern psychology, we built upon Fischer's view of the relation between state-dependent learning and amnesia as follows (Erickson & Rossi, 1974/1980, pp. 71–90):

Taken together these clinical and naturalistic investigations strongly suggest that hypnotic trance is an altered *state* of consciousness and amnesia, in particular, is a natural consequence of this altered state. Recent research in "state-dependent learning" lends experimental support to the general view of all amnesias as being "state-bound." We can now understand hypnotic amnesia as only one of a general class of verifiable phenomenon rather than a special case. Fischer (1971c) has recently summarized the relation between state-dependent learning and amnesia as follows:

Inasmuch as experience arises from the binding or coupling of a particular state or level of arousal with a particular symbolic interpretation of that arousal, experience is state-bound; thus, it can be evoked either by inducing the particular level of arousal, or by presenting some symbol of its interpretation, such as an image, melody, or taste.

Recently, some researchers had 48 subjects memorize nonsense syllables while drunk. When sober, these volunteers had difficulty recalling what they had learned, but they could recall significantly better when they were drunk again. Another scientist also observed amphetamine-induced excitatory, and amobarbital-induced, "inhibitory," state-dependent recall of geometric configurations. His volunteers both memorized and later recalled the configurations under one of the two drugs. However, while remembering from one state to another is usually called "state-dependent learning," extended practice, learning, or conditioning is *not* necessary for producing "state-boundness." On the contrary, a single experience may be sufficient to establish state-boundness.

Déjà vu experiences and the so-called LSD flashbacks are special cases of the general phenomenon of state-boundness. Note that neither focal lesions nor molecules of a hallucinogenic drug are necessary for the induction of a flashback—a symbol evoking a past drug experience may be sufficient to produce an LSD flashback.

It follows from the state-bound nature of experience, and from the fact that amnesia exists between the state of normal daily experience and all other states of hyper- and hypoarousal, that what is called the "subconscious" is but another name for this amnesia. Therefore, instead of postulating *one* subconscious, I recognize as many layers of self-awareness as there are levels of arousal and corresponding symbolic interpretations in the individual's interpretive repertoire. This is how multiple existences become possible: by living from one waking state to another waking state; from one dream to the next; from LSD to LSD; from one creative, artistic, religious, or psychotic inspiration or possession to another; from trance to trance; and from reverie to reverie (p. 904).

We would submit that hypnotic trance itself can be most usefully conceptualized as but one vivid example of *the fundamental nature of all phenomenological experience as "state-bound."* The apparent continuity of consciousness that exists in everyday normal awareness is in fact a precarious illusion that is only made possible by the associative connections that exist between related bits of conversation, task orientation, etc. We have all experienced the instant amnesias that occur when we go too far on some tangent so we "lose the thread of thought" or "forget just what we were going to do," etc. Without the bridging associative connections, consciousness would break down into a series of discrete states with as little contiguity as is apparent in our dream life.

According to this view, what we usually experience as our ordinary everyday state of awareness or consciousness is actually habitual patterns of state-dependent memories, associations, and behaviors. I have conceptualized "creative moments" in dreams, artistic and scientific creativity, and everyday life as breaks in these habitual patterns (1972/1985). The new experience that occurs during creative moments is regarded as "*the basic unit of original thought and insight as well as personality change.*" I have described the possible psychobiological basis of creative moments as follows (Rossi, 1972/1985, p. 158):

> Experiencing a creative moment may be the phenomenological correlate of a critical change in the molecular structure of proteins within the brain associated with learning (Kimble, 1965) or the creation of new cell assemblies and phase sequences (Hebb, 1963).

Erickson's use of psychological shock (Rossi, 1973/1980) to evoke creative moments during hypnotherapy as a means of breaking out of maladaptive patterns of state-bound learning will be explored in Chapters 4 and 5.

Meanwhile, experimental support for the essential identity between the processes of psychological dissociation and state-dependent learning was forthcoming from the Hilgards' research on the use of hypnosis in the relief of pain (Hilgard & Hilgard, 1975). The Hilgards expressed their view as follows (p. 183):

> Another approach to dissociated experiences is the peculiar action of certain drugs upon the retention and reinstatement of learned experiences, leading to what is called state-dependent learning. If learning takes place under the influence of an appropriate drug, the memory for that learning may be unavailable in the nondrugged state, but return when the person is again under the influence of the drug. This occasionally happens with alcohol: the drinker forgets what he said or did while intoxicated, only to remember it again when next intoxicated. Because the memory is stored, but unavailable except under special circumstances, this phenomenon has some characteristics of hypnotic amnesia. Presumably, when the site and nature of these effects become known, they may have some bearing on the physiological substratum for hypnosis.

In his neodissociation theory of hypnosis, Ernest Hilgard then integrated historical and modern, experimental and clinical data to document how the major classical phenomena of hypnosis can be conceptualized as forms of "divided consciousness" (Hilgard, 1977, pp. 244–245):

> If information acquired in one state, as under the influence of a drug, is forgotten in the nondrugged state, but recalled again in the drug state, that is an experimental illustration of a reversible amnesia. This arrangement is of course the paradigm of *state-dependent learning*. The literature has been reviewed by Overton, who is also one of the leading investigators in the field (Overton, 1972, 1973). . . According to Overton (1973), drug discrimination . . . may be based "on the dissociative barrier which impairs a transfer of training between the drug and the no-drug condition." *The concept of dissociation employed by Overton is consonant with neodissociation theory. That is, two types of behavior may be isolated from each other because of different available information.* (Italics added)

The next development in my understanding of the relation between hypnosis and state-dependent learning came in the early 1980s, when I experienced the similarities between the psychobiological characteristics of ultradian rhythms and the "common everyday trance" that Erickson utilized for hypnotherapeutic healing (Rossi, 1972/1985, 1981, 1982, 1986a). This led to the formulation of the ultradian theory of hypnotherapeutic healing, which was summarized as follows (Rossi, 1982, p. 23):

> The similarities between the behavioral characteristics of ultradian cycles (a multioscillatory system of psychophysiological processes involving many parasympathetic and right-hemispheric functions which have a 90-minute periodicity throughout the 24-hour day) and those of the "common everyday trance" led the author to propose a new state(s) theory of hypnosis. The background for this proposal developed over eight years of observing the clinical, hypnotherapeutic techniques of Milton H. Erickson, whose work appeared to utilize a similar 90-minute periodicity. The ultradian theory of hypnotherapeutic healing proposes that (1) the source of psychosomatic reactions is in stress-induced distortions of the normal periodicity of ultradian cycles, and (2) the naturalistic approach to hypnotherapy facilitates healing by permitting a normalization of these ultradian processes.

Extensive reviews of the research (Kripke, 1982) indicated that *the suprachiasmatic nucleus of the hypothalamus was probably a major regulator of these rhythms, which were sensitive to learning and conditioning by both psychological and physiological factors.* An independent verification of these findings came when I accidentally stumbled upon the remarkable work of Werntz (1981; Werntz, Bickford, Bloom, & Shannahoff-Khalsa, D., 1981), who found additional experimental evidence for the role of the hypothalamus as the source and mediator of ultradian rhythms in cerebral dominance, nasal dominance, and autonomic nervous system integration. The exciting theoretical implication of Werntz's work was its provision of an empirical link between Western psychophysiological research on altered states of consciousness and the Eastern yogic practices of ancient times (Rossi, 1986a). This developing rapprochement between Eastern and Western conceptions of the relationship between mind and body is further supported by Benson's independent line of research (1983a, b), which described the "relaxation response" in yoga, meditation, and prayer as having its healing source in an integrated *hypothalamic* response, resulting in a generalized decrease in sympathetic nervous system activity.

The next breakthrough in my understanding came about a year later when I read McGaugh's (1983) review of recent research on the neurobiology of memory and learning. This research reported that hormones released during periods of stress modulated memory and learning in the limbic system (specifically, in the amygdala and hippocampus). I immediately realized that: (1) these were the same hormones of the hypothalamic-pituitary-endocrine system that Selye had found to be the source of stress-related psychosomatic problems; and (2) the new neurobiological research on memory and learning, and Selye's classical psychosomatic research, were both essentially state-dependent memory and learning phenomena.

More recently, Izquierdo (1984) has independently reported laboratory research on "endogenous state dependency"; he confirms that memory depends on the relation between neurohormonal and hormonal states. According to Izquierdo, the first explicit statement regarding the endogenous state dependency hypothesis was made by Zornetzer in 1978 (p. 646):

> In normal memory formation the specific pattern of arousal present in the brain at the time of training may become an integral component of the stored information. The neural representation of this specific pattern of arousal might depend on the pattern of activity generated by brainstem acetylcholine, catecholamine, and serotonin systems. It is this idiosyncratic and unique patterned brain state, present at the time of memory formation, that might need to be reproduced, or at least approximated, at the time of retrieval in order for the stored information to be elaborated.

Zornetzer's psychobiological hypothesis appears to be the clearest fore-runner of what I am formulating here as the "state-dependent theory of mind-body healing and therapeutic hypnosis."

Although state-dependent memory, learning, and behavior (SDMLB) have been the subject of well-controlled experimental research for the past 40 years (Overton, 1978; Rossi & Ryan, 1986), they are less familiar than classical Pavlovian and Skinnerian operant conditioning. Therefore, it might appear on first acquaintance that SDMLB is an exotic and highly specialized form of learning that is a minor variant of classical or operant conditioning. Actually, the reverse is true: SDMLB is the broad, generic class of learning that takes place in all complex organisms that have a cerebral cortex and limbic-hypothalamic system; Pavlovian and Skinnerian conditioning are specific varieties of SDMLB. The pioneering investigators and their followers were unaware, for the most part, of the role of limbic-hypothalamic SDMLB factors in their early learning experiments.

Pavlov, for example, was not able to take into account all the subtle *internal* responses of stress in his dogs that were conditioned to salivate with the *external* paired association of powdered meat and a sound. Most current psychobiologically oriented researchers and theorists in memory and learning (Lynch, McGaugh, & Weinberger, 1984) are in general agreement (though with varying vocabularies) that there are at least two classes of *internal* response involved in the memory and learning of all higher organisms: (1) there is a specific locus of a memory trace on a molecular-cellular-synaptic level (Hawkins & Kandel, 1984; Rosenzweig & Bennett, 1984); and (2) there is an involvement of the amygdala and hippocampus of the limbic-hypothalamic system in processing, encoding, and recall of the specific memory trace that may be located elsewhere in the brain (Mishkin & Petri, 1984; Thompson et al., 1984). It is this second factor involving the limbic-hypothalamic system that engages memory, learning, and behavior with the subtle state-dependent factors that encode psychosomatic problems that are resolvable by therapeutic hypnosis and other methods of mind-body healing.

A careful comparison of the work of Selye and Erickson indicates that they were both dealing with the same basic phenomenon of *state-dependent memory and learning* as the genesis and resolution of psychosomatic problems: Selye from the perspective of physiological research; Erickson from the psychological perspective. Neither, however, was apparently aware of the concept of state-dependent memory and learning, and of how it could serve as the common denominator of their work.

I will present the work of Selye and Erickson in more detail in the next chapter. First, however, let us consolidate our understanding of the state-dependent theory of mind-body healing and therapeutic hypnosis with two illustrative clinical problems: traumatic amnesia and multiple personality.

Illustrative Case Examples

Traumatic Amnesia

In a recent doctoral dissertation on "Mood State-Dependent Memory and Lateralization of Emotion," Gage (1983) has described Erickson's pioneering role in developing state-dependent memory approaches to therapeutic hypnosis as follows (pp. 14–15):

> Milton H. Erickson, who investigated memory phenomena such as hypnotic hypermnesia, posthypnotic amnesia and posthypnotic suggestion, was an early pioneer in the area of mood SDM [State-Dependent Memory]. Although in his writings he never labeled his work "state-dependent memory," this was clearly the topic of some of his investigations. He perfected a method which would allow people who were amnesic for clinically relevant events to remember them in every detail. His method was based on a reorienting process which recreated the sights, sounds, sensations, thoughts and feelings surrounding the forgotten event (cf. Erickson, 1937, 1939). His "reorienting" is clearly the same process as that described by mood SDM.

A direct quotation from Erickson's report on the "Development of Apparent Unconsciousness During Hypnotic Reliving of a Traumatic Experience" will serve to illustrate this point. In this case, Erickson utilized age regression as a means of investigating the "psychic development" of a young man who had recently recovered from a psychotic episode (Erickson, 1937/1980, pp. 45–59):

> The experimental procedure consisted of training the patient to enter profound somnambulistic hypnotic trances, during which, by means of a series of hypnotic suggestions, he was disoriented completely and then reoriented to an earlier period of his life. When thus reoriented, by the employment of carefully worded systematic suggestions and questions, he was induced to relive past events in a chronologically progressive fashion, describing them in detail to the

experimenter as if they were in the course of actual development in the immediate present. An attending stenographer recorded in full the entire course of the experimental events, including the descriptive material. In every instance for which adequate data were available from sources other than the patient himself, it was found that events of the distant past were relived and recounted by the patient with remarkable vividness and with richness and accuracy of detail.

Study of the experimental findings disclosed an incident of peculiar interest, illustrative in an unusual fashion of psychosomatic interrelationships. This incident concerned the development of what appeared to be a state of unconsciousness as the patient relived the experience of a homicidal assault which had occurred two years previously, when he was 17 years old. All previous information concerning this assault consisted of the statement by the patient that he had been "taken for a ride" and beaten so badly that hospitalization had been necessary. He seemed to have complete amnesia for all informative details of this experience, including even the name of the hospital. Extensive and persistent questioning in the ordinary deep hypnotic trance, as well as in the normal waking state, secured only unimportant items, despite the fact that he seemed to be cooperating to the limit of his ability.

When the day of this event was reached in the hypnotic reliving of his past life, the patient expressed his fears over his employment as a police informer, vividly portraying intense anxiety concerning threatened criminal vengeance, and his entire behavior and appearance were suggestive of a most harried state of mind. When the hour of 4 p.m. was reached in his reexperiencing of the events of this day, he relived, with marked intensity of feeling, the scene of his being ordered into an automobile by two men whom he knew to be criminal characters and his fearful behavior during the course of a long drive, during which he pleaded piteously with his abductors in a terrified fashion. Finally, he reenacted his forced acceptance of a bottle of pop from the criminals, fearfully and hesitantly drinking from an imaginary bottle. As he swallowed, he grimaced, mumbled that it tasted bitter, asked if it was poisoned, and dodged and cowered as if evading a blow. His entire appearance continued to denote intense terror. Shortly after completing the act of drinking, he belched and suddenly looked bewildered. His pupils, which previously had been fluctuating constantly in size, became widely dilated, and fine lateral nystagmus developed. He then rubbed his eyes, complained that he could not see plainly, said that everything was getting dark and that he was dizzy, and began shaking his head as if to throw off something or to rouse himself. Questioning by the experimenter elicited the information that the patient felt himself becoming sleepy. It was noted that his speech, previously clear, was now thick and indistinct and that his appearance had changed from that of terror to that of somnolence.

At this time the patient was sitting on a couch, and every few seconds the experimenter had been testing him for the presence of catalepsy as an index of his continuance in the hypnotic state. After about two minutes of decreasing activity, during which the patient shook his head more and more slowly and mumbled with increasing inarticulateness, his eyes closed, despite his apparent effort to keep them open. Suddenly he gave a short, gasping grunt and collapsed, sprawling inanimately over the couch. Immediate examination by the experimenter disclosed complete loss of hypnotic rapport, with absence of the catalepsy which hitherto had been consistently present. Physically, there were sagging of the lower jaw and marked atony of the muscles of the legs and arms. Also, the patellar and pupillary reflexes, which are consistently present during hypnotic states, were absent. The respiration and pulse, which had been greatly increased during the state of terror, had decreased somewhat during that of somnolence. Now they were found to be markedly diminished in rate and so weak and faint as to be barely perceptible. In brief, the patient presented every appearance of being unconscious. However, before the blood pressure and accurate counts of the pulse and respiration could be taken, the patient seemed to be recovering. He stirred slightly and moaned, and catalepsy returned slowly. Shortly he opened his eyes and, after staring vacantly around, weakly closed them again. It was noted that the pupils were still widely dilated, that fine nystagmus was present, and that the eyes were not focused. The patient licked his lips repeatedly, moaned for water, and weakly rubbed his forehead, grimacing with pain as he did so. He paid no attention to the experimenter's insistent questions, "What's the matter? What's happening?" except to say, "It's dark, dark." This was followed by a second collapse, of slower onset than the first but apparently of the same character, with the same physical findings except that the respiration was deep and labored while the pulse was slow and firm. Repeated attempts were made by the experimenter to arouse the patient, but he remained unresponsive for several minutes. Finally, catalepsy returned, and the patient opened his eyes and stared about unseeingly. Nystagmus was absent, and the pupils were somewhat dilated but responsive to light. He twisted his head about, moaned, rubbed his neck as if it were painful, rubbed his forehead gently, grimacing as if with pain, and shivered constantly. Again, he licked his lips repeatedly and kept moaning for water. No response was made to the experimenter's insistent questioning except the monosyllables "light" and "woods." Now and then he put his hands to his ears, rubbed them feebly and mumbled, "buzzing."

Soon the patient seemed to recover to a considerable degree, and he again became fairly responsive to the experimenter's inquiries, which concerned the events he was reliving. There followed a relatively inadequate account, as compared with his initial communicativeness, of lying in a ditch alongside a road through a woods, of being cold, wet, and uncomfortable, and of suffering from intense thirst, roaring in the ears, headache, and a painful, bleeding wound on his forehead, from which he went through the act of wiping blood in a gingerly fashion. He also declared that it seemed to be morning.

From then, he recounted in a fragmentary fashion the experience of being picked up by some men and taken to a hospital. The reliving of the next two days was also disjointed and inadequate, but that of subsequent events was complete, during the course of which the name of the hospital was obtained.

This reexperience of a homicidal assault illustrates how state-bound information is generated by an altered psychophysiological state (particularly the alarm reaction of the autonomic nervous system and the endocrine system, leading to increased respiration, pulse, and blood pressure) that can be accessed via therapeutic hypnosis. Erickson accessed state-bound information by carefully retrieving the contexts and frames of reference in which it was embedded (Erickson & Rossi, 1979). As he said in the above case, "The employment of carefully worded systematic suggestions and questions . . . to relive past events in a chronologically progressive fashion" was an important key to the success of his procedure. These systematic questions and suggestions accessed the memory sets that enabled the patient to relive the traumatically isolated (amnesic) state-bound memories.

Erickson's manner of accessing state-bound memories by reviewing the context and sensory-perceptual cues surrounding their original acquisition was fundamentally different from the manner of traditional authoritarian hypnotism involving direct suggestion. For example, in the traditional procedure of inciting the subject to "Remember!" there was a reliance on the alleged "hypersuggestibility" of the hypnotic state. Erickson (1932/1980) found in his initial investigations, however, that *hypersuggestibility was not a characteristic of hypnosis.* He described it as follows (p. 495):

> In the writer's own experience . . . *hypersuggestibility was not no-ticed, although the list of individual subjects totals approximately 300 and the number of trances several thousand.* Further, a considerable number were hypnotized from 300 to 500 times over a period of years. Also, several of the subjects were immediate relatives with consequent in-timate daily contact, and they were trained to respond, in experimen-tation, quickly and readily to the slightest suggestion. *Far from making them hypersuggestible, it was found necessary to deal very gingerly with them to keep from losing their cooperation, and it was often felt that they developed a compensatory negativism toward the hypnotist to offset any in-creased suggestibility. Subjects trained to go into a deep trance instantly at the snap of a finger would successfully resist when unwilling or more in-terested in other projects.* Even when persuaded to give their consent against their original wishes, the induction of a trance was impos-sible. Nor were those subjects more suggestible to other people, since, when their services were "loaned" to the author's colleagues, the production of hypnosis in them, despite their extensive train-ing, was just as hard as it had been originally for the author. And the same thing was found true when the author "borrowed" sub-jects. In brief, *it seems probable that if there is a development of increased suggestibility, it is negligible in extent.* (Italics added)

The clause, "it was found necessary to deal very gingerly with them," is the key to a more adequate interpretation of therapeutic hypnosis as Erickson developed it. Hypnotic subjects are *hypersensitive*, not hypersug-gestible (Ellenberger, 1970, p. 115). It could be said that good hypnotic subjects have an easy access to their state-dependent experiences because of their sensitivity. This sensitivity is the quality that makes them amena-ble to accepting and carrying out suggestions if they are in a cooperative relationship with the hypnotherapist. It is also the quality that enables them to be more receptive to the subtle and often unrecognized nuances of hypnotic communication that have been called the "demand charac-teristics" (Orne, 1962) or the "minimal cues" (Erickson, 1964/1980, 1980b) of the hypnotic situation. Some particularly talented subjects can utilize their sensitivity to realign their sensory-perceptual and mental processes in a way that allows them to experience the classical phenomena of hypnosis and a variety of unusual and innovative state-dependent patterns of mind-body interactions.

Multiple Personality and State-Dependent Memory

In her Ph.D. dissertation, Jody Lienhart (1983) has formulated a state-dependent theory of multiple personality as exemplified by five well-documented cases (Sybil [Schreiber, 1973]; Chris Sizemore [Thigpen & Cleckley's *The Three Faces of Eve*, 1957; Sizemore, 1977]; Christina Peters [Peters, 1978]; Betsy [Brassfield, 1980, 1983]; and herself, Jody Lienhart [Brassfield, 1983; Putnam, 1982]). Lienhart had the opportunity to present an unusually thorough analysis of both the objective and subjective facts of each case, since she herself is one of them. She described the scope of her study and some of the theoretical assumptions she found support for, as follows (1983, pp. 6–7):

> Implicit in each of the studies of childhood trauma is the pervasive nature of paradoxical communication. Frequently, this double bind communication style appears during the formative, preverbal stages of childhood in which interpretation of these messages is confused. This results in insufficient experiential learning which would allow appropriate translation of the confused messages (Hilgard & Marquis, 1961).
>
> Characteristically, hypnosis is produced by paradoxical statements in which the messages are incongruent (Haley, 1963). Numerous studies have revealed that the processes of learning and recall differ under the hypnotic state than in normal "forgetting" (Hilgard, 1977).
>
> This study presents the theoretical assumption that multiple personality is developed through early childhood state-dependent learning. Furthermore, it is hypothesized that this learning occurs as a result of the hypnoidal effects of childhood trauma such as abuse and sexual molestation. The child, unable to translate the paradoxical nature of the messages he receives, fragments into a trance state. Furthermore, it is suggested that memories incorporated during each of these hypnoidal experiences are similar to knowledge acquired during state-dependent learning.

Under hypnosis, Lienhart was able to recall the critical incident of her own traumatic dissociation and the formation of a new personality before her fourth birthday, when she was seduced by her "Uncle Bulen". She provides an unusually vivid description of her subjective state of being confused and "hypnotically stunned" by this traumatic incident (1983, pp. 74–75):

> The actual incident which triggered the first personality fragmentation was an attempt by Bulen to force the child into an act of fellatio. Jo Ella certainly had no conception of why the erect penis was being shoved into her mouth. She could only respond to his ominous threats and the sensation of choking on this enormous "thing." She could neither cope with the awful fear nor could she flee from it. At this point, Jo Ella's mind simply blanked out the dreaded experience. It was as if she had completely separated from her body and had disappeared.
>
> Moments, or maybe even hours later, the figure of the small child could be seen huddled against the large stucco building. It was late afternoon and the chill of early autumn brushed through her home-made dress. But this was not the same Jo Ella who had earlier struggled against the powerful grasp of her favorite "Uncle Bulen." The new child, Jo Ella II, was later dubbed the Kid. All memory traces of the earlier incident had vanished.
>
> The Kid was a perfect mimic and could ape the original personality very precisely. But this child was a totally new person in almost every way. Her perception of her world had been irretrievably altered. The previous incident had left complete confusion in the child's mind and this "lost time" could not be re-established within its contextual setting. Neither was it possible to cope with the incident because there were no experiential counterparts with which to compare it. Jo Ella II was hypnotically stunned and yet unable to find any of the words which would have allowed her to deal with the experience, either for herself or others.

Lienhart evaluates her own case (1983, pp. 89–90):

> Jody's case history is replete with similar self-contradictions which bind the child into an unresolvable conflictual state. The good, generous and loving uncle becomes a person who is cruel and sexually exploitive. Since the early Jo Ella cannot reconcile these extreme polarities, she enters into a trance state which emotionally removes her from the scene. The emergent personality, Jo Ella II, is amnesic for the incident. Indeed, the only access to the encapsulated experience is through hypnosis or through its reemergence in a situation which may have similar contextual cues.

In this description of the formation of a multiple personality, we find the salient characteristics of the *state-dependent theory of therapeutic hypnosis: a situation of extreme psychophysiological distress results in an amnesia for the stressful incident that is reversible by hypnosis.* Jody's case, as well as others in Lienhart's dissertation, emphasizes another important feature required of an adequate state-dependent theory of therapeutic hypnosis: It illuminates *the process of falling into a spontaneous state of hypnosis under circumstances of traumatic stress* (Cheek, 1960); it also illuminates the role of the double bind or paradoxical communication in precipitating and maintaining the dissociated state. Lienhart's case well illustrates the role of therapeutic hypnosis in accessing the memories encapsulated by the traumatic process of state-bound learning so that they can be therapeutically reintegrated into the total personality.

Lienhart concludes her analysis with a formulation of the role of context and mental sets in making knowledge consciously available in one state and not another. We will quote a portion of her view because it serves as a bridge to the language of "memory cues" as it is used by experimental psychologists in state-dependent memory research. Lienhart's insight that knowledge is separated into intellectual and emotional sets is of particular significance, since it provides support for Erickson's hypnotherapeutic approach of accessing emotional and intellectual memories independent of one another when he felt he was dealing with traumatic processes in his patients (Erickson & Rossi, 1979). Lienhart concludes (1983, pp. 88–89):

> Just as hypnosis requires intense concentration rather than "sleep," the multiple has learned to concentrate totally on certain memories from the past. The underlying problem appears to be one of retrieval from an infinite number of memory sets. It is within the retrieval process that the perceptual distortions occur. This creates a chaotic confusion because the individual memory units are not encapsulated within the proper "sets" in an orderly fashion. Thus, a memory cue from one period of life is stored with the wrong "memory set." Consequently, certain stimulus cues may trigger one of the behavior response sets but within the wrong context or sequence. The process is crudely similar to the distortions, condensations and symbolic connections which occur during the dream state. Knowledge which is accessible in one state is not available during the altered state as it is integrated poorly and distributed more randomly within the range of recall of the dominant personality.

Another interesting feature demonstrated by multiples that is not well understood by researchers is the emotional detachment from the appropriate "intellectual" set. It would appear that some affective experiences are stored independently from their intellectual counterparts. As a result of this, an emotional unit from one set may attach itself to a constellation of cues which make up a totally different cognitive set.

The "infinite number of memory sets," each more or less state-bound, is what makes up the seemingly random patterns of associations that we experience as subjective consciousness in everyday life (Erickson, Rossi, & Rossi, 1976). Therapeutic hypnosis accesses these memory sets in a systematic manner to reactivate precisely those that are required for healing (Erickson & Rossi, 1979).

Recent theory and research on the phenomenon of multiple personality indicate that the subpersonalities can have different cognitive (Silberman, Putnam, Weingartner, Braun, & Post, 1985) and psychophysiological response patterns as well. Braun (1983a, b) has used the concept of state-dependent learning to account for the different memory systems in multiple personalities because "information which is encoded under one psychophysiological condition is best retrieved under the same psychophysiological condition" (1983a, p. 133).

In an objective study of multiple personality, Ludwig et al (1972) found that "the only dissociated functions among the different states of consciousness pertained to *emotionally laden* information, skills, and activities associated with each specific personality" (Ludwig, 1983, p. 94). Neutral information, skills, and activities unrelated to the emotional issues of any aspects of the multiple personality were not dissociated. This emotionally laden aspect of dissociated or state-bound information in both multiple personality and hypnosis points once again to the functional involvement of the limbic-hypothalamic system as the major mind-body connection (transducer) for emotional processes.

A Psychobiological Resolution of the Mind-Body Problem

If we take these views of recent psychobiological research to their logical conclusion, we have a pragmatic solution to the centuries' old mind-body problem—indeed, a resolution of the Cartesian dualism of mind and body. Mind and body are not separate phenomena, one being somehow spirit and the other matter. Mind and body are both aspects of one information system. Life is an information system. Biology is a process of information transduction. *Mind* and *body* are two facets or two ways of conceptualizing this *single information system*.

Most theories of mind-body relationships stop short at this point without saying anything more definite about *how* mind and body are connected and *how* they communicate. Here, we will not avoid this basic issue by omission or vague philosophical nostrums. The state-dependent theory of mind-body communication and healing can be expressed as four integrated hypotheses:

1) *The limbic-hypothalamic system is the major anatomical connecting link between mind and body.*
2) *State-dependent memory, learning, and behavior processes encoded in the limbic-hypothalamic and closely related systems are the major information transducers between mind and body.*
3) *All methods of mind-body healing and therapeutic hypnosis operate by accessing and reframing the state-dependent memory and learning systems that encode symptoms and problems.*
4) *The state-dependent encoding of mind-body symptoms and problems can be accessed by psychological as well as physiological (e.g., drugs) approaches— and the placebo response is a synergistic interaction of both.*

The major thrust of these hypotheses is that *mind-body information transduction* and *state-dependent memory, learning, and behavior* mediated by the limbic-hypothalamic system, are the two fundamental processes of mind-body communication and healing. Medical science has specialized in all the anatomical, physiological, and pharmacological methods of accessing and facilitating healing; that is, it has focused almost exclusively on the "body side" of the mind-body equation. In this chapter we have developed an experimentally based psychophysiological rationale for understanding how *psychological* factors can facilitate healing as well. State-dependent memory, learning, and behavior phenomena are the "missing link" in all previous theories of mind-body relationships. They bridge the mysterious gap between mind and body; they are the common denominator between traditional Western medicine and all the holistic, shamanistic, and spiritualistic approaches to healing that depend upon highly specialized cultural belief systems, world views, and frames of reference.

We are now in a position to explain the many forms of iatrogenic illness and healing that have been so difficult for Western medicine and psychology to understand. The state-dependent theory of mind-body healing can elucidate, for example, how even in our modern age, researchers (Dunlap, Henderson, & Inch, 1952) could have found that 30 percent of the 17,000 medical prescriptions they studied in England were actually placebos in the sense that the drugs did not have any specific physiological effect on the conditions for which they were prescribed. We can now understand how *any drug that alters any aspect of the body's sensory-perceptual or physiological responsiveness on any level can disrupt the more-or-less fragile state-dependent encoding of symptoms and thereby evoke a ''nonspecific'' but very real healing effect that we call the ''placebo response.''*

Let us now turn our attention to a more detailed study of the relationship between mind-body symptoms, state-dependent learning, and therapeutic hypnosis through a comparison of the pioneering research of Hans Selye and Milton Erickson.

4

Stress and Psychosomatic Phenomena:
Pioneering Work of Hans Selye
and Milton Erickson

D URING THE PAST HALF century, the study of stress and psychosomatic
phenomena has been the major stimulus for investigating mind-body
communication and healing. Our approach to this area will be to update
and integrate the work of two major pioneers: the physiologist Hans
Selye, and the psychiatrist and hypnotherapist Milton Erickson. These two
investigators contributed profoundly original observations to our understanding of psychosomatic phenomena: Selye primarily from his innovative physiological experiments on stress; Erickson primarily from his
open-ended, naturalistic investigations of spontaneous psychosomatic
dysfunctions during hypnosis. Integrating their work leads to a more comprehensive understanding of mind-body problems and the means of facilitating their resolution.

In this chapter we will review Selye's formulation of the *General Adaptation Syndrome* (GAS), which has been described aptly as the foundation
of psychosomatic medicine. We will use the concept of *state-dependent
memory and learning* and its natural consequent, *state-bound information and
behavior*, to update Selye's view of the GAS. Recent research that has
deepened our understanding of the functions of the hypothalamus then
will be used to integrate Selye's concept of the GAS with Erickson's view
of the experiential and psycho-neuro-physiological basis of hypnotherapy.

SELYE'S CONCEPT OF THE GENERAL ADAPTATION SYNDROME (GAS)

Selye acknowledged the influence of the great French physiologist,
Claude Bernard, in the evolution of his concept of the General Adaptation
Syndrome (1974). Bernard stated that one of the most characteristic fea-

tures of all life is its ability to maintain the *constancy of its inner milieu,* the environment within its skin. Walter Cannon (1932, 1953) later called this property *homeostasis:* the characteristic of maintaining a steady internal physiological state despite external changes in the environment. Life's response to any injury or disease could be characterized as an effort to maintain its homeostatic balance against the intrusion or change from the outside world. Selye's first original contribution was to show that whatever the source of *biological stress* intruding upon the organism, it would react with *the same pattern of response* to restore its internal homeostasis. He described his process of discovery as follows (Selye, 1974, pp. 24–27):

> In 1926, as a second year medical student, I first came across this problem of a stereotyped response to any exacting demand made upon the body. I began to wonder why patients suffering from the most diverse diseases that threaten homeostasis have so many signs and symptoms in common. Whether a man suffers from a severe loss of blood, an infectious disease, or advanced cancer, he loses his appetite, his muscular strength, and his ambition to accomplish anything; usually, the patient also loses weight, and even his facial expression betrays that he is ill. What is the scientific basis of what at that time I thought of as the "syndrome of just being sick"?
>
> . . . *How could different stimuli produce the same result?* In 1936, this problem presented itself again—under conditions more suited to exact laboratory analysis. It turned out in the course of my experiments in which rats were injected with various impure and toxic gland preparations that, irrespective of the tissue from which they were made or their hormone content, the injections produced a stereotyped syndrome (a set of simultaneously occurring organ changes), characterized by enlargement and hyperactivity of the adrenal cortex, shrinkage (or atrophy) of the thymus gland and lymph nodes, and the appearance of gastrointestinal ulcers.
>
> . . . It soon became evident from animal experiments that the same set of organ changes caused by the glandular extracts were also produced by cold, heat, infection, trauma, hemorrhage, nervous irritation, and many other stimuli. . . . This reaction was first described, in 1936, as a "syndrome produced by various nocuous agents" and subsequently became known as the *General Adaptation Syndrome* (GAS), or the *biological stress syndrome.* Its three stages—(1) the alarm reation; (2) the stage of resistance; and (3) the stage of exhaustion.

State-Dependent Learning and the General Adaptation Syndrome

The first two stages of Selye's GAS—the *alarm reaction* and the *state of resistance*—take on a profoundly new significance in the light of the more recent research in state-dependent memory and learning. The alarm reaction is characterized by the activation of the sympathetic nervous system, which stimulates the release of epinephrine and norepinephrine from the adrenal medullae. As we noted earlier, McGaugh's research (1983) demonstrated that these are the same hormones (among others) that modulate the retention of memory. *Learning and memory acquired during Selye's alarm reaction therefore tend to be state-dependent!* A person in a traumatic car accident experiences an intense rush of the alarm reaction hormones. His detailed memories of the accident are intertwined with the complex psychophysiological state associated with these hormones. When he returns to his usual or "normal" psychophysiological states of awareness a few hours or days later, the memories of the accident become fuzzy or, in really severe cases, as illustrated in the case of traumatic amnesia of the previous chapter, the victim may be completely amnesic. The memories of the accident have become "state-bound"—that is, they are bound to the precise psychophysiological state evoked by the alarm reaction, together with its associated sensory-perceptual impressions of the accident.

Gold (1984) recently validated this experimentally when he found that "a single injection of epinephrine results in long-lasting change in brain function. . . . The findings suggest that some hormonal responses may not only regulate neuronal changes responsible for memory storage but may also themselves initiate long-lasting alterations in neuronal function" (p. 379).

Selye's next stage, the stage of resistance, is the period during which psychosomatic symptoms become particularly evident and troublesome. In our car accident example, the psychosomatic response could be any part of the alarm reaction that was originally experienced—anxiety, pain, hysterical paralysis, headaches, ulcers, etc. The victim now is struck with a subtle "problem of adaptation" that traditional physical medicine often does not know how to deal with. This is especially the case when the initial cause of the stress (such as the car accident) has disappeared and yet the mind-body—having learned a new defensive (psychosomatic) mode of adaptation, continues with it. *The psychosomatic mode of adaptation was learned during a special (usually traumatic) state-dependent psychophysiological condition; it continues because it remains state-bound or locked into that special psychophysiological condition even after the patient apparently returns to his normal mode of functioning.*

Selye proposed a number of solutions for the psychosomatic problems manifested during this *stage of resistance*. Most typically, medication could be used to counteract the stressor hormones or, in extreme cases, surgery could remove the adrenals that produce the hormones. Selye frequently described this stage of resistance as being "stuck in a groove." That was his way of describing what we now recognize as state-bound psychophysiological behavior. Selye reasoned that if a shock could get one stuck in a groove, perhaps another shock could get one out again so that the person could "snap out of disease" (Selye, 1976, p. 9). He believed that the various forms of shock (electroconvulsive and insulin shock treatment for the mentally ill, psychological shock, etc.) were types of *nonspecific therapies* that counteracted many of the *nonspecific aspects* of the GAS. In a following section we will see how this understanding of the relationship between shock and the nonspecific approach to psychosomatic problems has an almost exact, though previously unrecognized, correspondence to Erickson's use of psychological shock as a general (nonspecific) approach to a variety of emotional problems.

State-Dependent Memory, Mood, and the Murder of Robert Kennedy

An unusually clear example of how a traumatic situation involving the heightened state of Selye's alarm reaction can generate state-bound information accessible by hypnosis is provided in the following description of the assassination of Robert Kennedy (Bower, 1981, p. 12):

> [This] illustration involves a talk I had recently with Vernard Diamond, a forensic psychiatrist who lives in the Bay Area, about a famous criminal case he dealt with—the case of Sirhan Sirhan, the man who assassinated Bobby Kennedy in Los Angeles in 1968. . . . Interestingly, Sirhan has absolutely no recollection of the actual murder, which occurred in the small kitchen of the Ambassador Hotel where he pumped several bullets into Kennedy. *Sirhan carried out the deed in a greatly agitated state and was completely amnesiac with regard to the event.* Diamond, called in by Sirhan's attorneys, hypnotized Sirhan and helped him to reconstruct from memory the events of that fateful day. *Under hypnosis, as Sirhan became more worked up and excited, he recalled progressively more, the memories tumbling out while his excitement built to a crescendo leading up to the shooting.* At that point Sirhan would scream out the death curses, "fire" the shots, and then choke as he reexperienced the Secret Service bodyguard nearly throttling him after he was caught. On different occasions,

while in trance, Sirhan was able to recall the crucial events, sometimes speaking, other times recording his recollections in automatic
writing, but the recall was always accompanied by great excitement.

The curious feature of the case was that material uncovered under
hypnosis never became consciously available to Sirhan in his waking state, and he denied that he committed the murder. Moreover,
he denied that he had ever been hypnotized by Diamond, denied
that it was his own voice on the tape recorder, and denied that it
was his handwriting—he alleged that Diamond must have hired an
actor or a handwriting specialist to mimic him. Sirhan eventually did
accept the theory that he must have killed Bobby Kennedy, ration-
alizing it as an act of heroism in the cause of Arab nationalism. But
his belief was based on "hearsay," much as is my belief that I was
born on a Wednesday evening—I must have been there but I sure
cannot remember it. (Italics added)

The generation of state-bound information in an extreme psychophysiological state of alarm is clearly evident in this case: "Sirhan carried out
the deed in a *greatly agitated state* and was *amnesiac* with regard to the event.
. . . Under hypnosis, as Sirhan became more and more worked up and
excited, he recalled progressively more, the memories tumbling out while
his excitement built to a crescendo leading up to the shooting." The
"greatly agitated state" was a heightened state of the psychophysiological
alarm response that was so extreme that Sirhan's memories became state-
bound: They were *dissociated* from his normal waking consciousness so
that he had a complete amnesia for the shooting. Hypnosis enabled Sirhan
to reexperience this extremely altered psychophysiological state, and with
it, "the memories [came] tumbling out while his excitement built to a
crescendo." This well-documented illustration of the intimate association
between the endocrine system, the alarm response, and state-bound information in the form of an amnesia that can be reversed under hypnosis
is typical of many examples. By accessing the heightened state of emotion in which these memories were state-bound, hypnosis was able to
retrieve them.

The objection could be raised that the extreme stress of the Sirhan Sirhan
case might be an exception in generating state-bound information; after
all, the situation is very different in more typical daily living where emotions and moods are of a milder nature. Bower (1981; Gilligan & Bower,
1984) has undertaken a series of experimental studies investigating this
generation of state-bound information by the emotional and mood states
typical of daily living. He used "hypnotically induced moods . . . to create

an experimental analog of affect-state-dependent learning" to measure memory and recall (Bower, 1981, p. 131). He found that when subjects learned material in a hypnotically-induced happy mood, they recalled it better when they were again in a happy mood. The same affect-state-dependent learning took place when a hypnotically-induced sad mood was the acquisition condition for learning.

Emotional states were also significant for recalling childhood memories: In a happy mood, subjects recalled more happy memories from childhood; in a sad mood, they recalled more sad memories. Bower's work demonstrates how emotions can generate state-bound information that is accessible by hypnotically-induced moods matching the acquisition condition in which the information was first encoded. Bowers formulated an "associative network theory of memory and emotion" to explain the "mood-state-dependent retrieval" that can be activated by physiological or symbolic verbal processes. Gazzaniga (1985) has discussed recent research in left and right cerebral hemispheric processes supporting the view that these associative "networks of the mind" can act as semiautonomous "modules" with many of the functional characteristics of the "unconscious" and with what we are calling here "state-bound information and behavior."

It is precisely in such interactions of the physiological and symbolic, demonstrated in the work of Bowers and Gazzaniga, that we recognize the type of mind-body connections most easily accessible by hypnosis. This experimental work, together with that of other investigators (Blum, 1967, 1972; Gage, 1983) thus provides a sound research base for the efficacy of therapeutic hypnosis, in which patients' associative networks and frames of reference are carefully accessed and utilized for resolving mind-body problems (Erickson & Rossi, 1979; Erickson, 1985).

ERICKSON'S HYPNOTIC INVESTIGATIONS OF PSYCHOSOMATIC PHENOMENA

Erickson's original contributions to the field of psychosomatic medicine are contained in four papers that were published together in the January 1943 issue of the journal *Psychosomatic Medicine* (1943a, b, c, d/1980). These papers on the *psychological* components of psychosomatic phenomena summarized the results of a decade of wide-ranging experimental and clinical hypnotic work that took place during the same time period when Selye was making his fundamental discovery of the *physiological* components. In a sense Erickson's and Selye's research was both complementary and reciprocal: Selye discovered the same physiological response to different stressors in what he termed the "General Adaptation Syndrome"; Erickson discovered psychologically different responses to the same stressor in what he termed "coincidental phenomena." Taken together, their work provides a comprehensive picture of the genesis and methods of resolving psychosomatic problems.

Viewed in isolation, Selye's work would imply that since different stressors all generate the same physiological syndrome (adrenal cortex enlargement, immune system suppression, and gastrointestinal tract ulceration), everyone should manifest the same physiological dysfunctions, whatever the source of stress (mental or physical). The fact that each individual actually manifests different physiological patterns indicates that there is another component to the stress response. This was called the "specific component" by Selye: It included the specifics of the physiological trauma (a knife wound and a burn both arouse the same GAS but each obviously has different physical and physiological features), as well as the psychological variations of those learned conditioned responses accumulated from the individual's life history. Selye, however, was silent on the subject of the dynamics of these conditioned psychological components. It is this unique pattern of psychologically conditioned responses within each individual (which makes up the state-dependent filter of Figure 1, p. 26) that Erickson explored in his studies of psychosomatic phenomena.

Erickson begins one of his early papers on the "Hypnotic Investigation of Psychosomatic Phenomena" with the following description of "coincidental phenomena" (1943c/1980):

> The purpose of this paper is to present an account of various psychosomatic interrelationships and interdependencies frequently encountered as *coincidental phenomena* during the course of hypnotic experimentation on normal subjects. . . . These *coincidental phenomena* are not those usual and expected changes in psychological, physiological, and somatic behavior that are essentially common to all hypnotic subjects in profound trances, such as alterations in reaction time, sensory thresholds, muscular tonus, and similar items of behavior. Rather, they are distinct from such psychosomatic manifestations of the hypnotic trance, and *they are in all probability expressive, not of the state of hypnosis itself, but of the interrelationships of hypnotically induced behavior and conditions* within the trance state. That is, after a profound trance state has first been secured, specific hypnotic instructions can then be given to the subject to elicit responses of a particular sort and in a chosen modality of behavior. *However, in addition to the behavior that is suggested, there may also be elicited, seem-*

ingly as coincidental manifestations, marked changes in one or another apparently unrelated modality of behavior. (pp. 145–146)

. . . Thus, for example, one subject rendered hypnotically deaf might show many changes in visual, motor, and other forms of behavior . . . while another subject rendered hypnotically color blind might show many disturbances of motor behavior but no changes in the auditory sphere. . . . Subjective feelings of nausea and vertigo invariably developed in one subject whenever a state of hypnotic deafness became well established for her. . . . Additionally she showed nystagmoid movements and pupillary dilation. . . . Another subject . . . with the onset of hypnotic deafness [experienced] an extensive anesthesia. Until this anesthesia was corrected he could not recover his hearing. . . . Several other subjects have shown a comparable inability to recover from induced behavior changes until the *coincidental developments* were first corrected. (pp. 148–149; Italics added)

. . . They [the coincidental developments] constitute essentially individual manifestations which occur under a wide variety of circumstances and many different associations. Furthermore they are not constant in their appearance for all subjects in the same situation. . . . However, the findings do tend to remain constant for the specific modality of behavior under investigation in the individual subject, although *repeated hypnotic experiences tend to lessen progressively the extent and duration of the phenomena likely to cause the subject discomfort.* (p. 146; italics added)

From the point of view developed in this section, we would characterize Erickson's "coincidental phenomena" as manifestations of the uniquely individual state-bound patterns of information and behavior that each person acquires as a result of his or her particular life history of experiential learning. These individual patterns are the basis of each person's unique repertory of hypnotic responsiveness, which can be utilized therapeutically. (These individual patterns may also be conceptualized as manifestations of the "creative unconscious" of each person.) When the person is subjected to undue stress over a period of time, these "coincidental phenomena" become the basis of the psychosomatic symptoms that express the experiential learnings encoded in the memory filters of the limbic system.

Erickson's finding that "repeated hypnotic experiences tend to lessen progressively the extent and duration of the [coincidental] phenomena likely to cause the subject [psychosomatic] discomfort" is the basis of one of his hypnotherapeutic approaches to mind/body dysfunctions. An example of Erickson's early use of this approach was presented in his paper called the "Hypnotic Investigation of Psychosomatic Phenomena: A Controlled Experimental Use of Hypnotic Regression in the Therapy of an Acquired Food Intolerance." A review of this case provides us with a clear example of how the state-dependent learning of a psychosomatic symptom and a phobic response (perhaps involving the autonomic nervous system, and especially the gastrointestinal component of Selye's GAS) can be resolved hypnotherapeutically (Erickson, 1943b/1980, p. 170):

> A subject in her early twenties was inordinately fond of orange juice and drank it at every opportunity. One day, because of gastrointestinal distress, she decided to try self-medication and proceeded to take castor oil, first mixing it with orange juice to disguise its taste. Unfortunately this concoction caused acute gastric distress: she became violently nauseated and she vomited repeatedly. Following this she went to bed. The next morning she felt much better and very hungry. She went to the kitchen to get her customary glass of orange juice. Quite unexpectedly she found that the sight, smell, and taste of orange juice caused immediate nausea and vomiting and she could not drink it.
>
> Instead of making a spontaneous recovery from this acute violent distaste for oranges, she continued to manifest it until it became almost phobic in character. She could not endure the thought of oranges in the refrigerator, and her family had to cease using them. Even the sight of oranges in fruit markets caused her to develop feelings of nausea.

Erickson reported that the origins of this conditioned gastrointestinal problem had another, highly emotionally charged determinant which resolved itself within a few days, and which he did not detail in his paper. The subject's conditioned distaste for orange juice persisted, however. This is very typical of psychosomatic problems and goes to the heart of the dilemma they present. The problem origins of a state-dependent pattern of memory and learning are often easily resolved, but the psychosomatic symptoms that they give rise to persist! The new dysfunctional pattern has become "functionally autonomous": It endures as a form of state-bound information and behavior that expresses itself independently and indeed frequently in seeming defiance of the conscious will/ego.

Because of the now-isolated character of the symptom, Erickson refused to treat it with direct hypnotic suggestion, even though the subject pleaded with him to do so. Instead he chose an indirect approach. At a social gathering one evening, the subject was persuaded by the guests to act as a hypnotic subject. Erickson then used her to demonstrate age regression, wherein she was reoriented to a period two years before she experienced her unfortunate association between orange juice, castor oil, and the highly charged emotional problem. After being in this age-regressed state for 20 minutes (a typical time period Erickson used to "set" a deeply somnambulistic hypnotic trance), she was able to join the guests in drinking orange juice without any adverse reaction. At no time was she given any direct suggestions to ameliorate or resolve her symptom. She was merely provided with an opportunity to drink orange juice, and she did so with pleasure. She was then awakened from trance with an amnesia for all that had taken place. During the remainder of the evening, "her facial expression was frequently puzzled and reflective, and she kept rolling her tongue about her mouth and passing it gently over her lips as if she were trying to sense some elusive taste." Several days later the subject reported that she had somehow "spontaneously unconditioned" herself and had regained her original liking for orange juice.

The salient feature of this case is how Erickson's indirect approach enabled the subject to reexperience her original liking for orange juice in an age-regressed state without interference from her learned negative gastrointestinal response. From the state-dependent memory and learning point of view, we would say that her age-regressed state-of-being bypassed the gastrointestinal symptom that was learned in a later state-of-being. When she was to once more experience her original liking for orange juice, the symptom was depotentiated or unconditioned (Rossi, 1973/1980; Erickson & Rossi, 1976/1980) without any interference from her conscious mind's negative expectation.

This form of hypnotherapy is very different from the classical approach of using direct suggestion to "command away" or inhibit a symptom. Erickson's indirect approach utilizes the mind's own naturalistic means of self-healing, without the intrusion of direct suggestions that could only be expressive of the therapist's limited view of how the cure "should" take place. The therapy takes place not by a hypnotic command imprinted on the subject's mind, but by circumventing what Erickson called "learned limitations" and accessing therapeutic response potentials that already exist within the subject. In this case, the learned limitation was a clear example of "a state-bound pattern of information and behavior" that encoded a distressing symptom which interfered with the subject's original response of enjoying orange juice. Erickson's indirect approach via age regression accessed her state-bound symptom in a permissive manner that allowed her own creative resources to do the actual healing. Later, I will provide additional case examples of how this type of therapeutic hypnosis can be more adequately conceptualized from our psychobiological perspective rather than from the traditional but misleading perspective of hypnosis as a programming of mind and behavior. Indeed, Erickson characterized programming as a "very uninformed way" of attempting to do hypnotherapy (Erickson & Rossi, 1979, p. 288).

In a little known or appreciated early paper on the nature of hypnotic psychotherapy, Erickson (1948/1980) outlined his rationale for a radically new concept of "trance" as a period of creative reorganization. He states it as follows (p. 38):

> The induction and maintenance of a trance serve to provide a *special psychological state in which the patient can reassociate and reorganize his inner psychological complexities* and utilize his own capacities in a manner in accord with his own experiential life. . . . Therapy results from an *inner resynthesis* of the patient's behavior achieved by the patient himself. It's true that direct suggestion can effect an alteration in the patient's behavior and result in a symptomatic cure, at least temporarily. However, such a "cure" is simply a response to suggestion and does not entail that reassociation and reorganization of ideas, understandings and memories so essential for actual cure. *It is this experience of reassociating and reorganizing his own experiential life that eventuates in a cure,* not the manifestation of responsive behavior which can, at best, satisfy only the observer.

Let us now turn our attention to a more detailed exposition of this creative approach to the reassociation and reorganization of mind-body problems, which I have described as a new language of mind-body communication and therapeutic hypnosis (Rossi, 1987).

5

The New Language of
Mind-Body Communication

IN THIS CHAPTER WE will focus on effective approaches for facilitating mind-body communication. We will learn how words, phrases, questions, and a variety of search strategies can access the problems encoded in state-bound memory and make information available for self-help. These approaches are all explorations of how we can best actualize human potential rather than manipulate and control behavior. Our work does *not* involve overt or covert conditioning, "influence communication," or programming. We do not even use "suggestion" in the conventional sense of putting an idea into another person's mind. Rather, we simply access state-dependent memory, learning, and behavior systems and make their encoded information available for problem-solving. The locus for control of the healing process remains within the patient at all times. The therapist is a facilitator, guide, and consultant.

Insofar as it is possible, we will always use the patient's own words, attitudes, and world view as the most desired route to accessing the problem areas. Our approaches are usually problem-centered because "problems" are paths to the person's "growing edge." Symptoms are often signals of the need for personal development. All of our therapeutic approaches actively involve the patients in taking action, even in the first session, that will move them quickly to better coping skills and a position of self-efficacy.

EVERY ACCESS IS A REFRAME

The basic premise for all the approaches outlined in this book is, "*Every access is a reframe.*" Each time we access the state-dependent memory, learning, and behavior processes that encode a problem, we have an opportunity to "reassociate and reorganize" or *reframe* that problem in a manner that resolves it. This premise is based upon the recent research in memory, learning, and cognition that was examined previously (Chapter 3; Lynch, McGaugh, & Weinberger, 1984). Memory does not operate like a tape recorder in which we simply play back exactly what we learned. Memory is always a constructive process whereby we actually synthesize a new subjective experience every time we recall a past event. Pribram (1986) expresses this active synthetic process of memory as follows:

> Images and other mental contents as such are not stored, nor are they "localized" in the brain. Rather, by virtue of the operation of the local brain circuitry, usually with the aid of sensory input from the environment, images and mental events emerge and are *constructed*. A similar mechanism involving the motor mechanisms of the brain can account for intentional, planned behavior. The evidence that such a mechanism exists is presented in *Languages of the Brain* and elsewhere (Pribram, 1971, 1976; Pribram et al., 1981). Much of my laboratory research has been involved in demonstrating that *brain function is active, not passive*, in its interactions with environment and elucidating the processes operative in this active aspect of mind. This research has shown that the *intrinsic cortex and limbic formations of the forebrain actively organize sensory input*, etc. (see review by Pribram, 1980). (Italics added)

Mind and nature are in constant change and creative flux. It is irritating to us when our memories of the same event are different from those of another person, and when even our memories change over time. These entirely natural differences and changes are the despair of our courts of law, which are based upon the rather naive view of a constant, unchanging, objective reality where "facts are facts" rather than the subjective constructions of our own minds. The law requires that a witness repeat the same story in the same way every time. The natural mind, by contrast, tends to repeat the same story with variations, seemingly seeking to constantly update and reframe "reality" in keeping with the new information and views it is spontaneously generating.

What is the despair of the law, however, is the opportunity of the psychologist! When the mind naturally reviews memories from slightly different perspectives, for example, it is spontaneously engaged in constructing alternate realities. This spontaneous construction of alternate realities has survival value in a constantly changing environment. People who do not recognize, welcome, and integrate these spontaneous changes are condemned to living an uncreative existence in an outmoded past (Rossi,

1972/1985). Most of us are unaware of how strongly we have been programmed to live in this way. We struggle in vain to preserve our past way of thinking, feeling, and doing until a symptom or problem becomes manifest evidence of our lack of adaptation to the current and ongoing changes that are taking place. Our symptom or problem is then our best guide to where "inner work" needs to be done to readapt and recreate ourselves. Each time we mentally review (access) what our problem is about, we can depend upon our mind to spontaneously reframe it in a slightly different way as it seeks an answer.

THREE-STEP ROUTINES FOR PROBLEM-SOLVING

At the Evolution of Psychotherapy Congress in Phoenix, Arizona, it was estimated that there are now over 300 different forms of psychotherapy (Rossi, 1987). All these therapies facilitate mind-body communication and healing to some degree. One could get lost in their bewildering complexities by trying to focus on all the nuances of difference between them. On the other hand, they all share the same three-step routine for problem-solving:

1) Therapist and patient initiate a communication process together;
2) They engage in some sort of therapeutic work; and
3) They hopefully have some criteria for problem resolution so they know when to discontinue the interaction.

In traditional hypnotherapy, the three steps go somewhat as follows:

1) Establish trust and rapport;
2) Offer therapeutic suggestions for creative inner work; and
3) "Wake up" the patient and ratify the resolution of the problem (Erickson & Rossi, 1979).

If the problem is not resolved, then carry out the same three steps again in another way, perhaps using different suggestions and patterns of inner work based upon what was learned from the first effort. The process is iterative: You do the three steps over and over, each time learning more about the patient's inner condition and resources, which then can be facilitated with greater effectiveness the next time around.

The three-step routines presented in this chapter range from the simple to the complex. They are easy to learn in the order in which they are presented, since experience with each builds the therapeutic skills needed to do the next one effectively. All of the routines are variations of a *basic accessing formula*, to which we will now turn our attention.

The Basic Accessing Formula

The essence of all the therapeutic approaches in this chapter can be found in what may be called the basic accessing formula. Hypnotherapists have used this formula in one way or another for centuries. It was analyzed and formulated by Erickson and Rossi (1976/1980) as the "implied directive." The basic accessing formula is fundamentally different from all previous forms of direct authoritarian suggestion in that it does not involve imprinting, conditioning, or programming the subject with the therapist's view of how problem-solving should take place. Rather, the accessing formula simply provides a framework for the patient's accessing of the state-bound encoding of his or her problem and facilitates information transduction so that inner healing can take place.

The basic accessing formula may be expressed in many different ways, but it always has three standard parts:

1) A time-binding introduction that initiates an inner search of state-dependent memory, learning, and behavior systems;
2) Accessing and transduction of the state-bound problems and symptoms;
3) An observable behavioral response signaling when the process of accessing and therapeutic transduction is completed.

When the patient responds to this inner accessing formula by quieting down and closing the eyes, we have an observable behavioral response indicating that inner work is taking place. This is an entirely natural and easily accepted approach to inner problem-solving, because it utilizes the typical everyday process we all experience when we turn inward momentarily to figure out how to deal with an issue. This expression of the accessing formula introduces and facilitates a process of reviewing memories associated with the problem. As will be seen, there are many expressions of the accessing formula that can facilitate new learning, the reframing of outmoded ideas, and the channeling of self-expression in more adequate ways for problem-solving.

Research on creative thinking (Rossi, 1972/1985) has demonstrated that the essence of the new is usually generated within us on an unconscious level. The conscious mind simply receives the new idea and subjects it to validation and integration with previous patterns of understanding. The

---

BOX 2 Basic Accessing Formula

1. *Time-binding introduction initiating inner search*
   As soon as your inner mind [creative unconscious, spiritual guide, etc.] knows

2. *Accessing state-bound sources of problem*
   that you can review some important memories related to the source of that problem,

3. *Observable behavioral signal of problem-solving*
   you will feel yourself getting more comfortable as your eyes close [the observable behavioral response] to review them.

---

basic accessing formula structures an opportunity for something new to happen on an unconscious level at the source of creativity. It is a way of focusing a patient's mental resources (e.g., state-dependent memories, sensory-perceptual associations, emotions, habits, and various patterns of learning, etc.) and directing them toward a creative state of problem-solving. Recent research in the neurobiology of learning (Rosenzweig & Bennett, 1984) suggests that new proteins are synthesized in appropriate brain cells during learning. We may speculate that the various forms of the accessing formula outlined in this and the following chapters actually "facilitate the internal synthesis of new protein structures that could function as the biological basis of new behavior and phenomenal experience" (Erickson, Rossi, & Rossi, 1976).

Let us now examine in detail some of the variations of the basic accessing formula that are particularly useful for clinical problems.

Accessing State-bound Resources for Problem-Solving

This general three-stage approach to problem-solving by accessing the patient's inner resources was originally described by Erickson and Rossi (1979, pp. 1–14) as a basic model for therapeutic hypnosis. It is being generalized here into a procedure that is useful for a wide range of problems that patients can resolve for themselves during a period of "inner work."

Stage 1: Readiness Signal for Inner Work. In this first stage of the approach, the therapist asks the patient to review the history and nature of the problem. This review begins *the activity of accessing and spontaneous reframing* that is characteristic of all memory processes. This review thus initiates the actual process of therapy, even though the patient may believe the problem is "only being talked about." In the positive atmosphere generated by the empathic therapeutic transaction, the patient will often experience a spontaneous partial remission of the symptom, or may gain some insights into how the problem might be resolved. These initial therapeutic explorations are, of course, supported by the therapist, who helps the patient recognize how the "inner mind" or "creative unconscious" is in a constant state of inner work, during which it is attempting, and even now succeeding with, various parts of the total problem-solving process. The patient is encouraged further, for example, by reviewing earlier life situations in which the patient or an acquaintance may have solved a similar problem.

The first stage of this approach reaches its climax when a positive therapeutic framework has been established and the patient now looks expectantly to the therapist for an "answer." The answer is supplied by introducing the patient to an internal problem-solving process, somewhat as follows:

> **"Now that you are ready to continue therapy on an even deeper level, you can begin by simply becoming more sensitive to yourself. [Pause]**
>
> **"When a deep part of your inner mind knows it can resolve that problem [pause],** *you will find yourself getting more and more comfortable, and your eyes will close."*

In the typical therapy situation, the patient already has sufficient cultural frames of reference to support this expectation that creative problem-solving can be initiated by a relaxed process of inner work and reflection. When the patient does, in fact, make a few bodily adjustments to get comfortable, and does, in fact, close the eyes as directed, the therapist has the observable behavioral responses indicating that the ideal internal psychobiological conditions for inner healing are being set in motion.

The phrase "getting more and more comfortable" is more than just a cliché—it initiates a shift in autonomic system balance from sympathetic toward parasympathetic dominance. It lowers the patient's overall psychobiological level of arousal (ARAS), as the proprioceptive and kin-

---

BOX 3 Accessing State-Bound Resources for Problem-Solving

1. *Readiness signal for inner work*
   When a deep part of your inner mind knows it can resolve that problem [pause], you will feel yourself getting more and more comfortable, and your eyes will close.

2. *Accessing and transducing state-bound resources*
   Now your inner mind can continue working all by itself to solve that problem in a manner that fully meets all your needs. [Pause]
   There are memories, life experiences, and abilities that your inner mind can use in many ways you may not have realized before.

3. *Ratifying problem-solving*
   When your inner mind knows that it can continue to deal effectively with that problem, you will find yourself wanting to move a bit [pause], and you will open your eyes and come fully alert.

---

esthetic input from all of the body muscles diminish. This tends to shift attention away from irrelevant external stimuli toward the internal state-dependent memory, learning, and behavioral systems that need to be engaged for problem-solving. Closing the eyes immediately enhances alpha wave (and eventually theta wave) generation in the brain, which is associated with creative sensing, feeling, and imagistic experience. This, in turn, means we have facilitated a shift from the rational and linear processes of left-hemispheric thinking toward the more primary, holistic processing characteristic of the right hemisphere, with its closer associations to the mind-body, limbic-hypothalamic information transduction system.

Instead of relaxing, closing the eyes, and turning inward, however, a patient may occasionally become more restless or distressed and alert. This indicates that the ideal therapeutic conditions for the first stage have not been met yet, suggesting that there may be another issue the patient needs to deal with before the creative process of problem resolution can begin. The therapist needs to reengage the patient with exploratory questions, somewhat as follows:

"I wonder if there are any other questions or problems you need to deal with first, before you do the inner work?"

This carefully worded exploratory question contains an important *implication*: The patient *will do* the inner work after first dealing with whatever other issue remains (Erickson & Rossi, 1979, 1980; Erickson, Rossi, & Rossi, 1976). This implication is also an instruction that facilitates the planning function of the prefrontal cortex. The creative inner work is being carefully organized and sequenced to follow whatever other issue remains. Once this has been accomplished, the therapist can again offer the *readiness signal for inner work*:

"When a deep part of your inner mind knows it can resolve that problem [pause], *you will feel yourself getting more and more comfortable, and your eyes will close."*

The first stage of establishing the readiness signal for inner work is thus an iterative therapeutic procedure: It is done over and over again, so as to immediately resolve any issue that interrupts the process of turning inward for a comfortable period of problem-solving. When the patient finally goes into comfort with eyes closed, the therapist can proceed with the second stage.

Stage 2: Accessing State-bound Resources. After the patient's eyes close, the therapist can allow a quiet period of inner work to proceed entirely on its own. It is valuable to carefully observe the patient during this brief period of time. Many different patterns of responsiveness may be evident. Sometimes the patient's eyelids flutter a bit just as they close, as is characteristic of a classical hypnotic induction. Occasionally the eyeballs will roll upward and/or squint toward the nose as the eyelids close. These movements have been cited by some (Spiegel & Spiegel, 1978) as an indication of a capacity for deep trance. After the eyes are closed, the eyelids may undergo momentary bursts of rapid, fine, vertical vibratory movements that may indicate the accessing of state-bound inner processes. Sometimes there are rapid left and right horizontal movements that suggest an inner landscape is being actively observed. Occasionally there may be large, slow, rolling movements of the eyeballs under the closed eyelids (Weitzenhoffer, 1971), which are again suggestive of deep states of altered experience. These eyelid movements all indicate that the patient is engaged in a search process which is ideal for this stage of inner work.

Sometimes the patient evidences simple quietude with no movements at all. Indeed, there seems to be an inverse relationship between the quality of inner work taking place and the degree of outer bodily activity (Erickson & Rossi, 1981).

The therapist may occasionally question patients about their inner experience when they manifest these different patterns of behavior. So little experimental research has been done in this area that we do not always know what individual patterns of response provide useful information about the therapeutic process. In any case, when the patient has been engaged in an inner process of self-involvement for a few minutes, we are ready for the second stage of *accessing and transducing state-bound resources*, that is supported somewhat as follows:

> **"Now** *your inner mind can continue working all by itself* **to solve that problem in a manner that fully meets all of your needs.** *[Pause]*
> *"There are memories, life experiences, and abilities that your inner mind can use in many ways you may not have realized before."*

These apparently casual statements contain implications that facilitate the problem-solving process in subtle ways. The clause, "Your inner mind can continue working all by itself," implies that there is a developing *dissociation* between the consciously driven activity of typical left-hemispheric thinking, in which one is engaged in willfully directing one's thoughts, and the self-organizing and autonomous primary process of the right cerebral hemisphere. There is a subtle depotentiation of the conscious mind's typical frames of reference and habitual patterns of activity (that may be reinforcing the problem), and a reinforcement of the more autonomous primary processing that holds the promise of creative problem-solving.

The second sentence, "There are memories, life experiences, and abilities that your inner mind can use in many ways you may not have realized before," is a means of accessing and transducing state-dependent memory, learning, and behavior systems that now need to be engaged for problem-solving. Ideally, patients should receive this most important facilitation in their own words, and in terms that are congruent with their personal belief systems.

Table 3 lists a variety of cognitive, emotional, sensory-perceptual, and behavioral signs that are indicative of significant involvement in the inner work of accessing and reframing the state-dependent memory and learning systems that encode problems. It is valuable to recognize these signs because they indicate when patients may be more available for therapeutic

TABLE 3 A partial listing of cognitive, emotional, sensory-perceptual, and behavioral signs of significant involvement with inner work and state-dependent phenomena.

Blushing or blanching of face	Sensory-perceptual distortions
Comfort, relaxation	Sleep stages
Emotional responses	Spontaneous altered state phenomena
Economy of movement	Age regression
Eyeball changes	Amnesia
Eyelid changes and closure	Anesthesia
Facial features relaxed	Catalepsy
Feeling distant (dissociated)	Hallucinations
Literalism	Illusions
Movements slow or absent	Time distortion
Retardation of blinking, startle, and swallowing reflexes	Speech minimal or absent
	Stretching
Pulse slowing	Tears
Pupillary changes	Time lag in motor and conceptual behavior
Respiration slowing	
Response attentiveness	Vocal changes
Sensory, muscular, and body changes	Yawning

This table is an adaptation of the "Indicators of Trance Development" in Erickson, Rossi, and Rossi, 1976.

change. When patients are in tears, for example, they are experiencing particular emotional states that will enable them to respond to questions and therapeutic approaches in a certain, often healing manner. A deeper state of relaxation or therapeutic catalepsy (outer body immobility with correspondingly intense inner work) can obviously enable some patients to be more receptive to those state-bound feelings, impulses, images, and ideas that can be of therapeutic value in helping them reframe their dominant but problem-plagued ways of thinking and being.

Stage 3: Ratifying Problem-Solving. The third stage of ratifying problem-solving and ending the therapeutic session is, like the first two stages, made dependent upon the patient's inner responsiveness to the therapist's "implied directives." When the therapist senses that a satisfactory amount of therapeutic work has been accomplished, this third stage may be initiated somewhat as follows:

"When your inner mind knows that you have resolved that problem to the fullest extent at this time, and that you can deal effec-

**tively with it, you will find yourself wanting to move a bit. [Pause]
"You will open your eyes and come fully alert."**

The patient usually stretches and readjusts his posture when the eyes
open. This spontaneous body reorientation is in part a response to the
therapist's words ("You will find yourself wanting to move"), and in part
an entirely natural and spontaneous orientation to state-dependent modes
of "normal" social relatedness in the world. Patients who have a talent
for experiencing deeper altered states traditionally associated with therapeutic hypnosis will often comment how they have been "out," "far
away," "really into it," "in a trance," or "felt drugged or hypnotized."
The world may seem brighter for a moment or two. There may even be
a sense of a loss or enhancement of the third dimension: The world seems
flatter or deeper for a few minutes. All these spontaneous reports of
altered states are accepted as an entirely natural and positive indication
of effective inner work; they are, as noted above, all indications of a deep
accessing of state-dependent phenomena that may be reframed for therapeutic change.

The patient usually makes some spontaneous remarks about the inner
experience and the constructive symptom/problem changes that have
taken place. This is entirely in keeping with the manner in which this third
stage of ratifying the therapeutic work was initiated with the words,
"When your inner mind knows that it can continue to deal effectively with
that problem, *you will find yourself wanting to move a bit.* [Pause] And you
will open your eyes and come fully alert."

These words imply that there will be no impulse to move until an increased ability to cope with the problem has been experienced. This implication, like all the other implications, gives the patient's unconscious
processes free choice—in this case, the freedom to complete the inner work
in its own way and make its own choice about when movement and
awakening will take place.

The phrase, "When your inner mind knows that it can continue to deal
effectively with that problem," contains a creative ambiguity that again
allows the patient's unconscious to make the most suitable choice in line
with its own best ways of functioning: It may have been able to completely
resolve the problem "here and now" in the therapy session, or it may
have to continue active inner therapeutic work after the session has ended.
Creative ambiguity facilitates free choice! We all function on many levels;
while apparently living our normal lives on one level and playing out
certain roles, we can be engaged in intense inner creative work and self-
reorganization on levels that are preparing for new roles and activities in
the future.

Incubating Mind-Body Healing

This variation of the Basic Accessing Formula derives from a number of different sources. Philosophers such as Vaihinger (1911) and the constructivists (Watzlawick, 1984) discuss the use of imagination via the "as-if" phenomena and self-fulfilling prophecies in the formation of our experiential reality and "fate." We are the victims of fate when we allow our unconscious, via its own autonomous creative process, to construct our future. If we have little or no relationship to these unconscious processes, we have no say in the construction of our future. We can take a hand in the construction of our future with inner work, however. Erickson, for example, developed what he called "pseudo-orientation in time" as a method whereby patients could generate their own futures by accessing and facilitating inner possibilities that existed only in embryonic form. Some clinicians are currently exploring the use of imaging as a major modality for facilitating the realization of positive self-fulfilling prophecies (Achterberg, 1985; Shorr, Sobel, Robin, & Connella, 1980) in mind-body healing. Other investigators are using other modalities, such as the "felt sense," which Gendlin (1978) describes as the essence of psychotherapeutic change.

Our approach is to utilize as many modalities of mind-body information transduction as are available to the individual. The accessing formula for *incubating mind-body healing* is an adaptation of Mills and Crowley's "Inner Resource Drawings" (1986), a drawing strategy they use with children. In their approach, the child is asked to draw (1) the problem as it is currently experienced; (2) the problem when it is resolved; and (3) how to get from the first to the second drawing. In work with adults, I have modified this approach by utilizing suggestion to stimulate an inner search in these three areas.

In the second half of this book, we will explore some of the physiological pathways by which these mind-body healing processes take place. From a psychobiological point of view, we may suppose that this accessing formula draws upon the imaginative and planning functions of the prefrontal cortex, as well as visually stored images of inner resources and problem-solving routines that may be encoded in previously inaccessible state-bound patterns. The frequent experience of emotional release that accompanies the insights and forgotten memories that come "spontaneously" to consciousness during this three-step routine are the typical signs of having accessed and therapeutically reframed state-bound patterns of memory, learning, and behavior. The psychological reorientation to a future when the problem is solved apparently adds a novel stimulus and therapeutic frame of reference that enables patients to break out of the

---

BOX 4 Incubating Mind-Body Healing

1. *Readiness signal for present problem review*
   When your inner mind is ready to review all aspects of that problem as you are currently experiencing it [pause], you'll find yourself getting more comfortable and your eyes will close. [Pause]
   Review, especially, all parts of it you don't know how to deal with yet.

2. *Incubating current and future healing*
   Now explore the future healing possibilities. How do you see yourself? How do you feel? What are you doing now that the problem is completely healed? [Pause]
   Now let your inner mind review how you are going to get from the present problem [pause]
   to the future when you are healed. [Pause]
   What are some of the steps you will take to facilitate your healing? [Pause]

3. *Ratifying mind-body healing*
   When your inner mind knows it can continue the healing process entirely on its own, and when your conscious mind knows it can cooperate with this healing [pause],
   you will find yourself stretching, opening your eyes, and feeling refreshed as you come fully alert.

"present problem frame" that has limited their access to their own inner resources.

Symptom Scaling and Prescription

This variation of the basic accessing formula introduces two new approaches: (1) *scaling* the currently experienced intensity of a problem by attaching a numerical value to it; and (2) *prescribing the symptom or problem,* whereby the patient is directed to carry out the seemingly paradoxical task of voluntarily making it worse. Our psychobiological orientation suggests that scaling may be a method of coordinating the languages and activities of the left and right cerebral hemispheres in relation to a problem. The right hemisphere may encode a problem in the analogical-metaphorical processes typical of emotions, body language, and dreams. In this form the problem may not be available to the more linear, logical and rational resolution routines of the left hemisphere. These left hemispheric processes may be accessed and associated with the problem by scaling it, since the left hemisphere is more facile with both numbers and words such as "more or less intense, better and worse."

By asking patients to *experience* the problem, we are presumably turning on right-hemispheric processes that have a readier access to the state-dependent encoding of the problem. By simultaneously asking patients to *scale* the problem, we are presumably activating and focusing more consciously directed left-hemispheric skills on the problem. By then asking patients "to make the problem worse and better" a number of times in fairly rapid succession, we are presumably asking them to coordinate left and right cerebral hemispheric activity in getting more and more experience in accessing and controlling the problem's experiential and behavioral manifestations.

A currently evolving principle of left-right hemispheric interaction is that some functions that are apparently indigenous in beginning their development in the right hemisphere gradually acquire supraordinate controls in the left hemisphere. The average person who simply enjoys listening to music, for example, utilizes predominantly the right hemisphere in this

---

BOX 5 Scaling the Symptom or Problem

1. *Symptom scaling and prescription*
   On a scale of 1 to 100, where 100 is the worst, what number expresses the degree to which you are experiencing that problem at this moment? Scale it right now.

2. *Problem prescription*
   Now let the problem get worse. Scale it. Now let the problem get better. Scale it. Etc.

3. *Ratifying the therapeutic response*
   [This therapeutic exercise is ended when the patient has made an obvious therapeutic gain by lowering the original scaling score of the problem, and by expressing confidence in being able to continue practicing this problem-solving routine for better and better resolution in the future.]

activity. A professional musician, however, has left-hemispheric dominance when occupied with music (Mazziotta, Phelps, Carson, & Kuhl, 1982; Phelps & Mazziotta, 1985). We could hypothesize that a patient who scales and rehearses a symptom that was originally encoded in the right hemisphere could be developing left-hemispheric control as he develops expertise in turning the symptom on and off. This would lead to the prediction that Positron Emission Tomography would find a shift from right- to left-hemispheric dominance as patients rehearsed and gradually gained control over problematic behavior. We would expect to find the same right-left hemispheric shift in subjects who learned to control symptoms via biofeedback.

Paradoxical Therapy. The so-called paradoxical aspects of this approach of problem and/or symptom prescription deserve further comment since paradox has generated so much interest recently as a new form of therapy (Seltzer, 1985; Weeks & L'Abate, 1982; Zeig, 1980a, b). From our psychobiological point of view, paradoxical therapy is not paradoxical at all: As we have seen, to prescribe a problem or symptom is actually the most direct path to accessing its psychobiological sources encoded within the state-dependent memory, learning, and behavior systems of the brain. Paradoxical therapy only seems paradoxical from a logical point of view wherein patients try to avoid the experience and expression of a problem in the hope that it will thereby "go away." Avoiding, resisting, or blocking a problem, however, only prevents one from accessing and therapeutically reframing it. When a problem or symptom "haunts" a patient, it is only because mind and nature are attempting to bring it up to consciousness so it can be resolved.

As was indicated earlier, research in the neurobiology of memory and learning indicates that the process of accessing and recall is not simply that—accessing and recall are always a synthetic process of reconstruction. As such, prescribing the symptom is actually a process of reconstructing it. When we ask a person to experience a symptom voluntarily rather than resisting it, we are drastically altering the internal dynamics and state-dependent memory and learning systems that allow the symptom to flourish. We have changed it from a dissociated and involuntary action to a voluntary action; we are undoing its state-bound character. When we ask a person to scale the intensity of the symptom, we are changing it further by adding a *novel, conscious, evaluative orientation* to it. This new evaluative orientation immediately potentiates problem-solving processes; it facilitates coping skills and self-efficacy; and the patient's ego is strengthened in its relationship to the formerly dissociated symptom.

The clinical effectiveness of these paradoxical approaches is supported by the fact that they are now used by so many different schools of psychotherapy (wherein they have been given different names). Most theorists in these different schools have expressed a sense of puzzlement as to why these approaches work, however. Since the paradoxical approaches make such exquisite sense from our psychobiological perspective, it may be worthwhile to review the many names and formulations that have been given to them. Our psychobiological approach may be seen as a common denominator underlying all the following (Seltzer, 1985, p. 20):

> From the psychoanalytic perspective, which includes the work of paradigmatic psychotherapists, we have inherited the descriptors "antisuggestion," "going with the resistance," "joining the resistance," "reflecting (or 'mirroring') the resistance," "siding with the resistance," "paradigmatic exaggeration," "supporting the defenses," "reductio ad absurdum," "reenacting an aspect of the psychosis," "mirroring the patient's distortions," "participating in the patient's fantasies," "out-crazying the patient," and "the use of the patient as consultant." From the vantage point of behavior therapy, we may appreciate paradoxical elements in such procedures as "blowup," "implosion," "flooding," "instructed helplessness," "massed practice," "negative practice," "paradoxical intention," "stimulus satiation," and "symptom scheduling." In gestalt therapy, an approach where the actual term "paradox" is rarely employed, the attempt to foster change paradoxically may be recognized in the therapist's cruel-to-be-kind suggestions to "stay with the [negative] experience," or to "exaggerate the feeling" (sensation, experience, speech, movement, etc.). Lastly, in the communication-systems school of therapy—by far the most vocal in endorsing and elucidating paradoxical strategies—we have the following miscellany of terms and titles: "the confusion technique," "declaring hopelessness," "exaggerating the position," "paradoxical injunction," "paradoxical instructions," "paradoxical rituals and tasks," "paradoxical written messages," "restraining (or 'inhibiting') change," "predicting a relapse," "prescribing a relapse," "positive connotation" (or "interpretation"), "reframing," "redefinition," and "relabeling," "symptom prescription" (or "prescribing the resistance, symptom or system"), "therapeutic paradox," and the "therapeutic double bind." R.P. Greenberg, in an article intriguingly subtitled, "The Power of Negative Thinking" (1973), refers generally to several of the above methods as "anti-expectation techniques," which should

serve as a reminder of the point made earlier that the paradoxical essence of all these methods is in their apparent irrationality *from the perspective of the client*.

Our simplified approach to "scaling and problem prescription" may be enriched by the special points of view and vocabulary of all these ways of accessing and therapeutically reframing symptoms and problems.

Information Channeling and Transduction

Psychoanalysis seeks to resolve symptoms and problems by analysis; behaviorism deals with them by conditioning and extinction. Our psychobiological approach seeks to channel and transduce symptoms and problems into creativity. An infinite range of therapeutic creativity and healing can be explored via the ideodynamic channeling and transduction of symptoms and problems. All of the sensory-perceptual modalities are involved: vision and imagery, audition, proprioception-kinesthesia, smell, taste, and all possible combinations of these as they are expressed in significant aspects of mind-body communication and human identity. Box 6 illustrates some of the basic channels for the transduction of a number of these state-dependent modalities.

In Chapter 2 we touched upon Bernheim's original formulation of the *ideodynamic* as the basic mechanism of information transduction in hypnosis. In Chapter 4 we reviewed Erickson's hypnotic investigations of "coincidental phenomena" as spontaneous occurrences of intermodal sensory transformations in the etiology of psychosomatic symptoms. Mishkin's memory and learning research (1982) reviewed in Chapter 3, as well as current investigations in the "multichannel integrations of nonverbal behavior" (Siegman & Feldstein, 1985), provides a new experimental research base for studying how information is transmitted, transduced, and sometimes "stuck" in a state-bound form so that it becomes what people ordinarily label as a problem or a symptom.

C.G. Jung was one of the early explorers in depth psychology who used intermodal information transduction as a therapeutic method. He called this process of integrating conscious and unconscious elements the "transcendent function" (Jung, 1960, pp. 67–91). When Jung's patients became overwhelmed with emotions, he sometimes would have them draw a picture of their feelings. Once the feelings were expressed in the form of imagery, the images could be encouraged to speak to one another. As soon as a dialogue could take place, the patient was well embarked on the pro-

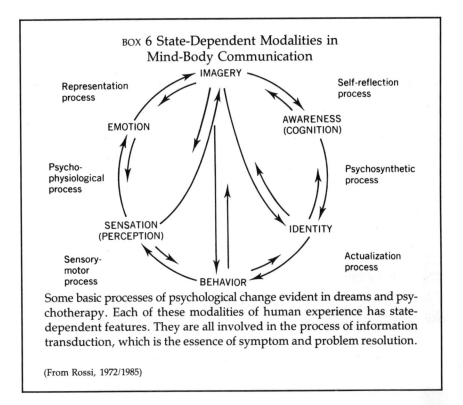

BOX 6 State-Dependent Modalities in
Mind-Body Communication

Some basic processes of psychological change evident in dreams and psychotherapy. Each of these modalities of human experience has state-dependent features. They are all involved in the process of information transduction, which is the essence of symptom and problem resolution.

(From Rossi, 1972/1985)

cess of reconciling different aspects of his dissociated psyche. Jung described his approach as follows (Jung, 1960, pp. 81–83):

> *In the intensity of the emotional disturbance itself lies the value, the energy which he should have at his disposal in order to remedy the state of reduced adaptation.* Nothing is achieved by repressing this state or devaluing it rationally.
>
> In order, therefore, to gain possession of the energy that is in the wrong place, he must make the emotional state the basis or starting point of the procedure. He must make himself as conscious as possible of the mood he is in, sinking himself in it without reserve and noting down on paper all the fantasies and other associations that come up. Fantasy must be allowed the freest possible play. . . .
>
> The whole procedure is a kind of enrichment and clarification of

the affect, whereby the affect and its content are brought nearer to consciousness, becoming at the same time more impressive and more understandable. This work by itself can have a favourable and vitalizing influence. At all events, it creates a new situation, since the previously unrelated affect has become a more or less clear and articulate idea, thanks to the assistance and cooperation of the conscious mind. *This is the beginning of the transcendent function, i.e., of the collaboration of conscious and unconscious data.*

The emotional disturbance can also be dealt with in another way, not by clarifying it intellectually but by giving it visible shape. Patients who possess some talent for drawing or painting can give expression to their mood by means of a picture. . . . Visual types should concentrate on the expectation that an inner image will be produced. As a rule such a fantasy-picture will actually appear— perhaps hypnogogcially—and should be carefully observed and noted down in writing. Audio-verbal types usually hear inner words, perhaps mere fragments of apparently meaningless sentences to begin with, which however should be carefully noted down too. . . . Such persons have little difficulty in procuring the unconscious material and thus laying the foundation of the transcendent function.

There are others, again, who neither see nor hear anything inside themselves, but whose hands have the knack of giving expression to the contents of the unconscious. Such people can profitably work with plastic materials. Those who are able to express the unconscious by means of bodily movements are rather rare. The disadvantage that movements cannot easily be fixed in the mind must be met by making careful drawings of the movements afterwards, so that they shall not be lost to the memory. Still rarer, but equally valuable, is automatic writing, direct or with the planchette. This too, yields useful results.

We now come to the next question: what is to be done with the material obtained in one of the manners described? To this question there is no *a priori* answer; it is only when the conscious mind confronts the products of the unconscious that a provisional reaction will ensue which determines the subsequent procedure. Practical experience alone can give us a clue. So far as my experience goes, there appear to be two main tendencies. One is the way of *creative formulation*, the other the way of *understanding*. (Italics in original)

This quotation comes from Jung's paper, "The Transcendent Function," which he worked on for 40 years (between 1916 and 1957) before he consented to its publication. One could say that it represents the essence of his psychotherapeutic methodology. From the psychobiological point of view being formulated in this book, I would say that Jung is describing a process of channeling and transducing into consciousness the state-bound information that encodes symptoms and problems by ''whatever sensory-perceptual-expressive modality is most natural to the patient.'' His methods can be seen as the generally unrecognized forerunners of the use of similar techniques in gestalt therapy, transactional analysis, cognitive and behavior therapy, psychosynthesis, and all the more recent forms of analogy and metaphor in Ericksonian psychotherapy (Lankton & Lankton, 1983; Mills & Crowley, 1986; Zeig, 1985).

The ideodynamic channeling and transduction of problems and symptoms are thus the psychobiological basis of a wide variety of current forms of psychotherapy. Because of this, most schools of psychotherapy can easily utilize the accessing formulas outlined in this and the following chapters. The first stage in this approach is to identify the modality in which the patient's problem is state-bound. One very inhibited patient, for example, continually opened and closed her hands in an absent-minded manner while giving a halting account of her problem. It was difficult to get a clear account, but it was obvious that she was attempting to integrate many complex inner and outer issues about whether or not she should have a child. I utilized her spontaneous hand movements to channel the exploration, transduction, and integration of her issues, as is indicated in Box 7.

This apparently simple example illustrates a number of significant points about the inner accessing and resolution of problems that patients have difficulty expressing. In traditional psychoanalytic theory, this patient's behavior would be called ''resistance.'' From a psychobiological perspective, however, so-called resistance is a problem in accessing state-bound information and transducing it into a form in which it can be utilized for problem-solving. The first statement, ''You are dealing with many issues that are difficult to express,'' is an obvious truth that the patient found easy to accept. As such, it initiated a cooperative therapeutic framework by recognizing her current experiential reality. I then utilized an ongoing portion of her experiential reality by noticing her spontaneous body language—the opening and closing of her hands (the proprioceptive-kinesthetic modality) as she struggled to express herself in words (the linguistic-verbal modality). This body language was a channel of self-expression already well associated with the state-bound information that was having difficulty reaching the verbal modality.

I therefore utilized this strong body language when I initiated a chan-

---

BOX 7 Problem Channeling and Transducing to
Facilitate Self-Expression

1. *Recognizing the current experiential situation*
    You are dealing with many issues that are difficult to express.
    [Pause]

2. *Channeling and transducing state-bound information*
    So when you feel yourself closing in on an important issue, let
    your hands close as you get a hold of it. Review it quietly in
    your own mind first. [Pause]

3. *Expressing and ratifying problem resolution*
    When you have the words and ideas that can help you resolve
    that issue, you'll find those hands opening. [Pause]
    And you can tell me just enough about it so I can help you fur-
    ther with the next issue.

---

neling and transduction with ''So when you feel yourself closing in on
an important issue, let your hands close as you get a hold of it.'' This
metaphor of ''closing in'' and ''getting a hold of'' channels and transforms
her body language into verbal terms. As such, this simple statement tends
to facilitate an intermodal transduction from the kinesthetic to the verbal
modality.

The third stage of expressing and ratifying problem resolution was initiated with another form of the accessing formula, ''When you have the
words and ideas that can help you resolve that issue, you'll find those
hands opening.'' The patient is allowed to do her inner work of accessing
and problem resolution entirely on her own; she is learning and rehearsing
more effective ways of working with herself.

The next sentence, ''And you can tell me just enough about it so I can
help you further with the next issue,'' directs her to a more focused form
of self-expression in order to advise the therapist about the next issue
needing resolution. Thus, the entire procedure is patient-centered and
iterative: There is an absolute minimum of analysis and interpretation by
the therapist; the patient generates, step by step, whatever conscious
insights are needed to facilitate further problem-solving.

Ideomotor Signaling

One of the most popular methods of accessing and resolving problems in therapeutic hypnosis today is via ideomotor signaling. There are two basic approaches: (1) the original naturalistic or utilization approach of Milton H. Erickson (1961/1980), and (2) the more highly structured approach of Cheek and LeCron (Cheek & LeCron, 1968; LeCron, 1954). Erickson's naturalistic style was to utilize whatever form of ideomotor mannerisms were already being expressed by a patient. If a patient tended to nod or shake his head spontaneously in a seemingly unconscious manner during the therapy session, for example, Erickson would recognize the movement as an ideomotor signal from a nonverbal level of mind-body responsiveness. Other natural ideomotor mannerisms might be expressed through the eyes (blinking or squinting during stress) and movements of the arms, legs, or hands. In the last section I utilized a patient's absentminded opening and closing of her hands as a naturalistic approach to ideomotor signaling that was particularly suitable for her.

The more highly structured approach of Cheek and LeCron, by contrast, uses a standard form of ideomotor finger signaling for all patients. Responses of "yes," "no," "I don't know," and "I don't want to answer," are assigned to the different fingers of the patient's hand. This is followed by a series of questions that can be answered with the finger signals. The questions are designed to access the source of the problem and find a resolution of it. A typical approach involves patients in a structured form of age regression in which they are asked to reorient themselves to a time before the problem became manifest. The therapist then asks a series of questions that can be answered by the finger signals to facilitate a careful, detailed review of all the sensory-perceptual learnings, attitudes, and frames of reference that contributed to the source of the problem and to its current maintenance.

In Box 8 I have outlined a way of introducing ideomotor *finger* signaling that is acceptable to most patients. As indicated, all questions are phrased so they can be answered with a simple yes or no finger signal. Cheek and LeCron (1968) give more examples of how a series of questions can be phrased to deal with a variety of clinical problems. Box 9 illustrates how ideomotor *head* signaling can be introduced as an interesting variation. Again, all questions are phrased so that a simple nod or shake of the head is sufficient to answer the question.

In a series of richly documented clinical papers, Cheek (1957–1981) has responded to the criticism that his ideomotor approach encourages pa-

---

BOX 8 Ideomotor Finger Signaling to Access
and Reframe Problems

1. *Identify yes/no finger signal*
   Review a happy or deeply satisfying memory and let's see
   which finger lifts, lifts up, sort of by itself, to signal yes.
   [Pause as patient identifies the yes finger by lifting it.]
   Now review an unhappy experience and discover which finger
   lifts to signal no. [Pause until patient identifies the no finger.]

2. *Access source and maintenance of problem*
   Let your inner mind take you back to a time before your experience of the problem, and then let that yes finger signal just so
   I'll know you're there. Will it be okay to go over it all, step by
   step, start to finish, just what's happening as you experienced
   the problem the first time?
   [This is followed by a series of questions that can be answered
   with yes or no finger signals to identify the state-bound experiences and feelings associated with the original acquisition of
   the problem. This is then followed by yes or no questions to
   identify current attitudes and circumstances that maintain the
   problem.]

3. *Ratify conditions for problem resolution*
   Will it now be okay for you to be completely free of that problem? Or is there a date in the future when you can see yourself
   free of it?
   [If necessary, this is followed by a series of questions to ascertain all the conditions the total personality needs to realize for
   problem resolution.]

---

tients to confabulate answers that please the therapist. He has formulated
a three-point criteria for evaluating the psychobiological validity of the
patient's therapeutic involvement with this procedure, which he discussed
as follows (Cheek, 1981, pp. 89–90):

With newer hypnotic techniques using repetitive subconscious
review below conscious, verbal levels of awareness, it is possible to
reveal cause and effect relationships between sensory input and
resulting responses. My conclusions have been drawn in consulta-

tion with more than 3,000 surgical patients and 15 men and women who have been unconscious due to head injury. . . .

Can we trust the information offered with ideomotor investigative methods? We know that hypnotized people are peculiarly able to fabricate information, either to please a hypnotist or to permit their escape from having to relive a very traumatic experience. This ability seems to rest at higher, more conscious levels of thought. It does not seem to occur at deeper horizons of awareness. We can trust the information when its eventual conversion to verbal reporting has followed this sequence:

1) We witness physiological signs of distress. Frowning, accelerated breathing, and pulsation of neck vessels tell us that something is stressful, but the hypnotized subject does not "know" what is happening when we ask.

BOX 9 Ideomotor Head Signaling to Access
and Reframe Problems

1. *Identify yes and no ideomotor head signals*
   When your unconscious is ready to review the sources of that problem, you'll find *your head nodding yes.* **As you review some of the negative consequences of that problem,** *your head can shake no.*

2. *Access source and maintenance of problem*
   When you have returned to a time just before the onset of that problem, your head can nod. [Pause]
   And will it be okay to review how you experienced it the first time? [This is followed by a series of questions to identify the state-bound experiences associated with the original acquisition of the problem and the current circumstances and attitudes that maintain it.]

3. *Ratify conditions for problem resolution*
   Will it now be okay for you to be free of that problem [or see a date on a calendar when you will have resolved it satisfactorily]? [This is followed by a series of questions to ascertain all conditions that the total personality needs to realize for problem resolution.]

2) An ideomotor signal identifies the beginning of the experience *after* we see the physiological changes. If asked about the event, the subject will continue his verbal level ignorance of the event.

3) Verbal reporting is possible after a variable number of subconscious scanning of the event. If the event is relatively nonthreatening, it may be quickly reported. [On one occasion] it took 13 reviews of the entire operation before my first success in retrieving a memory.

If there is any question about the validity of a report, we have found we can ask for an answer to the question, ''Does the inner part of your mind agree with what you have just told me?'' I would not place any weight on evidence offered by a confirmed alcoholic, drug addict, or pathological liar using ideomotor methods, nor would I trust evidence offered by a criminal suspect. My studies of anesthetic experiences have not included people in these categories.

From the point of view developed in this book, I would say that Cheek's physiological, ideomotor, and verbal levels are examples of state-bound patterns of information that had become dissociated from each other. Psychosomatic symptoms are expressions of these dissociations; therapy is achieved by facilitating information transduction between them. It is evident from Cheek's above statement that his repetitive questioning evokes recursive inner searches on the ''deeper,'' state-dependent psychobiological levels until the sought-for material is transduced into the verbal level. Because this method specializes in the facilitation of recursive processes, it is most ideally suited for treatment of traumatic situations. As we have seen, trauma induces an altered state wherein memories are encoded in a state-bound form that is frequently not available to ordinary ego consciousness. Cheek has investigated a variety of traumatic or altered-state situations that produce such state-bound effects: critical illness (1969), childbirth (1975, 1976), general anesthesia (1981), accidents (1960), dream states (1965), frightening sexual experiences such as rape (1960), and the death or serious injury of a loved one (1960). Cheek's approach is particularly applicable in situations where highly directive, short-term, and exploratory efforts are needed to quickly access symptoms and the effects of trauma that reach deeply into the psychophysiological levels of memory storage, imprinting, and learning. The highly emotional responses that are frequently obtained when traumatic material is uncovered with this approach require careful clinical management by well-trained therapists. In Chapter 7 an example of Cheek's work will be presented to illustrate its highly variable and creative characteristics in accessing and transducing mind-body problems associated with the effects of stress on the autonomic and endocrine systems.

Ultradian Approaches to Healing

The most recent psychobiological approach to mind-body communication and healing utilizes ultradian rhythms. Elsewhere I have presented data detailing the similarities between many of the cognitive and behavioral characteristics of these rhythms and the "common everyday trance" (Rossi, 1982, 1986a). Since much of the theory and practice of using these psychobiological rhythms for healing has been covered in these papers, we will simply outline an accessing formula utilizing the rhythms in this section.

Since ultradian rhythms occur at 90-minute intervals, their subtle behavioral manifestations will be apparent to the observant therapist during most therapy sessions that last at least that long. For example, when it is observed that the patient is spontaneously entering a quiet or inner-directed mood, one can be fairly certain that an ultradian resting phase is being experienced. The therapist can facilitate and utilize the healing potentials of this "ultradian break" by simply commenting on it in an approving manner, and by allowing the patient's unconscious to do some quiet inner work for five to 20 minutes without attempting to sustain the outer dialogue. If the ultradian resting phase is unrecognized and ignored, then this is the period of the therapy session during which the patient typically manifests "resistance" in the form of many otherwise unaccountable symptoms (moodiness, partial withdrawal, irritability, tongue slips, memory gaps, and the types of "mistakes" we all make when we are tired and need to rest). While it is always of value to understand the psychodynamic implications of these "resistances," it is also wise to recognize them as the behavioral signs of the need to allow the unconscious to do its own inner healing work.

Practical, clinical illustrations of this ultradian approach will be presented in the second half of this book. Meanwhile, it is important to note that, because the cognitive, emotional, and behavioral manifestations of ultradian rhythms are so similar to manifestations of altered states and hypnosis, there will be a natural temptation for therapists to "suggest" or evoke these behaviors even when they are not present. Indeed, this is what most hypnotherapists do: they "suggest" or "condition" the patient to go into hypnosis when *they* are ready, rather than when the patient's unconscious (and physiology) is ready. This highly directive approach is often successful because ultradian rhythms are very flexible in their manifestation; they can be "skipped" and their cycle lengths easily changed in most individuals. This more typical hypnotherapeutic approach apparently works well enough much of the time. I believe, however, that when the hypnotherapist is too arbitrary in imposing his own, rather than

---

BOX 10 The Ultradian Accessing Formula

1. *Recognizing and facilitating natural ultradian rhythms*
   I notice your body seems to be getting quieter in these last few moments, and you're not saying much as you look out the window [or whatever withdrawal behavior the patient is manifesting]. I wonder if that means your unconscious is ready to enter a comfortable period of therapeutic healing? [Pause]
   If it is, you'll find yourself getting even more comfortable, with your eyes closing.

2. *Accessing and utilizing ultradian healing*
   You can continue allowing that comfort to deepen, just as you do when you enjoy taking a break or a much needed nap. [Pause]
   You may or may not be aware of just how your unconscious is doing exactly what it needs to do to deal with the issues that can be best resolved at this time. [Allow a five- to 20-minute period of quiet inner work.]

3. *Ratifying continuing ultradian healing and coping*
   When your unconscious knows it has dealt with that issue to the fullest extent possible at this time, [pause]
   and when your conscious mind knows it can recognize and allow you to continue this inner healing a few times a day when it feels natural,
   [pause]
   you'll find yourself wanting to stretch and open your eyes, coming fully awake, alert, and refreshed.

---

the patient's, timing for hypnotic work, it can set off resistance and paranoid reactions. It is now a question for empirical research to determine whether patients have a better overall clinical response to therapeutic hypnosis when their natural ultradian rest rhythms are utilized rather than ignored.

A careful review of all the boxed outlines in this chapter clarifies how they are all variations of the basic accessing formula that was introduced in the beginning. They all use the same three steps: a suitable introduction, a period of inner work, and a final ratification of the value of the therapy accomplished. The variations of this basic three-step approach are ways of increasing the therapist's flexibility in adapting to the particular needs of each individual patient. The following chapters will provide further examples of how each of these variations may be used for accessing and resolving a broad range of psychobiological problems.

SECTION II

The Psychobiology of Mind-Body Healing

6

An Overview of Mind-Body
Communication and Healing

SAVANTS HAVE DEBATED whether mind can move mountains. In this volume we explore the more humble question of whether mind can
move molecules. In the preceding chapters I surveyed the central role of
the limbic-hypothalamic system in mediating and modulating emotional-
ly-laden psychobiological processes. Here I document in greater detail the
relationship between the anatomy and functions of the limbic-hypothalamic
system and the development and resolution of psychosomatic problems.
Evidence is presented to support the view that psychosomatic problems
can be most adequately conceptualized as dysfunctions encoded within
the state-dependent learning of the limbic-hypothalamic system of mind-
body information transduction.

In this and the following chapters, we examine the four major systems
of mind-body information transduction modulated by the limbic-hypothalamic system: the autonomic, endocrine, immune, and neuropeptide systems. The basic thrust of current research in psychobiology is in studying
how all four of these systems communicate with each other in sickness
and in health. We explore the anatomy and functions of each of these four
systems successively and examine some of the mind-body symptoms,
problems, and diseases that have been found most closely associated with
each. Insofar as it is possible, we review case studies illustrating some of
the innovative hypnotherapeutic approaches that are currently being developed to deal with the types of mind-body healing typical of each system.

THE ANATOMY AND FUNCTIONS OF HYPOTHALAMUS

One seeks in vain for clarity regarding the basic anatomy and functions
of the hypothalamus! Each medical textbook seems to picture something
different, depending upon which functions are being discussed and which

99

methods are being used (Ganong, 1985; Guyon, 1981; Kandel & Schwartz, 1985; Ornstein & Thompson, 1984). The hypothalamus does not appear to be a discrete, easily identifiable organ as are the heart, the lungs, or the cerebral hemispheres. Rather, the hypothalamus is a locus of tissues with seemingly vague boundaries at the base of the forebrain. It is made up of many important nuclei or centers of mind-body transduction and regulation. The functions of many of these nuclei, as depicted in Figure 2, are so different from one another that they seem to be entirely independent processes, accidentally thrown together in close proximity. What appears on first view to be "accident," however, is assuredly only a sign of our ignorance of nature's significant design. In fact, a careful study of the functions of these nuclei indicates that they are all concerned with the regulation of our internal environment via the autonomic, endocrine, immune, and neuropeptide systems.

The hypothalamus is an incredibly small area of the brain for such an important set of functions: It is about the size of a pea and weighs but

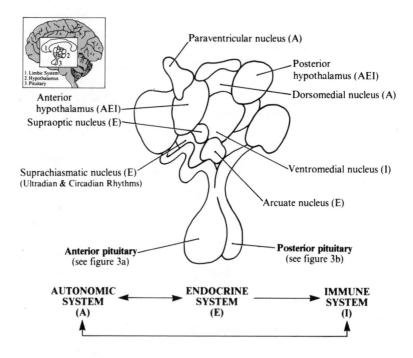

FIGURE 2 Some functions of the hypothalamus as the source of mind/body transduction to the autonomic (A), endocrine (E), and immune systems (I).

a few grams! Figures 2, 3a, and 3b illustrate how the hypothalamus is the central focus of the limbic system in the brain. The word *limbic* means *border*; it was originally used to describe the border between the "higher" mind functions of the cerebral cortex and the "lower" structures of the brain involved with the regulation of emotions and body physiology. The hypothalamus receives signals from all parts of the nervous system so that it functions as a central information exchange concerned with the well-being of the entire body.

Guyon has described the central role of the hypothalamus as follows (1981, pp. 700–701):

> The hypothalamus lies in the very middle of the limbic system. It also has communication pathways with all levels of this system. In turn, it and its closely allied structures, the septum and mammillary bodies send output signals in two directions, (1) downward through the brain stem mainly into the reticular formation of the mesencephalin, pons, and medulla, and (2) upward toward many areas of the cerebrum, especially the anterior thalamus and limbic cortex. In addition, the hypothalamus indirectly affects cerebral cortical function very dramatically through activation or inhibition of the reticular activating system that originates in the brain stem.

The hypothalamus is thus the major output pathway of the limbic system. It integrates the sensory-perceptual, emotional, and cognitive functions of mind with the biology of the body. *Since the limbic-hypothalamic system is in a process of constantly shifting psycho-neuro-physiological states, all learning associated with it is, of necessity, state-dependent.*

The Hypothalamus and the Autonomic Nervous System

The hypothalamus has been called the "head ganglion" of the autonomic nervous system because it is the major integrator of the body's basic regulatory systems (hunger, thirst, sex, temperature, heart rate, blood pressure, etc.). This is of central significance for our concepts because the autonomic nervous system has been regarded traditionally as the major means by which therapeutic hypnosis achieved its biological effects. The autonomic system is itself made up of two branches: (1) the *sympathetic system* that is involved in the energizing or alarm response whereby heart rate, blood pressure, respiration, etc., are stimulated; and (2) the *parasympathetic system* whereby the same functions are relaxed. Recently some researchers (Bulloch, 1985) have included the *entric system* (which is primarily concerned with the internal regulation of the stomach, intestines, etc.) as a third branch of the autonomic nervous system. The entric system usually carries out its functions semi-independently of the autonomic system, however. Since it is primarily regulated by the newly recognized messenger molecules of the *neuropeptide system,* we will discuss it under that heading.

THE HYPOTHALAMUS AND THE ENDOCRINE SYSTEM

Most of us are familiar with the pituitary as the "master gland" of the endocrine system that regulates all the other hormones of the body. The hypothalamus mediates the information that governs even the pituitary, however. When a person encounters pain, for example, the thalamus serves as a sensory relay station that transmits a portion of the signal directly to the hypothalamus even before the pain is experienced consciously. This is true for all other sensations as well, with the exception of olfactory signals, which are transmitted to the hypothalamus through the amygdala. Even the concentrations of nutrients, electrolytes, water, neurotransmitters, and hormones in the blood and cerebrospinal fluid can excite or inhibit the various feedback control centers in the hypothalamus that regulate the internal environment of the body either directly or via the pituitary. From the other side of the limbic border, the realm of "mind" can influence the hypothalamus by the excitatory or inhibitory neural impulses of the cerebral cortex that are converted into pituitary regulation by the specialized neurons of the hypothalamus.

How much is really known today about these specialized neurons of the hypothalamus—about how mind and body actually communicate on a cellular and molecular level? We all know that the philosophically inclined have debated this problem for centuries, but do we have any real facts about it today? Surprisingly, the answer is a definite *yes.* Figures 3A and 3B are illustrations of the mind-body transducers that function on the cellular level between the hypothalamus and the pituitary.

Whatever mind may be, most of us have a fairly reliable hunch that it is intimately associated with the activity of the $2^{100,000,000,000,000}$* connections among the nerve cells of the brain. Whatever the body may be, most of us recognize it at base as flesh, blood, glands, bone, and the way all of these tissues are regulated by hormones, and so forth. Figures 3A and 3B illustrate two types of nerve cells in the hypothalamus that have become

---

* This is the number two multiplied by itself a hundred million times. According to Carl Sagan (1977), this means that *there are more possible mental states in each person's brain than there are atoms in the known universe!*

specialized into mind/body transducers. They receive electrical impulses of mind (the cerebral cortex) on one end just like any conventional nerve cell of the brain; on the other end, however, they discharge a "releasing factor" or hormone to regulate some tissues of the body.

For example, Figure 3A illustrates how nerve cells in the *arcuate nucleus* of the hypothalamus produce hormone-releasing factors that are released into a local bloodstream to the anterior pituitary. From the anterior pituitary an endocrine hormone *prolactin* is then secreted to turn on milk secretion in a woman's breasts. Figure 3B illustrates how cells from the *paraventricular* and *supraoptic nuclei* of the hypothalamus transduce nerve impulses from higher cortical sources into mind-modulating effects on the production of the hormones *vasopressin* and *oxytocin*. These are stored in the posterior pituitary cells until they are released into the general bloodstream to regulate the kidneys and other organs during stress. *Many such cells from the different nuclei of the hypothalamus transduce the neural information of mind into the somatic processes of the body via the pituitary and endocrine system.*

This understanding of how these neurons in the hypothalamus transduce neural information of mind into hormonal messenger molecules of the body is called *neurosecretion*; it is the central concept of modern *neuroendocrinology*. The existence of such *neuroendocrinal information transducers* is the basic reason for conceptualizing the new field of psycho-

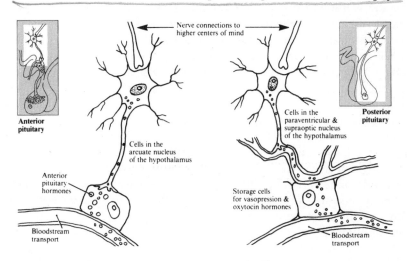

FIGURE 3A
Mind/body connections from higher centers of mind to hypothalamus, to anterior pituitary, and to remainder of body.

FIGURE 3B
Mind/body connections from higher centers of mind to hypothalamus, to posterior pituitary, and to remainder of body.

biology as a branch of information theory. It is the key insight that unites biology and psychology within the single framework of information theory in a manner that makes mind-body communication and healing an empirical science rather than a pious hope.

THE HYPOTHALAMUS AND THE IMMUNE SYSTEM

The most recently recognized regulatory function of the hypothalamus is its influence on the immune system. Our understanding of this central modulation of the immune system is still so new that it has not yet been incorporated into the standard texts of psychophysiology and medicine. The pioneering work of Ader (1981) and Stein, Schleifer, and Keller (1981), among others, however, has begun to uncover the actual psychophysiological mechanisms whereby the hypothalamus can alter both cellular and humoral immune activity in its anterior and posterior nuclei. We will explore some current views on the mind modulation of these processes in a later section on cancer, rheumatoid arthritis, and asthma.

THE HYPOTHALAMUS AND THE NEUROPEPTIDE SYSTEM

Neuropeptides are the messenger molecules that are formed when information is transduced from neural impulses of mind into hormones of the body (described earlier as *neuroendocrinal information transduction*). The concept of the neuropeptide system of mind-body communication is so new that much of its anatomy and functioning is a matter of speculation among a relatively small vanguard of researchers. It is well-known, however, that the hypothalamus is a central hub of neuropeptide activity. This system appears to overlap the autonomic, endocrine, and immune systems, in that they all apparently utilize neuropeptides as "messenger molecules" to communicate within themselves and with each other. Because these "messenger molecules" travel throughout the body in so many different ways, the neuropeptide system has incredibly pervasive and flexible patterns of communication. *The neuropeptide system may thus be the most multifaceted channel for information transduction and the expression of state-dependent memory and learning.* We will explore a number of speculations about its possible role in the "body image," sexuality, emotions, and the mediation of some of the so-called mysterious phenomena of hypnosis that remain unexplained even today.

7

Mind Modulation of the Autonomic Nervous System

HYPNOSIS HAS LONG BEEN recognized as an effective means of modulating the autonomic nervous system (Braun, 1983b; Crasilneck & Hall, 1959, 1985; Gorton, 1957, 1958). Most investigators, however, have had little to say about the actual psychobiological processes involved. An initial approach to exploring these processes is diagrammed in Figure 4, which illustrates some of the major anatomical and functional relationships between mind, hypothalamus, and the autonomic nervous system.

In general, mind influences of the cerebral cortex reach the hypothalamus via its associated limbic system structures, the hippocampus, amygdala, and thalamus. The hypothalamus then mediates these mind influences to the autonomic nervous system via the lower brain stem control centers, which serve as relay stations to the sympathetic and parasympathetic nervous systems. Stimulation in appropriate areas of the hypothalamus, for example, can activate the sympathetic system control centers of the heart strongly enough to increase the arterial blood pressure by more than 100 percent. Other hypothalamic centers can control body temperature by regulating blood flow to or from the surface of the skin, increase or decrease salivation and gastrointestinal activity, and cause bladder emptying.

The vital processes of all the organs regulated by the autonomic nervous system are subject to the influences of state-dependent learning via their association with the hypothalamic-limbic system, which feeds our life histories of experiential learnings into them. In other words, *all the organs illustrated in Figure 4 can respond psychosomatically.* During times of stress, state-bound patterns of information may be generated in the regulation of any individual organ or combination of them. These patterns may then become manifest as the unfortunate responses that we call "psychosomatic problems." To understand how this is possible, it will be necessary to look

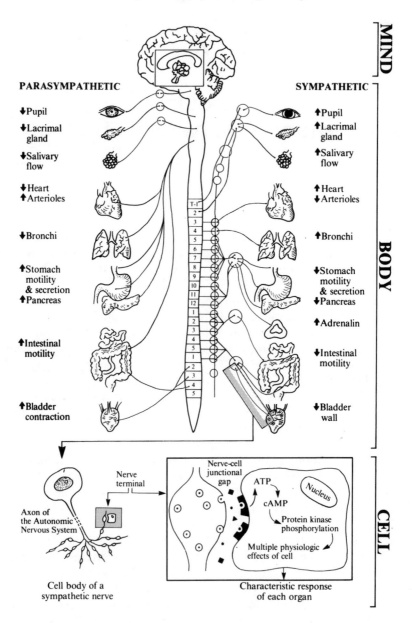

FIGURE 4 Mind modulation of the autonomic nervous system and its two branches, the sympathetic (activating) and the parasympathetic (relaxing), down to the cellular level.

at how mind modulates the biochemistry within the individual cells of each organ regulated by the autonomic nervous system.

MIND MODULATION OF CELLULAR ACTIVITY
VIA THE AUTONOMIC NERVOUS SYSTEM

Weiner (1977) has commented on the general state of disbelief and apathy regarding what we now know about how the mind and central nervous system actually modulate the complex chemical machinery of each living cell in the body. It took more than a few centuries for humanity to believe and utilize the implications of Copernicus's finding that the earth revolves around the sun and not vice versa. Likewise, it seems as if it will take more than a few decades, if not centuries, for most people to understand and learn to use the mind's ability to facilitate healing at the cellular and biochemical levels.

Figure 4 is an overview of the three-stage process whereby mind modulates the activities of the cells via the autonomic nervous system. *Stage one* consists of mind-generated thoughts and imagery (neural impulses) in the frontal cortex (Achterberg, 1985). In *stage two* these mind-generated impulses are filtered through the state-dependent memory, learning and emotional areas of the limbic-hypothalamic system, and transduced into the neurotransmitters that regulate the organs of the autonomic nervous system. The autonomic nervous system finally branches into the sympathetic (activating) and parasympathetic (relaxing) systems. The sympathetic system terminal nerve endings secrete the neurotransmitter *norepinephrine* (usually) to activate receptors on the cells of the organs they modulate (the heart, lungs, pancreas, intestines, etc.), while the parasympathetic system terminal nerve endings secrete *acetylcholine*. These neurotransmitters initiate the *third stage* in the process of information transduction from the thoughts, images, and emotions of mind to the biochemical responses within the individual cells of the tissues and organs of the body. This final stage of the process runs somewhat as follows:

1) The neurotransmitters are messenger molecules that signal the tissues of each of the body's vital organs by first binding with receptors in their cell walls. This process is illustrated in the lower portion of Figure 4, where neurotransmitters can be seen crossing the "nerve-cell junctional gap" and fitting into the receptors of the cell wall. This changes the molecular structure of the receptor.

2) Since the receptor is a part of the cell wall, the change in its molecular structure can alter the permeability of the cell wall to various ions

(sodium, potassium, calcium, etc.). These ionic changes alter the electrical properties of the cells to promote activities characteristic of each cell.

3) Another way the receptor can transmit information is by activating an enzyme in the cell membrane such as *adenylcyclase*. This enzyme, in turn, initiates the formation of *adenosine triphosphate* (ATP) and *cyclic adenosine monophosphate* (cAMP)—the so-called second messenger system—which then initiates and energizes the characteristic metabolism of each cell.

Although this outline of the three stages provides only the barest sketch of hundreds of incredibly complex biochemical reactions, it is sufficient to illustrate our major point: *Mind modulates the biochemical functions within the cells of all the major organ systems and tissues of the body via the autonomic nervous system.* Later we will trace the analogous routes by which the endocrine, immune, and neuropeptide systems can also transduce information from mind to molecules in the appropriate cells of the body.

The Psychobiology of Healing at the Cellular Level: Tissue Regeneration and Cancer

At a recent conference on neuroimmunology Melnechuk outlined how the autonomic nervous system plays an important role in the psychobiology of healing as it operates at the cellular level (1985, pp. 57–58):

> It should also be recalled that nerves, the immediate source of neurotransmitters, play a trophic (growth) role in the emergence of at least some organs during embryonic growth and development. In later life, nerves are also known to play a role in the continuous development of taste buds and in the regeneration of the adrenal gland and other tissues. Since nerves go everywhere in the body, the neurotransmitters they release may play a lifelong role in the metabolism, biosynthetic activity, and division of all cells. Neurotransmitters would do this either as trophic factors in themselves, as some evidence suggests, or additionally, as I propose, by modulating the activity of the growth factors effective in the tissues they innervate.
>
> In the latter case, they would affect either the growth factors themselves, or their receptors, or the second messengers triggered by the growth factors in their target cells. It is worth sketching this elaboration because oncogenes, the genes whose expression can cause can-

cer, seem to code for variants of growth factors, growth-factor receptors, and their second messengers. Accordingly, psychoneural modulation of oncogenic growth factor activity may help explain so-called spontaneous and miraculous cancer remissions. . . .

Positive emotions appear to have specific biochemical correlates, which in turn have specific effects on tissues and diseases. Since the autonomic nervous system, which is affected by emotions, appears to secrete not only the long-familiar catecholamine neurotransmitters [e.g., epinephrine, norepinephrine, dopamine] but also the newly recognized peptide neurotransmitters, it can in principle deliver quite specific profiles of messengers to individual tissues. Recently, sensory nerves have been found to secrete peptide neurotransmitters at their peripheral ends, so they too could affect tissue growth.

From this perspective, then, in which the nervous system releases neurotransmitters that modulate growth factors, the brain, as the organ of emotions and attitudes, seems to be in a position to dispatch appropriate mixtures and amounts of growth-modulating neurotransmitters and hormones to particular sites.

It is evident from this quotation that psychobiologists are finally beginning to discover the actual biochemical steps by which mind can modulate molecules at the cellular and genetic levels, thereby explaining the mysteries of spontaneous healing, the placebo response, and so-called miracle cures. The challenge for hypnotherapists is to determine how to facilitate healing at these specific biochemical stages within the cells, as they are illuminated by basic research. While we are still very far from being able to do this, the following sections touch upon some pioneering studies in this area.

MIND MODULATION OF BLOOD FLOW AND THE AUTONOMIC NERVOUS SYSTEM

Barber (1978, 1984) has brought together a fascinating overview that demonstrates how therapeutic hypnosis can be effective in healing a wide variety of apparently unrelated mind-body problems. This suggests that the phenomena of focused attention, imagery, biofeedback, and therapeutic hypnosis all operate by altering the direction of blood flow. Altering blood flow by directed thinking, imagining, and feeling is one of the basic, common factors in the resolution of most, if not all, mind-body problems.

The following well-documented list expands upon Barber's work by detailing the healing processes that can be facilitated by the mind modulation of blood flow to the various tissues and cells of the body:

1) Warming and cooling different parts of the body to deal with headaches (Barabasz & McGeorge, 1978; Barber, 1978, 1984; Erickson, 1943c/1980);
2) Controlling blushing and blanching of the skin (Barber, 1978, 1984; Erickson, 1980c);
3) Stimulating the enlargement and apparent growth of breasts in women (Barber, 1984; Erickson, 1960a/1980; Williams, 1974);
4) Stimulation of sexual excitation and penile erection (Barber, 1978, 1984; Crasilneck, 1982);
5) The amelioration of bruises (Barber, 1984; Cheek, 1962a);
6) Controlling bleeding in surgery (Banks, 1985; Cheek, 1969);
7) Minimizing and healing burns (Barber, 1984; Cheek, 1962a; Moore & Kaplan, 1983);
8) Producing localized skin inflammations similar to previously experienced burns (Barber, 1984);
9) Curing warts (Johnson & Barber, 1978; Ullman, 1959);
10) Producing and curing diverse forms of dermatitis (Barber, 1984; Ikemi & Nakagawa, 1962);
11) Ameliorating congenital ichthyosis (Barber, 1984; Mason, 1952, 1955);
12) Aiding coagulation of blood in hemophiliacs (Banks, 1985; Barber, 1984);
13) Ameliorating the alarm response (Cheek, 1960, 1969; Rossi, 1973/1980);
14) Ameliorating hypertension and cardiac problems (Benson, 1983a, b; Gruen, 1972; Schneck, 1948; Wain, Amen, & Oetgen, 1984; Yanovski, 1962);
15) Ameliorating Raynaud's disease (Conn & Mott, 1984; Jacobson et al., 1973);
16) Enhancing the immune response (Black, 1969; Hall, 1982–83; Lewis, 1927; Mason, 1963).

The next step is to identify the actual psychobiological mechanisms that govern the processes of blood flow hypothesized to underlie this diverse array of healing. Here, however, we rapidly reach the limits of our current understanding. To comprehend even these limits, we first need to review what is definitely known about the control of blood flow. The regulation of blood flow is usually considered under three headings: (1) autonomic nervous system, (2) humoral systems, and (3) local tissue controls. We will consider each in turn.

1) *Autonomic Nervous System*. With its branches in the sympathetic and parasympathetic systems, the autonomic nervous system regulates blood flow by dilating or constricting blood vessels. This regulation takes place primarily via the action of neurotransmitters at sympathetic nerve endings located on the arteries, arterioles, metarterioles, veins, and venules (but not on capillaries and their sphincters). The parasympathetic system, by contrast, has only a minor role in the regulation of blood flow: Its only important effect takes place via the vagus nerve, which can decrease heart rate and contractility.

There are important characteristics of this autonomic nervous system control: It can occur quite rapidly (it begins within one second and reaches full development in five to 30 seconds), and it can regulate large parts of the body simultaneously. The entire system usually acts automatically on an unconscious level under control of the vasomotor center in the brain stem. This automatic control center, however, is subject to mind modulation via the limbic-hypothalamic system, which can send excitatory or inhibitory information to it. Many parts of the cerebral cortex can modulate the controls of the vasomotor center, usually via the limbic-hypothalamic system. These parts include the motor cortex, the anterior temporal lobe, and especially the frontal cortex with its capacity for utilizing and directing the psychobiological expression of learning encoded within the limbic system. Many parts of the cerebral cortex dealing with a variety of sensory-perceptual processes (imagery, kinesthesia, audition) can initiate the routes by which state-dependent memory and learning can be funneled through the limbic-hypothalamic system to modulate blood flow by the autonomic nervous system.

One of the major effects of the autonomic nervous system on blood flow that is mediated by the hypothalamus is the alarm response. When suddenly exposed to a personal danger, strong patterns of stimulation to the hypothalamus are transduced into powerful vasodilation and/or constriction of blood supply to muscles and glands. Arterial blood pressure rises, heart output increases, and the blood system becomes ready to supply oxygen and nutrients to the tissues that need them. This alarm response is one of the "mass action" effects of the autonomic nervous system on blood flow. It is of great value in preparing the body to meet emergencies, but it leads to stress and associated psychosomatic problems if continued for an unreasonably long period.

2) *Humoral Control of Blood*. Humoral control refers to the substances such as hormones, ions, and other factors in the body fluids that can regulate blood flow. A number of hormones that are part of the endocrine system (to be outlined later) can be turned on by the autonomic nervous system. The sympathetic branch of the autonomic nervous system, for example, can stimulate the adrenal medulla (center of the adrenal glands) to secrete two such hormonal agents, epinephrine and norepinephrine, that are distributed throughout the body to regulate blood flow by constricting or dilating blood vessels. Norepinephrine constricts most of the vascular systems of the body. Epinephrine has a similar effect on most tissues, except for its mild vasodilation of skeletal and cardiac muscles when blood is needed (particularly during the alarm response).

This humoral control over blood flow lasts longer than the faster but shorter-acting direct stimulation by the release of neurotransmitters at the sympathetic system nerve endings, which act on the major endocrine organs illustrated in Figure 4. When this longer-acting, humoral mechanism gets out of control, however, it leads to excess and continued stress, eventually resulting in the psychosomatic problems associated with Selye's General Adaptation Syndrome.

3) *Local Tissue Controls of Blood Flow*. As we get closer to the local control systems which determine how much blood reaches the individual cells of tissues via the arterioles and capillaries, our knowledge of the possibilities of mind modulation grow even dimmer. It has been mentioned that arterioles are innervated directly by the sympathetic nervous system and indirectly by epinephrine and norepinephrine released into the blood by the adrenal medulla. Arterioles are thus subject to mind modulation via the hypothalmic-autonomic route. Capillaries, on the other hand, are more closely regulated by the local tissue needs for oxygen and nutrients. The mechanism of this control is the small muscular *precapillary sphincter* that surrounds the origin of the capillary.

There are two major theories regarding the regulation of these precapillary sphincters: the vasodilation theory, and the oxygen demand theory (Guyon, 1981). The vasodilation theory proposes that the greater the rate of metabolism, the greater the release of local vasodilators (such as carbon dioxide, lactic acid, and adenosine phosphate) that open the precapillary sphincters, metaterioles, and arterioles. Adenosine is a particularly important dilator at this level because it is released by heart cell muscles when coronary blood flow becomes too little; thus, insufficient release of adenosine could be related to the incidence of cardiac problems. The fundamental role of adenosine triphosphate (ATP) as the "second messenger system" within the cells of the body that transduces mind information from the cortical-limbic-hypothalmic-autonomic pathway is diagrammed in Figure 4.

The oxygen demand theory is also known as the "nutrient demand" theory since many nutrients are also involved. The locus of action in this theory is on the precapillary sphincters, which are continually in vasomotion and whose openings are approximately proportional to the metabolic needs of the tissues. I am not aware of any proposed mind-modulating effects at this level, although one could speculate that the appetite and thirst control centers of the hypothalamus could be involved through processes not yet well understood.

A pioneering research effort in the voluntary and hypnotic control of oxygen in the tissues was recently performed by Olness and Conroy (1985). They found that children (ages seven through 17) who were experienced in self-hypnosis were able to increase oxygen in their tissues (as measured continuously by a Novamatrix transcutaneous monitoring system). One child even voluntarily *decreased* the oxygen level. The authors of this study do not discuss the psychophysiological mechanisms involved, but they conclude that their study documents voluntary control over this aspect of autonomic nervous system functioning.

Hypnotherapeutic Approaches to the Autonomic System

An important example of the mind modulation of cellular activity via the autonomic nervous system occurs when its sympathetic branch signals the adrenal medullae (center of the adrenal glands) to secrete epinephrine and norepinephrine into the bloodstream to activate the alarm response throughout the body. Coping with this alarm response is of great importance during accidents, life emergencies, and medical interventions (such as surgery) in which the victim's or patient's fear could contribute to excess blood loss, hypertension, cardiac problems, and even physiological shock. Reassurance from any responsible person (doctor, nurse, medical aide, helpful bystander) can greatly mitigate the stress-induced aspects of the emergency by attenuating the sympathetic alarm reaction and substituting the calming effects of the parasympathetic system. In this section we will review a number of hypnotherapeutic approaches that have been used successfully in a wide variety of clinical practices dealing with the alarm response.

1) *Controlling Bleeding During Surgery and Hemophilia.* Banks (1985) has recently reported how hypnotic suggestion can be used to control bleeding

during acute gastrointestinal hemorrhage, angiography (X-ray studies of blood vessels), and embolization (intentional injection of vessel blocks into arteries feeding an abnormality). Banks recognizes that stress and confusion during these medical procedures are in themselves sufficient to induce a state of heightened sensitivity wherein the patient is receptive to suggestions without the formal induction of hypnotic trance. During the angiography procedure, for example, excess bleeding can be stopped or turned on again with the following suggestions (Banks, 1985, p. 80):

> "This may seem strange, but has anyone asked you to stop bleeding yet?"
>
> The patient's quizzical look and verbal response of "no" elicited the following short verbalization:
>
> "Then why don't you stop bleeding? *Now!* I know it *sounds* like an unusual request, but it really would help us to help you; and after all, you really have been controlling bleeding—all of your life—probably without knowing consciously what you have been doing. You get cut or scratched and you *stop bleeding*, just like you increase your heart rate when you get frightened, and you slow it down when you relax—you *do it* but you don't know how. So you don't need to *consciously* know how you stop your bleeding but it will help us if you just *let it happen . . . now!*"
>
> If it is later required to turn bleeding back on, the doctor suggests the following:
>
> "So far you have really done well. You have stopped your bleeding completely. But in order to show what *was* bleeding, you now need to *undo* whatever it was that you have done. You don't need to know how, but just let it go ahead and bleed, *now*, so we can see if we have found the correct spot."

These simple but well-formulated requests take advantage of a number of indirect hypnotic suggestions summarized by Erickson and Rossi (1980). The reader can recognize how these requests are actually a variation of our basic accessing formula: (1) There is a time-binding introduction of "Why don't you stop bleeding? *Now!*"; 2) there is an accessing of state-dependent unconscious processes that can control bleeding "if you just let it happen"; and 3) there is a recognizable behavioral response that ratifies the inner process when the bleeding actually stops.

Banks asks why a hemophiliac patient can stop bleeding from a tumor that should not respond to normal physiological controls, as follows (1985, p. 85):

Does he produce a spasm in normal feeding arteries? . . . Activate clotting factors? Neither hemophiliacs nor physicians who work with them have a logical explanation of *how* they achieve their dramatic results without demonstrable circulating factor VIII [a blood factor needed for normal blood coagulation but absent in hemophiliacs]: we can do no better.

From the theoretical perspective of this book, one could infer that the limbic-hypothalamic-autonomic system is the route by which hemophiliacs achieve their results: The sympathetic branch of the autonomic system could constrict the blood vessels and thus shut off the blood flow.

2) *Ideomotor Signaling for Accessing Problems Associated with Surgical Anesthesia, Accidents, Critical Illness.* David Cheek (1959) made a number of original discoveries on the ''Unconscious Perception of Meaningful Sounds During Anesthesia as Revealed Under Hypnosis.'' A typical example of his work was reported as follows (Cheek, 1957, p. 109):

This 27-year-old dentist volunteered for investigation of his appendectomy at the age of 15. He stated that he had always wondered if a ''ghost'' surgeon had done the operation but had never known just why he felt this. He was curious to find out if his impression was correct, and it was the impression of the writer that the curiosity was free of malevolence.

During the induction the subject related his sensation of light trance to that experienced after he had been knocked unconscious during a football scrimmage at the age of 16. Asked if there were another experience which felt similar, he indicated a ''yes'' with his finger and regressed back to the induction of anesthesia for his appendectomy one year earlier. This equating of the hypnotized state with previous experiences of delirium or with unconsciousness from diabetic coma or chemical anesthesia has been frequent in the writer's experience.

Q: ''Where are you now?''
A: ''I think I'm in the O.R. [operating room]—I'm not going down very well.'' (Respiratory rate jumps from 14–28.)
Q: ''Are you scared?''
A: Finger: ''No.''
Q: ''Do you hear any sounds?''
A: ''The fan is going—they are talking back and forth—not to me.''

Q: "Is there anything that worries you?"
A: Finger: "Yes." Verbal: "No."
Q: "Would it be all right to hear it consciously?"
A: Finger: "Yes." Verbal after a pause: "You better cut here."
Q: "Where does it come from?"
A: "It seems to be coming from Sobie" (the family physician). The subject is now urged to go back over this and give the exact words as though he were replaying the record.
A: "I think we better cut here."
Q: "Is there anything after that that disturbs you?"
A: "Yes" (with finger after pause of ten seconds). Verbal: "It seems like they can't find it. 'It's tucked under'—that comes from the doctor on the left side of the table" (Sobie). After another pause (25 seconds), "Come on, we got to get this out of here."
Q: "Whose voice is that?"
A: "It doesn't seem to be Sobie. He seems to be on the left and somebody else is on the right, and somebody is down at the foot."
Q: "Does this statement frighten the deep part of your brain?"
A: Finger: "No."
Q: "Does the deep part of your brain feel anything?"
A: Finger: "No." Verbal: "Just a little hyper-awareness of the lower right quadrant." (Note the later-orientation choice of words.)
Q: "Do you feel any discomfort while they are looking?"
A: Verbal: "No."

When now asked to indicate the next thing, he states that nothing is being said, but he senses a feeling of relief and he knows they have found the appendix.

A little later the subject says, "Now the light is right over my head. It didn't use to be over my head. It's brighter. I guess they must have taken the mask off or something."

Q: "Are they finished?"
A: Finger: "No."

He now seems disturbed because, although they have talked as though finished with the surgery, they decide to put another clamp on the skin.

This illustration of the ideomotor finger signaling method of accessing state-bound information encapsulated from normal waking consciousness by chemical anesthesia reveals a number of interesting features. The first is that the patient's respiratory rate jumped from 14 to 28. This indicates that an important psychobiological shift was taking place as the traumatic memories of the operation were beginning to be accessed under hypnosis. Another significant feature of this finger signaling example was the conflict between the ideomoter and verbal levels. Thus in response to Cheek's question, "Is there anything that worries you?" the finger signaled "yes" while the patient answered "no." Such conflicting responses are the reason why Cheek uses three levels of psychobiological responsiveness to assess the degree of therapeutic involvement and validity of his clinical investigations. Let us review these three levels again in the context of the above illustration.

1) The first level typically involves increased perspiration, respiration, and heart rate. These are all indications of autonomic system arousal and, together with McGaugh's (1983) work cited earlier on the hormonal and neuroendocrinal encoding of life experience, would be the basis of this first level of psychobiological responsiveness. Responses on this level can be regarded as involuntary.
2) The second level is the ideomotor finger signal itself, which is usually experienced by subjects as moving in an autonomous and involuntary manner. Some subjects, however, experience the movement as partially voluntary; others simply do no know whether or not it is completely involuntary.
3) The third level is that of verbal report. Many subjects experience this as completely voluntary; others are less sure; and for some, it even seems to be involuntary.

I would describe these three levels as interacting patterns of state-bound information. Because of the traumatic acquisition conditions under which the limbic-hypothalamic autonomic nervous system encoded this information, it is not available to the person's usual associative networks of consciousness. The normal processes of information transduction have broken down. Cheek's finger signaling approach to accessing this state-bound information is a unique way of reestablishing the process of information transduction between the physiological, ideomotor, and verbal levels.

Cheek has his subjects review the state-bound memories at the ideomotor level a number of times before attempting to obtain a verbal report. It is tempting to speculate that this need to "review" is actually a procedure for accessing and reactivating Hebb's (1949) "cell assemblies and phase sequences" (1949) and Gazzaniga's "mind modules" (1985) that encode the state-bound information in neural associative networks. Repeating the accessing and reactivating process increases the probability that transduction between the physiological and verbal levels will be reconnected. Confirmation of Cheek's general ideomotor approach to accessing and reframing traumatic memories is currently appearing in numerous research programs. Barnett (1984), for example, has recently reported the results of a ten-year study of "the role of prenatal trauma in the development of the negative birth experience." In this study he has used the finger signaling method to access memories that could be implicated in a wide range of functional disorders, including alcoholism, anxiety, depression, asthma, phobias, nail-biting, sexual dysfunction, and marital problems.

From the area of laboratory research, Cheek's work on the unconscious perception of meaningful sounds during surgical anesthesia was confirmed in animal research by psychobiologists Weinberger, Gold, and Sternberg (1984). They found that anesthetized experimental animals could learn the conditioning of an auditory signal when they received a dose of epinephrine to put them in a state of heightened psychophysiological arousal. These researchers suggested that since epinephrine is an important neurotransmitter, it functions to consolidate memory storage. This is a striking confirmation of McGaugh's work quoted earlier on the psychobiological encoding of state-bound information.

In human research Henry Bennett (1985), a psychologist at the University of California at Davis, is confirming that unconscious learning during surgery can influence its outcome and the rate of recovery. Clearly, more work with humans under controlled conditions is needed to explore the parameters, limitations, and further possibilities in this area.

THE PSYCHOBIOLOGY OF COPING:
CONVERTING NEGATIVE THREAT INTO POSITIVE CHALLENGE

The ability to cope with stress is currently emerging as one of the most significant factors in the psychobiology of health and illness (Gentry, 1984). Most schools of psychotherapy consider enhanced coping skills as a goal and criterion of the effectiveness of the therapeutic work. Selye's pioneering work on the psychobiology of stress, of course, is the source of this current recognition of the significance of coping. In the later stages of his work, Selye (1974) differentiated between the type of stress that caused illness, and the type of stress—"eustress"—that was life-enhancing. This distinction corresponds nicely with the views of humanistic psychologist Abraham Maslow (1962), who divided human motivation into two branches: (1) *deprivation motivation* that engendered negative feelings and illness because of a lack of the basic necessities of life, and (2) *being motivation* that enhanced life with positive feelings of love, joy, hope, and happiness.

The psychobiological basis of this distinction between negative and positive emotions in response to stress has recently been investigated by a number of researchers (Holroyd & Lazarus, 1982; Lazarus & Folkman, 1984). They found a significant difference in the body's response to "threat" (stress) and "challenge" (eustress). Threat is associated with two factors: (1) an increase in the blood level of catecholamines (epinephrine and norepinephrine, secreted from the adrenal *medulla* in response to sympathetic stimulation described earlier as the alarm response of the autonomic nervous system); and (2) the release of cortisol into the bloodstream by the adrenal *cortex* (signaled by the pituitary gland sending ACTH to the adrenal cortex, as illustrated in Figure 1). Challenge, on the other hand, is associated only with an elevation in catecholamine levels.

In a study on the biochemistry of self-efficacy (or coping), Bandura (1985) found that there was an elevation in catecholamine levels in patients who were experiencing a phobia. He then found that the greater their sense of being able to cope with their phobia, the lower their catecholamine levels. The greater the sense of self-efficacy, the less stress is experienced and the lower the catecholamine levels remain. This suggests a basic principle of psychobiological therapy: *Convert the negative stress of threat into a positive coping experience of challenge.* This novel way of conceptualizing the therapeutic aim of the various forms of the basic accessing formula is illustrated in Box 11.

A hypnotherapeutic approach to phobias based on a variation of our basic accessing formula (originally described as the "three-stage utilization approach to hypnotherapy" in Erickson & Rossi, 1979) was utilized by Nugent, Carden, and Montgomery (1984) "in an effort to validate both the approach and the supposition that creative unconscious processes can thus be accessed and utilized therapeutically." The purpose of their "standard suggestion form" was to "access and direct creative unconscious processes toward the creation and implementation of satisfactory solutions to recurrent problem behaviors" (p. 201). In three experimental cases, they found that a single hypnotherapeutic session was sufficient to resolve sleep disturbance problems and phobias for hypodermic needles. Their

---

BOX 11 Converting Negative Threat to Positive Challenge

1. *Readiness signal for inner work*
   **You will know when you are ready to explore how you can
   deal more effectively with that problem [pause]
   when you find yourself getting more comfortable with each
   breath you take [pause]
   and your eyes may even close as you focus on it.**

2. *Reframing threat into challenge*
   **You can comfortably review all aspects of your problem that are
   most threatening [pause]
   and wonder how you will successfully resolve each as a worthwhile challenge.**

3. *Ratifying problem-solving*
   **And when you know that you can continue that constructive
   approach [pause],
   you'll find yourself ready to stretch, awaken, and share just
   one or two effective ways you will enjoy using to meet those
   challenges.**

---

therapeutic approach to a phobia for needles in one college subject they
call "B" was described as follows (Nugent, Carden, & Montgomery, 1984,
pp. 202–203):

> Following our pre-induction talk a trance induction was initiated.
> B responded to the internal visualization induction by rapidly de-
> veloping a deep trance. She was then given the creative task of find-
> ing a way she could remain awake and alert during future pro-
> cedures involving needles. We gave this task via a "standard"
> suggestion form used in all applications of our procedure: "Now
> your unconscious mind can do what is necessary, in a manner fully
> meeting all your needs as a person, to insure that (*desired therapeutic
> outcome*), and as soon as your unconscious knows that you will
> (*desired therapeutic outcome*), it can signal by (*appropriate ideomotor
> signal*)." The specific suggestion given B was: "Now your uncon-
> scious mind can do what is necessary, in a manner fully meeting all
> your needs as a person, to insure that *you remain comfortably awake*

and alert anytime you receive an injection in the future, and as soon as your unconscious knows you will *remain comfortably awake and alert when receiving an injection,* it can signal by *lifting your right hand into the air off the chair.''* This suggestion was our communicative effort to access and direct unconscious processes to the creation and implementation of altered behavioral responses to injection. Three minutes after this suggestion was given, B's right hand lifted jerkily into the air. She was then awakened and experienced a complete amnesia for the trance period.

It would now be desirable to determine the relative effectiveness of using this hypnotherapeutic formula to lower catecholamine levels in comparison with the behavioral approach described by Bandura.

ULTRADIAN RHYTHMS AND THE AUTONOMIC NERVOUS SYSTEM

The discovery of the ultradian rhythms that regulate many functions of the autonomic and endocrine systems is a recent research milestone that has important implications for the development of new approaches to therapeutic hypnosis (see Rossi, 1982, 1986a). In this section we will outline some implications of the ultradian-autonomic link; in the next chapter we will deal with the ultradian-endocrine relationships.

The concept of dominance in the functioning of the cerebral hemispheres has a long tradition in physiology and medicine (Gazzaniga, 1985). Until the present time it was presumed that hemispheric functioning was not only specialized in function but also fixed in time. A series of studies during sleep (Goldstein, Stoltzfus, & Gardocki, 1972; Gordon, Frooman, & Lavie, 1982), however, indicated that there were natural, 90-minute ultradian rhythms in hemispheric dominance that might affect psychological functioning. Every 90 minutes during sleep, for example, most people experience a period of dreaming (REM sleep). Klein and Armitage (1979) then found that there were natural, 90-minute oscillations of ultradian rhythms in the mental activity and cognitive style of normal subjects when they were awake: Left- and right-hemispheric dominance tended to alternate with this ultradian periodicity.

The next experimental step was taken by Debra Werntz (1981), who found that these ultradian rhythms in cerebral hemispheric dominance were contralaterally associated with similar alternations in the nasal breathing cycle. That is, when the left nostril was open and taking in air, the right cerebral hemisphere had an EEG pattern indicative of greater activity, and vice versa. In a subsequent study (Werntz et al., 1981), she found that changing nasal breathing from one side to the other also changed cerebral hemispheric dominance! Not only was the nasal breathing rhythm a natural, non-invasive window on cerebral hemispheric activity, but voluntarily induced changes in airflow between the left and right nostrils could be used to change the locus of activity in the left and right cerebral hemispheres in the highest levels of brain and mind! She and her colleagues outlined a theory of these relationships with the autonomic nervous system as follows (Werntz et al., 1981, pp. 4–6):

> We feel that the correlation of the nasal cycle with the alternation of cerebral hemispheric activity is consistent with a model for a single ultradian oscillator system and imposes a new conceptual understanding for the nervous system. . . . We propose an even more complete and integrated theoretical framework which incorporates an organization for all ultradian rhythms and their regulation by the autonomic nervous system, most specifically the integration of autonomic and cerebral hemispheric activity. It could be suggested at this point that there might be some basis to believe that the "separate forms of intelligence" localized in each hemisphere require an increased metabolic support of the contralateral side of the body in terms of the overall bias they might serve. *In this context, the nasal cycle can be viewed as an easily measureable indicator or "window" for this framework.*
>
> . . . . Thus the whole body goes through the Rest/Activity or Parasympathetic/Sympathetic oscillation while simultaneously going through the "Left Body-Right Brain/Right Body-Left Brain" shift. This then produces ultradian rhythms at all levels of organization from pupil size to higher cortical functions and behavior. . . . It is important to note that this represents an extensive integration of autonomic and cerebral cortical activity, a relationship not previously defined or studied. We propose that as the nasal cycle probably is regulated via a centrally controlled mechanism, possibly the hypothalamus, altering the sympathetic/parasympathetic balance, this occurs throughout the body including the brain and is the mechanism by which vasomotor tone regulates the control of blood flow through the cerebral vessels thereby altering cerebral hemispheric activity.

For thousands of years the Eastern yogis have claimed they could regulate their states of consciousness by regulating their breathing in the practice they called *pranayama* (Rossi, 1985, 1986a). They have also claimed that their supposedly miraculous control over their body physiology was related to the conscious regulation of their breathing rhythms. Since these feats of mind-body control deal primarily with the autonomic nervous system, Werntz's work may provide a theoretical and empirical bridge to the ancient yogic traditions.

Conversations with David Shannahoff-Khalsa (1983) of the Jonas Salk Institute of La Jolla, California, suggested that an exploration of any mind-body state or problem involving the autonomic nervous system could be undertaken safely and easily by shifting cerebral hemispheric dominance via the nasal breathing rhythm. I have detailed several methods for shifting hemispheric dominance in this way previously (Rossi, 1986a,b). My favorite method is to simply lie down comfortably on one side of my body or the other. Lying on the right side, for example, causes the right nostril to become congested, while the left nostril opens within a few minutes. This, in turn, reflexively tends to activate the right cerebral hemisphere. By lying on the left side, the left cerebral hemisphere is activated.

Preliminary explorations with this simple method as outlined in Box 12 have yielded fascinating experiential results. A functional headache due

---

BOX 12 Shifting Cerebral Hemispheric Dominance and
Mind-Body States

1. *Identifying nasal dominance and mind-body state*
   When you are experiencing a mind-body state you would like to explore and transform, first determine which nostril is clear.

2. *Shifting nasal and hemispheric dominance*
   Lie on your side, with the clear nostril downward. This will shift reflexively your cerebral dominance within a few minutes to the hemisphere on the downward side. Simply receive and wonder about the sensory, perceptual, emotional, cognitive, or symptomatic shifts taking place all by themselves within the next five to 20 minutes.

3. *Ratify hemispheric and mind-body shifts*
   In an upright position, notice that the formerly blocked nostril is now clear, and vice versa. Record the mind-body changes that accompanied this nasal-cerebral hemispheric shift and study the characteristic patterns of your responses to guide yourself further.

to simple stress or overwork, for example, often can be made to change its intensity and location relatively quickly simply by shifting the nasal rhythm fron one side to the other. Some patients have reported that pain can be shifted ideodynamically into a feeling of pleasant warmth, coolness, or whatever, by shifting sides. Moods, negative affects, and body discomfort can be imaged and reflected upon with more meaningful insight after five or six minutes of playing with one's sensory transformations in this manner. Elsewhere I have published some of my personal experiences of accessing profound, autohypnotic states of "lucid somnambulism" by shifting to right-hemispheric dominance during ultradian rest periods (Rossi, 1972/1985).

In his book, *Meditation and the Art of Dying* (1979), Dr. Usharbudh Arya has described an interesting relationship between the nasal cycle, sexual orgasm, and the highest states of bliss in *samadhi*. According to ancient yogic literature, both nostrils are open during sexual orgasm, and during the deepest meditative states of *samadhi*. The ectasy of this form of meditation he describes is due to "upward implosions . . . of kundalini . . . so that celibacy becomes easier and more enjoyable than sex." It remains for Western science to assess these observations.

These preliminary observations on the relationships between the autonomic nervous system, cerebral hemispheric dominance, and behavior open an extremely wide range of interesting possibilities for developing new psychobiological approaches to therapeutic hypnosis, mind-body healing, and the facilitation of human potentials. Another look at Figure 4 at this point will provide the reader with an overview of the profound scope of many of the approaches touched upon in this chapter: figure 4 illustrates a complete path of information transduction, mediated by the autonomic nervous system, that exists between mind, body, and molecular processes within each cell of the body. This path of information transduction is being modulated constantly and automatically on an involuntary, unconscious level by the state-dependent encoding of memory, learning and behavior from our experiences of everyday life. Continuing research and clinical practice will reveal the avenues by which we can learn to facilitate these mind-body processes of communication in a more voluntary manner. In the next chapter we will extend these possibilities by exploring what we already know about the mind modulation of the endocrine system.

8

Mind Modulation of the Endocrine System

THE ENDOCRINE SYSTEM is comprised of many organs located throughout the body that secrete hormones into the bloodstream to regulate cellular metabolic functions, such as the rates of chemical reactions for metabolism, growth, activity level, sexuality, etc. Figure 5 illustrates how some of the major organs and functions of the endocrine system can be influenced by mind modulation processes via the limbic-hypothalamic system. Virtually all these organs of the endocrine system can either mediate or be the loci of psychosomatic problems.

The pituitary gland at the base of the brain is the "master gland" of the endocrine system: It sends out hormones as "messenger molecules" to regulate all the other hormone-producing organs of the body (see Figure 5). The pituitary, in turn, is modulated by the limbic-hypothalamic system. As indicated earlier, the hypothalamus is comprised of many nuclei or nerve centers that act as receiving stations to pick up information about the *internal environment* from the blood and cerebrospinal fluid, and about the *external environment* from the sense organs. The limbic-hypothalamic system is the major center for integrating this information with the processes of mind, and then transducing this newly integrated information to the pituitary, which in turn regulates all the other organs of the endocrine system. The actual cells of the hypothalamus that transduce the nerve impulses of mind into the secretions (hormonal-releasing factors) that regulate the pituitary were illustrated earlier in Figures 3A and 3B (p. 103).

Within the past decade a revolutionary series of discoveries about the multiple roles of many endocrine hormones has transformed our understanding of memory, learning, and behavior (Guillemin, 1978; Henry, 1982; Snyder, 1980). The traditional role of hormones in regulating meta-

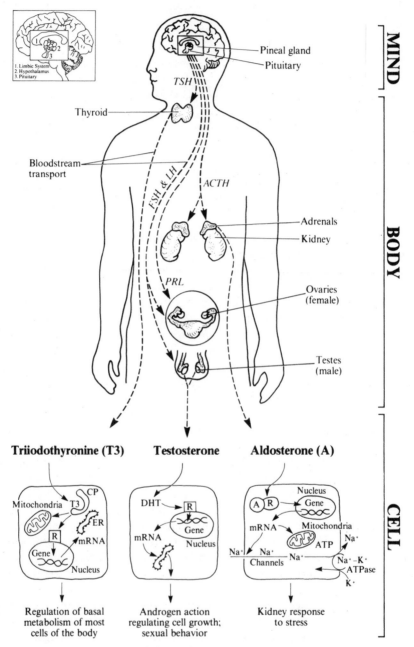

FIGURE 5 Mind modulation of the endocrine system, with three examples at the cellular level of the still theoretical ''mind/gene connection.''

bolic functions of the body is currently being supplemented by a growing realization of how they also may function as neurotransmitters and neuro-modulators that facilitate mind-body communication at many levels within the brain itself. This is possible because the cell receptors that are activated by these hormones are present in brain tissues as well as in body tissues. Table 4 lists a number of endocrinal hormones that operate on cell recep-tors in both brain and body.

The most extraordinary development that has taken place recently in the field of endocrinology involves the discovery of the new class of pituitary hormones called the *endorphins* and *enkephalins*. These hormones have many regulatory functions of psychological interest, including the modulation of stress, pain, moods, sexuality, appetite, addictions and substance abuse, work and sports performance, as well as the basic pro-cesses of learning and memory (Davis, 1984).

The discovery of the endorphins is so new that there is still no general agreement about their physiological classification. Margules (1979), for example, has postulated that the endorphin system represents a new divi-sion of the autonomic nervous system that is basically concerned with the "conservation and expenditure of bodily resources and energy in antici-pation of famine or feast" (p. 155). This view is supported by many lines of evidence, including the distribution of endorphins throughout the body and many brain areas (hypothalamus, pituitary, nucleus raphe magnus, periaquaductal grey), as well as in the spinal cord and gastrointestinal tract.

Since a major biosynthetic source of one of the major endorphins (β-endorphin) and enkephalins (meta-enkephalin) comes from the same mother molecule as the adrenocorticotropic hormone (ACTH) in the an-terior pituitary, however, many authorities now consider this entire system to be part of neuroendocrinology. β-endorphin has the same secretory release dynamics from the pituitary as ACTH: It is basically released into the bloodstream in response to stress (physical, emotional, cognitive, and imaginative), as well as in response to natural daily (circadian) biorhythms. It is important to recall the psychobiological source of the endorphin hor-mones when evaluating the meaning and implications of the many still contradictory claims concerning the functions of the endorphin system.

Since many of the multiple functions of hormones are mediated either directly or indirectly by the limbic-hypothalamic-pituitary system, they are accessible to mind modulation and hypnotherapeutic intervention. That is, although hormones usually function autonomously, we now know that their activity is modulated by significant life experiences and encoded in the form of state-dependent memory, learning, and behavior. Rosenblatt (1983) has pointed out that whenever a receptor for a drug is

TABLE 4 The multiple functions of some hormones that have related functions in mind and body

---

1) As described earlier, Selye discovered that *corticotropin releasing factor (CRF)* is a hypothalamic hormone which mediates the release of ACTH by the pituitary, which in turn tells the adrenal cortex of the body to release cortisol into the bloodstream. This is the traditional role of hormones acting on receptors in cells of the body's organs as described by classical endocrinology. Recently, however, it has been discovered that there are receptors for CRF and ACTH in brain cells which can mediate stress-like behavior and psychological variables such as attentiveness, memory, and learning (Izquierdo, 1984; McGaugh, 1983; Rigter & Crabbe, 1979).

2) *Cholecystokinin (CCK)* is a hormone that is active from the esophagus in the throat to the small intestine. It modulates gall bladder contraction, pancreatic enzyme, and motility of the gastrointestinal tract. Receptors for CCK also exists in brain cells,however, where it controls satiety (probably by its action on the hypothalamic control centers). Thus, it may become important in future treatment of obesity (Kissilef et al., 1981). This, of course, also suggests a psychobiological route by which mind may modulate appetite. Candace Pert (1986), Chief of Brain Biochemistry for the National Institute of Mental Health, speculates that CCK also may mediate what people mean when they speak of "gut feelings."

3) *Insulin* was first known to be a hormonal secretion of the pancreas involved in carbohydrate metabolism by increasing the uptake of glucose by cardiac, muscle, liver, and adipose tissue, etc. Recent physiological studies of its receptors in the brain, as well as behavioral studies, indicate that it modulates eating behavior by direct effects on cerebral capillaries (Pert et al., 1985).

4) *Gonadotrophin-releasing hormone (GnRH)* from the hypothalamus stimulates the release of pituitary hormones such as gonadotrophins, lutenizing hormone (LH), and follicle-stimulating hormone (FSH), that in turn stimulate growth and regulate the physiology of sexual processes. When receptors in the brain of rats are activated by GnRH, they show sexual behavior and posturing.

5) *Vasopressin or antidiuretic hormone (ADH)* is released from the posterior pituitary when it receives appropriate posterior signals from the hypothalamus. In classical endocrinology, vasopressin was studied for its regulation of kidney action, water balance, and urine flow. Now it is also being recognized for its effects as a vasoconstrictor in regulating blood flow. When cell receptors in the brain are activated, however, vasopressin has been found to enhance memory and learning (McGaugh, 1983). There is also a relationship between circadian rhythms and ADH levels in the cerebrospinal fluid. All of this research suggests that the different levels of learning and memory that occur throughout the 24-hour cycle may be related to ADH fluctuations in its access to many different brain tissues.

---

present in the brain or elsewhere in the body, that means there are *endogenous substances* (usually hormones) which are intended by nature to interact with these receptors. This was the important lesson taught by the discovery of the endorphins, which were discovered only when researchers looked for them after the receptors for the opiate drugs (heroin, morphine, etc.) had been identified in the brain.

The autonomic, endocrine, immune, and neuropeptide systems all operate by activating receptors on the surfaces of the individual cells of the tissues of the body. These receptors are like locks that must be opened to turn on the internal activities of the cells' cytoplasm (and even their genes). The neurotransmitters of the autonomic nervous system, the hormones of the endocrine system, and, as we shall see later, the immunotransmitters of the immune system, all function as "messenger molecules" or keys that open the receptor locks on the surface of the cells. *This messenger molecule and cell-receptor communication system is the psychobiological basis of mind-body healing, therapeutic hypnosis, and holistic medicine in general.* If each cell of the body is like a miniature factory, its receptors are locks on the doors. The autonomic, endocrine, immune and neuropeptide systems are communication channels whereby mind may activate genes and the internal cellular machinery. The genes, of course, are the ultimate blueprints for building, organizing, and regulating how the cellular machinery works.

Incredible as this may seem, we already have some understanding of a number of the psychobiological routes by which mind modulates gene action. We touched upon Melnechuk's (1985) view of how mind could modulate gene action via the limbic-hypothalmic-*autonomic* system route in the last chapter. In the next section we will outline a more well-documented route by which mind can modulate gene activity via the limbic-hypothalamic-*endocrine* system.

THE MIND-GENE CONNECTION VIA THE ENDOCRINE SYSTEM

When I first began to discuss the *mind-gene connection* (Rossi, 1985) as a means by which hypnotherapeutic approaches could be developed to modulate gene activity, my conjectures were greeted as a novel form of science fiction. Genes seem so inviolate, with 60,000 or so of them apparently carefully guarded within the microscopic nucleus of each living cell of the body. We usually think of genes as resting quietly until the chromosomes suddenly spring into action in the process of cell division. The actual facts are quite different: Many genes are in a process of continuous, dynamic equilibrium with cellular metabolism. This genetic-cellular equilibrium is, in turn, modulated by neurotransmitters and hormones that ultimately come as messengers from the central nervous system.

A general model of the mind-gene connection requires a survey of the entire series of transduction processes that take place from mind and neural events, to blood, tissue, and cellular processes, and finally to the molecular activity of genes within the nucleus of each cell. In Figure 5 this transduction process is divided into three stages.

Stage one consists of mind operating in the area of the anterior frontal cortex (Achterberg, 1985) as the generative locus for organizing imagery in healing and health. These frontal lobe processes are then filtered through the individual's repertory of experiential life learnings encoded in state-dependent memory, learning, and behavior processes of the limbic-hypo-thalamic system.

Stage two is the transduction of these learnings by the hypothalamus into the hormone-releasing factors that regulate the endocrine's pituitary gland (see Figures 3A and 3B, p. 103). The pituitary in turn releases a host of hormones which regulate the entire endocrine system of the body, as illustrated in Figure 5.

Stage three takes place on the cellular level when these hormones turn on the cAMP system or pass directly to the nucleus of the cell to activate gene processes. Genes are involved in providing the information for build-ing new proteins, which in turn serve as structural elements of the cell or as building blocks for enzymes that facilitate the basic biochemical pro-cess of each cell.

This is the three-stage process which I term the *mind-gene connection*. Let us now review an example of this process at the cellular level to illustrate how thyroid and steroid hormones, modulated by mental stress, actually regulate gene action.

Mind modulates gene activity via the cortical-limbic-hypothalamic-pi-tuitary axis, which, as we have seen, is a basic information transduction route for psychosomatic processes. The pituitary sends hormones to glands such as the adrenal cortex and the ovaries and testes, which in turn secrete steroid hormones that penetrate into the cells and direct the genes to synthesize proteins. These proteins then function as structural elements, enzymes, or vehicles that activate other cellular functions. The sequence of information transfer within the cell runs somewhat as follows.

1) While most hormones require a special receptor mechanism on the cell wall to initiate the process of transfer into the cell, the steroid hormones have a special ability to pass directly into the cytoplasm within the cells.

2) Once within the cell, the steroid hormone enters the cytoplasm (the

basic matrix of the living substance of the cell) where it binds with a *specific receptor protein*.

3) This hormone-receptor protein complex is then able to move into the nucleus of the cell where the genes reside.

4) The hormone-receptor complex undergoes transformations that activate a specific set of structural genes on the DNA strand to form "messenger RNA."

5) The messenger RNA then diffuses through the nucleus back into the cytoplasm, where it serves as an information template that tells the ribosomes ("factories" of the cells) how to sequence a series of amino acids into new peptides and proteins. Many of the peptides formed in this manner facilitate communication within the cell as well as between cells, tissues, and the autonomic, endocrine, and immune systems.

Figure 5 illustrates how hormones modulated by mind ultimately influence gene activity in a way that is significant for three levels of behavior: (1) thyroid hormone regulation of our basal metabolism and general level of activity; (2) androgen (testosterone) hormonal regulation of sexual and aggressive behavior, and (3) the stress-mediating effects of adrenal cortical hormones (e.g., aldosterone) on kidney function. Each follows the type of five-stage sequence outlined above, with significant variations as illustrated in Figure 5.

Thyroid hormones play a vital role in regulating the metabolic processes of practically all the tissues of the body. General levels of body activity, emotional tension, and health are all a function of how the thyroid regulates the metabolic machinery of the cells. It is now known that the thyroid operates by acting directly upon the genetic material within the nucleus of each cell. One of the proposed mechanisms by which its hormones enter the cell is illustrated in Figure 5. After entering the cell, one of the thyroid hormones (triiodothyronine, or T3) binds to a cytoplasmic protein (CP) that concentrates it. T3 then binds directly to receptors on the nuclear membrane to gain entry to the genetic material. Messenger RNA (mRNA) is then generated and transported out to the cytoplasm, where it is used as a template by the ribosome "factories" located on the endoplasmic reticulum (ER) to produce the proteins and enzymes characteristic of the cell's functions. T3 can also bind to receptors on the mitochondria of the cell to mediate energy, oxygen, and other metabolic functions.

Androgens. Testosterone is an example of an androgen hormone from the endocrine system that regulates sexual libido. It has been implicated in a wide range of behaviors ranging from normal assertiveness to criminal aggression. It enters the cells and operates directly upon the genetic material by following the general five-stage paradigm described above, with the variations illustrated in Figure 5. After testosterone enters the cells, it is converted into dihydrotestosterone (DHT), which is accepted by the receptor on the nuclear membrane and transported to the genetic site of action. Again, mRNA is produced and enters the cytoplasm to guide the formation of new proteins for the androgen actions of cell growth, and so forth.

Adrenal Hormones. Aldosterone is a hormone secreted by the adrenal cortex under the influence of stress. Aldosterone has many sites of action throughout the body. The effect of aldosterone on the renal tubular cells of the kidney are illustrated in Figure 5. The cytoplasm of the renal tubular cells contain a *specific receptor protein* that binds the aldosterone hormone and carries it to the genes to produce the new proteins. Within 45 minutes, the new proteins within the renal cells promote sodium reabsorption from the tubules and potassium secretion. This is an example of the vital "sodium-potassium pump" that is basic to many different systems of the body. A chronic excess of aldosterone and other hormones secreted by the adrenal cortex (e.g., cortisol), however, has been implicated in many forms of hypertension and in Selye's "Diseases of Adaptation."

Selye (1976, pp. 170–171) has listed the following "Diseases of Adaptation" due to stress: "high blood pressure, diseases of the heart and of the blood vessels, diseases of the kidney, eclampsia, rheumatic and rheumatoid arthritis, inflammatory diseases of the skin and eyes, infections, allergic and hypersensitivity diseases, nervous and mental diseases, sexual derangements, digestive diseases, metabolic diseases, cancer, and diseases of resistance in general."

It is beyond the scope of this volume to provide further detail about the incredibly complex psychobiological processes involved in each of these mind/body dysfunctions. Medical and psychological specialists are needed to focus on the details of each illness to elucidate the actual psychobiological processes involved. Once these are clarified, we can proceed to create the new hypnotherapeutic approaches of the future that will access and utilize the specific mind-body processes needed to facilitate healing. Current hypnotic approaches do not yet make use of what is outlined here regarding the mind-gene connection. As we learn to use these incredible advances in psychobiological understanding, a great renaissance of hypnotherapeutic methodology can take place.

PSYCHOBIOLOGICAL "CLOCKS" AND MIND-BODY PROBLEMS

As indicated earlier, a salient though still generally unrecognized feature of the regulation of the endocrine system by the hypothalamic-pituitary-adrenal axis is the periodic nature of this regulatory process. We are all familiar with some of the basic rhythms of life: the monthly reproductive rhythm in women, the circadian (24-hour) rhythm of sleep and wakefulness, and the ultradian rhythms (1½-hour) we began to explore in the last chapter. It is now recognized that all these rhythms are ultimately regulated by neuroendocrinal sources in the brain—primarily in the hypothalamus, the pituitary, and the pineal gland. There is also much to suggest that even the entire life cycle of life and death is regulated by hormonal messengers. Because of this fact, the process of aging is included in our discussion. Since these life rhythms are regulated by the same hormones that modulate memory and learning, we can expect to find state-dependent memory and learning phenomena associated with all the interesting aspects of life we touch upon.

ULTRADIAN RHYTHMS, THE ENDOCRINE SYSTEM, AND PSYCHOSOMATIC PROBLEMS

The endocrine system is mediated in a rhythmical manner by nerve centers in the hypothalamus. These "suprachiasmiatic nuclei" of the hypothalamus (Figure 2) function as biological "clocks" (Poirel, 1982) that regulate both the circadian and ultradian rhythms governing a variety of biological processes mediated by the autonomic and endocrine systems. In Chapter 7, I described how ultradian rhythms modulate autonomic nervous system activity. Here I describe how ultradian and circadian rhythms regulate endocrine system activity. Because there are many mind-body functions that are modulated by both the autonomic and endocrine systems (such as stress reactions and activity levels), some of the material of this chapter will overlap with and extend the concepts presented earlier.

Dement and Kleitman (1957) found that a 90-to-120-minute ultradian rhythm was a "basic-rest-activity-cycle" (the BRAC hypothesis) which ran continuously throughout the 24-hour day. In his monumental work on sleep and wakefulness, Kleitman (1963) concluded that this basic-rest-activity-cycle was due to an endogenous oscillation that had profound implications for physiology and behavior. One implication can be found in the typical pattern of our work-day activity, which appears to fall into 90-minute ultradian rhythms: Begin work at 9:00 a.m.; take a break mid-morning, around 10:30 a.m.; have lunch 90 minutes later at noon; return to work at 1:00 p.m. and have mid-afternoon break at 2:30 or 3:00 p.m.; then cocktail time, dinner time, and so forth. Even during sleep, a prominent ultradian rhythm is found in the 90-to-120-minute periodicity of dream (REM) sleep. In a recent summary of ultradian cycle research, Kripke noted how many of these behavioral and psychological processes are associated with endocrine metabolism as follows (1982, p. 336):

The wealth of phenomenology which has been uncovered in pursuit of the BRAC hypothesis should console any investigator troubled that the hypothesis remains controversial. Dramatic behavioral cycles have been discovered, both in man and lower primates, and perhaps these cycles have important ethologic functions. Cycles in fantasy, hemispheric dominance, and perceptual processing have been described. The significance of these cycles in both normal and pathologic psychologic functioning deserves our attention. *Episodic hormone secretion seems to be a fundamental property of endocrine metabolism, and it is somehow related to the REM cycles.* The suggestion that the pituitary is only responsive to intermittent releasing hormone stimulation is particularly exciting, for it suggests one way in which ultradian cycles may be a functional necessity. (Italics added)

One of the most interesting recent theories about the genesis of psychosomatic problems is that *they result from the behavioral disruptions of the ultradian rhythms that modulate both autonomic and endocrine system functioning.* Orr, Hoffman, and Hegge (1974), for example, reported that most humans manifest a stable ultradian rhythm when under quiet conditions. When their subjects were overstressed with extended performance tasks (e.g., monitoring complex panel meters), however, their ultradian rhythms underwent major disruptions in amplitude and patterning. In association with earlier experimental work with rhesus monkeys, these investigators concluded that psychosomatic responses (heart rate alterations, gastritis, ulcers, asthma, dermatological problems) were a consequent of the continual disruption of the body's natural ultradian cycles. As is typical of psychosomatic problems arising from real-life stress, they found that there were highly individualized patterns in this disruption process: ''The same stressor can produce quite different physiological and behavioral responses patterns in different subjects . . . and there appears to be no simple relationship between a physiological response and specific behavioral response'' (p. 1000).

Work by Friedman (1972, 1978) on oral drive rhythms in obesity-bulimia and by Friedman, Kantor, Sobel, and Miller (1978) on neurodermatitis provides further confirmation of the genesis of psychosomatic problems in the disruption of ultradian rhythms. This interruption of ultradian rhythms was accomplished by keeping experimental animals in continuous activity on treadmills—which is analogous to humans' disrupting their normal ultradian rhythms by not taking a rest break every 90 minutes or so.

The lack of determinism or specificity in psychosomatic illness has been a basic problem that has puzzled researchers and clinicians alike (Weiner,

1977). Generally, individual differences in psychosomatic responses to the same stressor are attributed to vague genetic, constitutional, and conditioning factors (Selye, 1976). Our focus on the role of state-dependent learning and memory suggests a more exact answer to this problem of so-called "indeterminancy" in psychosomatic illness. As with all mind-body connections, psychosomatic problems are highly individualized expressions of the learnings and life experiences of each person that have been encoded as state-bound information and behavior. Because the sources of this state-bound information are not easily available to the associations and frames of reference of our habitual patterns of awareness, we tend to be amnesic for the reason underlying the problem.

The research on ultradian rhythms of the endocrine system suggests another nonspecific approach to psychosomatic problems that already may be the common denominator in many of the broadly used and frequently effective psychotherapeutic approaches generally described as hypnosis, autogenic training, meditation, relaxation training and the relaxation response (Benson, 1975, 1983a, b). Elsewhere (Rossi, 1982, 1986a) I have described how many of the behaviors associated with the rest phase of ultradian rhythms are identical with Erickson's behavioral observations of readiness for the "common everyday trance." This led to the hypotheses (1) that Erickson was actually using the rest phase of the ultradian rhythms to achieve deeply therapeutic trances; and (2) that self-hypnosis in particular could be most effective during this period (Rossi & Ryan, 1986).

I have summarized the relationship between the genesis of psychosomatic problems by the stress-induced disruption of the body's natural ultradian rhythms and their resolution via hypnosis as follows (Rossi, 1982, p. 26):

> The implications of this association between disruptions of the ultradian cycle by stress and psychosomatic illness are profound. If the major proposal of this section is correct—that therapeutic hypnosis involving physiological processes is actually a utilization of ultradian cycles—then we can finally understand in psychophysiological terms why hypnosis traditionally has been found to be an effective therapeutic approach to psychosomatic problems: *Individuals who override and disrupt their own ultradian cycles (by ignoring their natural periodic needs for rest in any extended performance situation, for example) are thereby setting in motion the basic physiological mechanisms of psychosomatic illness*. Most of this self-induced stress could be conceptualized as left-hemispheric processes overriding their ideal balance with right-hemispheric processes and associated parasympa-

thetic functions. *Naturalistic therapeutic hypnosis provides a comfortable state wherein these ultradian cycles can simply normalize themselves and thus undercut the processes of psychosomatic illnesses at their psychophysiological source.*

Simply experiencing a comfortable therapeutic trance can normalize our basic-rest-activity-cycle and its associated regulation of many endocrinal and autonomic system ultradian rhythms that control our basic metabolism. This normalization process can be regarded as the essence of the nonspecific approach to therapeutic hypnosis. In practical clinical work (Erickson & Rossi, 1979), there is always a balance between specific and nonspecific hypnotherapeutic approaches. As we gain increasing knowledge of each, we can proceed with greater confidence and effectiveness.

Taking a Break and the Common Everyday Trance: A Case Study

The following case reported to me by Connie Crosby, M.S.W., during her internship at the C. G. Jung Institute of Los Angeles, illustrates this point:

> A middle-aged, Caucasian woman, whose major source of distress was a feeling of inadequacy in every respect, reported that she had gone to her doctor complaining of a strong, persistent smell of ammonia whenever she urinated. The doctor responded by telling her to cease wearing pantyhose and to wash her genital area more frequently. The patient was outraged because, as she said, the smell of ammonia was coming from an internal, not an external, source. How dare this doctor insinuate that she was not fastidious!
>
> She then discussed a second source of discomfort for her, which centered around her secretarial job. She complained that she worked too hard and was not appreciated for it. She was very faithful about *"never"* leaving her desk. She stated, with evident pride, that she urinated before leaving for work and then not again until she returned home. In the next breath she castigated herself for her tendency to daydream and for her inability to concentrate upon the task at hand. Consequently, much of her time at work was unproductive.
>
> Putting the two issues together, I asked her how much water she drank. She replied, "None! Water has not passed my lips for years. I hate it. Besides, if I drank water, I'd have to leave my desk—and who would answer the phone?"
>
> I then explained that people require a break at least every 90

minutes in order to work efficiently. In addition, I suggested that the strong smell of ammonia might be due to a highly concentrated urine and that to heal her body she needed to drink 64 ounces of water daily. But, knowing the patient, I couched my statement in terms of improving her job performance: In order to eliminate day-dreaming and work more effectively, she *had* to leave her desk for a few minutes every 90 minutes. She would then find herself return-ing to work with full concentration. One way to ensure that she made time for breaks was to drink water from a carafe she was to place on her desk. Her body would then remind her to get up by an urgent need to urinate. *To become a truly conscientious secretary, she had to urinate at least every 90 minutes!*

After objecting for a few minutes, the patient agreed to try my plan. Weeks later she reported that the smell of ammonia had disap-peared entirely and that, oddly enough, she was actually enjoying her job. Furthermore, she had received a bonus and a compliment from her boss. To top it off, this lonely woman had also made a friend in the ladies' room at work; they have since gone to the movies together.

Overt hypnosis was not used in this case, nor was the patient told that she was experiencing the "common everyday trance" when she let herself take a break, drink, urinate, and daydream every 90 minutes. The simple reframing of "taking a break" into "increased work efficiency," however, introduced enough change to profoundly influence many levels of her functioning—all the way from the biochemical to the social. We will now review how ultradian rhythms can be used more specifically to enhance self-hypnosis and posthypnotic suggestion.

Self-Hypnosis Utilizing State-Dependent Learning in Ultradian Rhythms

I originally developed the ultradian approach to self-hypnosis by the curious route of trying to maximize the effectiveness of posthypnotic sug-gestion. One of Erickson's basic views about hypnotherapy was that posthypnotic suggestions were most effective when they were associated with "behavioral inevitabilities." It is inevitable that the patient will "wake up" soon, walk out of the office, go home, eat, sleep, dream, work, etc. Erickson would associate therapeutic posthypnotic suggestions with those inevitable daily behaviors mediated by the endocrine system that he felt were most personally meaningful for the individual patient (Erickson & Rossi, 1979). What could be more inevitable than the fact that everyone exercises his or her own unique pattern of slightly altered states via natural ultradian rhythms throughout the day? I have outlined a number of approaches for utilizing these slightly altered states (that Erickson called the "common everyday trance") to enhance the effectiveness of posthypnotic suggestion and self-hypnosis. All of these approaches depend on the state-dependent learning and memory aspect of giving suggestions and training during a specific period of the patient's natural psychobiological ultradian rhythms.

One of the simplest of these approaches is to notice during a clinical interview when the patient's behavior indicates that the rest phase of an ultradian rhythm is being experienced. As described in Chapter 5, the patient will appear to be in a quiet moment of reflectiveness or inner reverie: the body becomes immobile; reflexes such as eye blinking or swallowing may be slowed or absent; the eyes may manifest a "far away" look and simply close spontanously for a moment or two; heart beat and respiration are slowed, and so forth. (See Rossi, 1986a, for a detailed discussion of the minimal cues indicating how the experience of this rest phase of the ultradian rhythms is similar to self-hypnosis.)

The essence of Erickson's "naturalistic approach" was to utilize this quiet moment for a hypnotic induction with a therapeutically motivating statement such as, "If it's okay for you to continue to explore that issue [or whatever] just as you are, your unconscious will let those eyes close as you continue comfortably." The therapist then simply observes with quiet expectancy. If the eyes do not close after a moment or two, another therapeutic alternative may be offered, such as, "But if there is another issue that is more important, you'll find yourself getting a little restless for a moment or two until it pops into your conscious mind."

These two statements taken together comprise a naturalistic and therapeutic double bind: Whichever alternative is chosen helps the patient move in a therapeutic direction. When the eye-closing alternative is chosen, one can be fairly certain that conditions conducive for state-dependent learning in hypnotherapy are being facilitated. Posthypnotic suggestions then can be associated with similar periods throughout the patient's normal day, when it is appropriate to "take a break and let your eyes close for a few moments to allow your unconscious to review what you need in order to continue your therapeutic progress."

Many people find that the rest phase of their ultradian rhythm is the best time to meditate or do self-hypnosis. An ultradian approach to self-hypnosis utilizes natural psychobiological rhythms that are more deeply rooted in the state-dependent matrices of personality than the artificially conditioned processes characteristic of all other methods. I recommend that patients simply close their eyes and tune into comfort, wherever it may be in their bodies. During such naturalistic rest periods I find it of value to avoid any form of verbal self-suggestion that might distort the self-healing needs of the total personality. I simply suggest that patients ''allow your unconscious to do its own work in its own way.''

I do recommend, however, that patients *wonder* how their unconscious will resolve whatever problem they want to deal with. *Wondering* is another of those words such as *comfort, relaxation,* and *sleep* that has a specific ideodynamic significance that goes well beyond the cognitive meaning. When we tune into comfort, relaxation, and sleep, we are facilitating state-dependent parasympathetic responses and the restorative and healing effects associated with them. I would hypothesize that the word *wondering* tends to facilitate a degree of dissociation from the person's habitual ego controls, which in turn may facilitate some of the creative and mythopoetic aspects of right-hemispheric processing. Since the right hemisphere has closer associative ties to the limbic-hypothalamic system, *wondering* may

---

BOX 13 Naturalistic Self-Hypnosis:
The Ultradian Healing Response

1. *Recognizing and facilitating the ultradian healing response*
   When you're tired, irritable, or simply feel the need to take a break, recognize it as a moment of opportunity to facilitate your natural ultradian healing response.

2. *Accessing and utilizing inner resources*
   Explore where the comfort is in your body. [Pause]
   Notice how it spreads and deepens, as you idly wonder about how your unconscious can utilize therapeutically your previous life experiences of optimal healing and being able to deal with current problems all by itself.

3. *Ratifying continuing ultradian healing and coping*
   After a while you'll notice that you're awake and aware of yourself, but somehow you were not a moment ago. You look at the clock and notice that 10 to 20 minutes have gone by that you cannot account for. Recognize the comforting, healing changes that have taken place and resolve to do this again, a few times a day, whenever you need to.

be used as a nonrational and nondirective approach to facilitating a healing relationship with one's unconscious processes. Wondering absent-mindedly about a personal problem during the comfort of a psychobiological ultradian rest period is a natural way of accessing and spontaneously reframing and resolving the state-bound encoding of the problem.

Since so many psychosomatic disorders have been found to be exacerbated by the psychobiological stress of disrupted ultradian rhythms, we can regard this form of naturalistic hypnosis as a general approach that could supplement any other orthodox form of treatment. I have discussed how lucid dreaming (LaBerge, 1985), lucid somnambulism, and profound self-therapeutic states of identity transformation are not uncommon among those who have practiced this naturalistic form of ultradian self-hypnosis (Rossi, 1972/1985).

CIRCADIAN RHYTHMS, THE ENDOCRINE SYSTEM, AND AFFECT DISORDERS

While the daily 24-hour sleep-awake rhythm has been studied extensively for decades, it is only recently that the human circadian system has been found to consist of at least two oscillating rhythms that are normally in a homeostatic relation to each other. One rhythm controls the daily regulation of temperature, cortisol secretion, and REM sleep. The other rhythm controls sleep and the endocrine hormones released during sleep, such as growth hormones and prolactic. Life conditions that disturb these rhythms lead to the breakdowns in optimal functioning we associate with jet lag, work-shift alterations, and stress-induced changes in the sleep cycle.

One of the major theories of endogenous depression is that it is related to phase disruptions between the two circadian rhythms. Four classical features of depression that could have their source in disrupted circadian phase sequencing are as follows (Wehr, 1982):

1) *Early morning awakening* in which one of the circadian rhythms is out of phase with the other in the day-night cycle;
2) *Diurnal variations in mood* wherein patients feel worse in the morning after awakening and better in the evening just before bedtime;
3) *The cyclicity of mania and depression* with its associated state-dependent memory and learning features;
4) *The seasonality of mania and depression,* with depression usually occurring in the spring and mania occurring commonly in the summer.

Great variations in these characteristics are found in individual patients and careful case studies are required to determine effective treatment by altering the timing of the sleep cycle, exposure to extra artificial light in the morning and evening, etc. The relationship between light and endogenous depression is traceable to the fact that there are separate neural channels linking the retina of each eye directly to these suprachiasmatic nuclei in the hypothalamus (Bloom, Lazerson, & Hofstadter, 1985). These suprachiasmatic nuclei of the hypothalamus act as pacemakers for the entire endocrine system.

A more definite common denominator between the affect disorders mediated by the limbic-hypothalamic-pituitary-endocrine system and hypnosis is that they both involve state-dependent phenomena. It has been found that the cognitive processes of manic-depressive patients manifest typical state-dependent memory and learning characteristics. These patients were able to recall verbal information learned during their manic state better during their next period of mania; likewise, information learned during depression was recalled better when they were depressed again (Weingartner, Miller, & Murphy, 1977). Similar findings on "affect state dependency" have been found in normal volunteers and in depressed patients who were subjected to therapeutic alterations of their mood and biological rhythms through sleep deprivation (Weingartner & Murphy, 1977). These findings have led clinicians to explore the clinical implications for state-dependent learning in psychotherapy (Reus, Weingartner, & Post, 1979).

A popular hypnotherapeutic method that we can now recognize in retrospect as contingent upon such affect state dependency encoded by endocrine system hormones (McGaugh, 1983; Izquierdo, 1984) is what Watkins has called the "affect bridge." In an exploration of the history of problematic emotions and ego states, Watkins (1978, 1980) had his patients "go back in time to when you last experienced that emotion." When a series of memories is recalled through this affect bridge, one arrives at the forgotten traumatic source of a personality problem that had previously been unavailable to the patient. The affect bridge functions as a state-dependent pathway to the encoded source of a problem that can now be accessed and reframed therapeutically.

TRANSFORMATIONS IN WOMEN'S CONSCIOUSNESS: THE ROLE OF HORMONAL RHYTHMS

We have seen how hormones from the endocrine system are fundamentally involved in the modulation of memory, learning, and consciousness itself. Since there are so many hormonal changes during a woman's monthly reproductive cycle and during pregnancy, childbirth, and nursing periods, we would expect that some state-dependent phenomena would become manifest. While a recent computer search on the relationship between menstruation and pregnancy, on the one hand, and memory, learning, emotions, attitudes, and behavior changes, on the other, produced thousands of references, none was focused specifically on state-dependent phenomena. A careful reading of these papers, however, reveals many state-dependent effects that were not recognized as such by the authors. In this section we will review only a few of the hormonal rhythms that are known to produce subtle but significant effects on the creative transformation of women's consciousness.

Progesterone and Endorphin in the Monthly Cycle

One of the first reports of such effects involves the hormone progesterone, which was found to facilitate state-dependent behavior (Stewart, Krebs, & Kaczender, 1971). Large quantities of progesterone are released monthly when it is necessary to increase the blood supply to the uterine wall to prepare for the egg's implantation if pregnancy should occur. Progesterone is also a messenger molecule that normally is involved in feedback to the pituitary, which it signals to inhibit the secretion of luteinizing hormone when the ovulation process is completed. Since progesterone has been shown experimentally to produce state-dependent effects, it is at least theoretically possible that its shifting concentration in a woman's body could modulate memory, learning, attitudes, emotions, and personality.

β-endorphin, which is one of the neuropeptide hormones of the endocrine system most strongly associated with endogenous state-dependent effects (Izquierdo, 1984), has been implicated recently in the regulation of luteinizing hormone in women with normal periods (Blankstein et al., 1981). The investigators hypothesize that stress-related distortions in the central nervous system release of β-endorphin are related to amenorrhea (lack of menstruation), and perhaps other menstrual disorders such as premenstrual syndrome (PMS) and dysmenorrhea (painful menstruation).

Hypnotherapy has a long history of successful intervention in menstrual disorders (Crasilneck & Hall, 1985). Leckie (1964) reported that in 25 cases of dysmenorrhea, 80 percent of the patients were freed of the symptom, usually with the presentation of simple, direct suggestions. Erickson (1960b/1980) employed more complex psychodynamic approaches to resolving many forms of menstrual distress that served important psychological needs in women. He reported that menstruation could be skipped, precipitated, interrupted, or prolonged as a function of emotional stress. Crasilneck and Hall (1985) believe that, quite apart from psychodynamic factors, the effectiveness of therapeutic hypnosis in dealing with a variety of menstrual disorders "may lie in calming the patient and allowing more normal functioning of the usual hypothalamic regulation of the menstrual cycle" (p. 361).

Oxytocin and Memory of Labor

Oxytocin is a hormone that is releasd from the uterus in massive amounts during labor. It is also secreted by the posterior pituitary to modulate lactation and maternal behavior. It is interesting to note that two basic hormones released by the posterior pituitary apparently have opposite effects on memory: vasopressin, as was outlined earlier, has an enhancing effect on memory and learning; oxytocin has the reverse effect in producing amnesia. This effect of oxytocin is regarded by some researchers (Weingartner, 1986) as responsible for the amnesia that usually cloaks a woman's memory of her experience of giving birth.

Many women feel cheated by this memory loss of one of the most significant experiences of their lives, and have consulted hypnotherapists for help in recovering their memory of the event. One such hypnotherapeutic effort was recorded and published in verbatim detail by the author (Erickson & Rossi, 1979, pp. 282–313). The remarkable feature of this case was that as the woman gradually recovered bits and pieces of her memories of giving birth to her child, she spontaneously reorganized her own personal identity. She recovered many earlier traumatic and amnesic memories that had become associated with the process of giving birth. She experienced a spontaneous personality maturation with the retrieval of the lost memories. This is a clear example of the guiding psychobiological premise of our approach as discussed in Chapter 5: *Every access is a reframe*. In this case, the reframe involved a profound transformation in the woman's consciousness of herself as a total person.

Postpartum Depression

A recent critical analysis of the scientific literature on postpartum depression (Hopkins, Marcus, & Campbell, 1984) indicates that there are three distinct varieties of it:

1) *Postpartum Maternity Blues*. This is apparently a short-lasting depressive alteration in mood that lasts from 24 to 48 hours. It occurs in 50-to-80 percent of women and is characterized by episodes of tearfulness and crying that may be associated with poor sleep (with its

consequent alterations in the circadian rhythms discussed above), stress, irritability, and anger.

2) *Postpartum Depression.* About 20 percent of women experience mild to moderate depressive episodes that can last six to eight weeks after giving birth, though the condition may persist for a year in some.

3) *Postpartum Psychosis.* This is a relatively rare reaction that occurs after one in a thousand births.

Because of the profound neuroendocrinal changes that take place during childbirth and parturition, many researchers have postulated a biological basis for these disorders. The wide prevalence of the maternity blues suggests that it is a "normal" psychobiological response. An association between menstrual problems and postpartum depression, however, suggests that women who have difficulty in physiologically compensating for the relatively minor hormonal changes of the menstrual cycle or who are biologically hypersensitive to subtle endocrinological changes, will have even greater difficulty adjusting to the dramatic decrease in placental steroid output during parturition (Dalton, 1971). The tremendous variability in individual reactions to the life stress of the entire birth process suggests the importance of considering the role of attitude, understanding, and social support in these depressive episodes.

A Psychobiological Hypothesis

One of the most peculiar myths among some psychoanalysts of the past generation was that when a woman in analysis became pregnant, the analysis might as well cease. It was believed that during pregnancy women would take an artificial "flight into health" and so be resistant to the hard work of undoing psychodynamic repressions. It took me many years to overcome this pejorative view of the situation. Indeed, women do experience profound emotional and personality shifts during pregnancy, but the shifts can involve a truly valuable and nonresistant process of permanent personality transformation and maturation.

The psychobiological perspective suggests an unexpected and highly controversial hypothesis that could be misunderstood and abused all too easily. I will state it nonetheless: *The pervasive hormonal shifts women experience during their critical periods of psychobiological transformation (puberty, menstruation, pregnancy, childbirth, nursing, menopause) lend a certain flexibility to their state-dependent memory, learning, attitudes, and emotional systems, so that they may be more open and available to personality change and transformation during these periods.* As is always the case with change, it can be for good or ill. When the change is unsupported and misunderstood, it can lead to maladaptation, depression, and illness; when the change is welcomed as an opportunity for personality growth and transformation, a more adequate state of consciousness and development can take place (Rossi, 1972/1985).

There is a vast and interesting literature on the role of traditional customs, rituals, and symbolism as support systems for women during their critical periods of psychobiological transformation (Brown & Graeber, 1982; Harding, 1955; Markowitz, 1985). It remains as a fascinating possibility for future research to explore how this psychobiological perspective can be used for facilitating feminine psychology. Moreover, its counterparts in masculine psychology may be even more subtle.

The Psychobiology of Relationship

Interest is developing in the role of psychobiological rhythms in relationships. Some investigators have suggested that the synchronization of biological rhythms in men and women could facilitate relationships. Leonard (1981), for example, has described relationship exercises that have been used to teach couples to synchronize rhythms. Circadian and ultradian research suggests that partners who work, eat, and sleep together find that their biological rhythms are in "sync," so that they are often in the mood to make love together as well. When partners are stressed so that their work, eating, and sleeping rhythms are askew, however, their relationship can suffer greatly (Chiba, Chiba, Halberg, & Cutkomp, 1977).

Biological Clocks and the Aging Process

Recent theoretical developments in the study of the aging process have emphasized how biological clocks of the hypothalamus operate by modulating the activity of the autonomic, endocrine, and immune systems. Since the hypothalamic-pituitary-endocrine axis plays the predominant role in most of these theories, however, we will discuss the aging process in this chapter focusing on the endocrine system.

Walford (1983) has integrated much of the experimental data on aging into a comprehensive three-stage theory that corresponds very closely to the three levels we have used to organize our overviews of mind-body communication in Figures 4 (p. 106) and 5 (p. 126) and will use in Figures 6 (p. 151) and 7 (p. 184) as well. It will be helpful to summarize our three levels of mind-body communication as an introduction to discussion of Walford's theory. Our three levels are as follows:

1) The basic mind-body transducer is the limbic-hypothalamic system of the brain.
2) Messenger molecules (neurotransmitters and hormones) are the vehicles for communicating information between all the major systems of mind-body regulation (the autonomic, endocrine, immune, and neuropeptide systems) and their central integration and control center in the limbic-hypothalamic system.
3) The limbic-hypothalamic system ultimately modulates the biochemical processes at the genetic and molecular levels within each living cell of the body.

Walford's theory of the aging process uses a similar outline as follows (1983, pp. 89–92):

One theory holds that the "clock" of aging lurks in the hypothalamus, a pea-sized area of brain a bit posterior to a spot midway between your ears. It regulates hunger, rage, sleep, sexual desire, and to some extent, development and aging. Dr. Caleb Finch at the University of Southern California has detected significant decreases in neurotransmitter chemicals in the hypothalamus from old compared to young animals. Released at a nerve ending and picked up by receptors on the adjacent nerve cell's surface, the neurotransmitters are a class of brain chemicals which transmit impulses from one nerve to the next. The hypothalamus and its transmitters regulate the pituitary gland hanging nearby from the base of the brain. When instructed to do so by the hypothalamus, the pituitary releases a bevy of important hormones such as growth hormone, ACTH, thyroid-stimulating hormone, and others. Hormonal variations programmed by the hypothalamus and carried out by the pituitary may induce the onset of aging, just as other variations within the same axis bring on puberty. . . .

The endocrine system is altered with age not only in its primary hormone levels but in the numbers of receptors located at the surfaces of cell membranes, and within the fluid space inside the cell. Many hormones must first react with cell receptors in order for their message to influence the program of the cell. . . .

The sequence is: hormone receptor→second messenger→cell nucleus→turning on of the appropriate genes. The loss of many types of receptors from the cells of old animals interferes with this progression.

Notice that we are gradually progressing from a molecular level (like DNA repair) to a systems level. There may well be two kinds of aging clock, one in the brain's hypothalamus orchestrating growth and development, another in each individual cell, the two clocks roughly synchronized and providing what is designed to be a fail-safe system. I shall be outlining experiments at the systems level involving either the endocrine or immune machineries that lead to rejuvenation of many features of aging—but not to extension of maximum life span. A two-clock model might explain the reason for what appears at first sight a stubborn paradox.

At a systems level the neuroendocrine and immune systems have been regarded, not necessarily as clocks, but as pacemakers for aging. The cause of aging is at a deeper, molecular level, but the way the molecular disarray manifests itself in sagging tissues, wrinkled skin, gray hairs, and declines in nearly all bodily functions is via the hormonal or immune systems, and probably both.

The prominent role of all the major hormones of the endocrine system is evident in Walford's theory of the aging process. His discussion of how the aging process can be slowed down in a practical manner emphasizes the biological role of exercise and nutrition in modulating the endocrine "pacemakers" of aging. Walford does not deal with the psychological implications of the fact that the biological clocks of the hypothalamus which regulate the endocrine system are so easily modified by our attitudes, thoughts, and emotions, as we have seen in this chapter. Although he recognizes the same three major levels of information transduction that are illustrated in Figures 4, 5, 6, and 7, Walford's focus is on the biological rather than the *psycho*biological.

As we have seen in previous chapters, research on stress is the principal way in which researchers have been able to measure the effects of psychological factors on the biological. Research on the psychobiology of aging uses this same route. Stress reduction is currently seen as the most practical psychological path to life extension (Groer, Shekleton & Kant, 1979). Since the biological clocks of the aging process are located in the hypothalamus, it is natural to use the limbic-hypothalamic route as a psychobiological approach to facilitating life extension.

As indicated previously, Benson (1983a, b) has gathered extensive cultural and experimental data to support his view that the "relaxation response" in yoga, meditation, prayer, and hypnosis has its psychosomatic healing source in facilitating an integrated hypothalamic response that reduces stress. While Benson has emphasized the role of the hypothalamus in regulating the sympathetic branch of the autonomic nervous system, the data presented in this book indicate that a well-integrated hypothalamic response will also optimize the functioning of the endocrine, immune, and neuropeptide systems. Because all of these systems of mind-body communication are modulated by the biological clocks of the hypothalamus, the ultradian relaxation response outlined in Box 13 (p. 139) may be the most practical, effective, psychobiological means we have at present for accessing and potentiating healing and rejuvenation of mind-body processes.

A well-integrated limbic-hypothalamic system response at the psychotherapeutic level means that we are marshalling the appropriate state-dependent memory, learning, and behavioral processes encoded by hormones of the endocrine system that are needed to facilitate restoration and healing. This is most simply accomplished by using whatever variation of the basic accessing formula is appropriate for a given clinical situation. The accessing formulas all seek to enhance a healing process of ideodynamic information transduction.

We may suppose that encoded in the limbic-hypothalmic system are experiential modes for optimal functioning, as well as the problematic patterns we have discussed. These optimal patterns are undoubtedly associated with happy memories of health, well-being, joyful experiences, creative work, and effective coping. They are the *raw material* or *inner repertory of resources* that our accessing formulas seek to utilize in healing. The fundamental task for each individual is to learn how to access and utilize his or her own unique inner repertory of psychobiological resources that can ultimately modulate biochemical processes within the cell. In the following two chapters, we will review how current experimental and therapeutic work with the immune and neuropeptide systems is beginning to demonstrate the exciting possibility of mind modulation of cellular responses to facilitate healing.

9

Mind Modulation of the Immune System

THE MOST RECENTLY researched, exciting, and complex mind-body relationship concerns the role of the central nervous system, early life
experience, emotions, and learning in modulating the immune system.

Medical history has always taken note of the anecdotal evidence for the
seemingly anomalous miracle cures and faith healings that have been reported from time to time (Ellenberger, 1970). Anthropologists have collected
data on the healing rituals and practices of "nature medicine" that seemed
a mixture of herbal and faith healing. Now psychologists such as LeShan
(1977) and Achterberg (1985) have assembled empirical evidence pointing
to the role of mind and belief in achieving these healing effects. Until
recently there has been no systematic scientific approach to these issues.
The research of Ader and the "new immunologists," however, has created
an unprecedented bridge between mind and body: Their experimental
research demonstrates how behavioral conditioning can inhibit or enhance
immune system response (Ader, 1981, 1983, 1985; Ghanta, Hiramoto,
Solvason, & Spector, 1985; Solomon, 1985).

The immune system has been recognized only recently as a third major
regulatory system of the body, on equal par with the autonomic nervous
system and the endocrine system. In this chapter we will outline just
enough of the basic facts about the immune system to give us access to
new ways of thinking about how hypnotherapeutic approaches can be
developed to facilitate its optimal functioning.

ANATOMY AND FUNCTIONS OF THE IMMUNE SYSTEM

The anatomy and functions of the immune system are simple to understand in a general way but incredibly complex and still mysterious in their
particulars. Most textbooks begin by defining the immune system in terms

of its function of resisting almost all types of invading organisms or toxins that could damage the body. There are two basic types of immunity: *innate* and *acquired*.

We are born with *innate immunity*, which provides a general, *nonspecific defense* against all invaders. The skin, along with the acid secretions and digestive enzymes of the stomach, provides a first line of innate immunity. The second line of defense is within the blood, where there are white blood cells and numerous molecules (e.g., lysosomes, basic polypeptides, and certain proteins) that can attack and destroy many types of invading pathogens. White blood cells are forms of innate immunity that function as mobile units to destroy foreign invaders within the bloodstream. White blood cells are also called *lymphocytes* since they concentrate themselves in the lymph system of the body. Figure 6 illustrates where the major centers of immune system tissue are concentrated and some of their communication networks with the autonomic and endocrine system.

The adult human has about 7,000 white blood cells per cubic millimeter of blood. There are many types of white blood cells, with typical percentages as follows: neutrophils, 62%; eosinophils, 2.3%; basophils, 0.4%; monocytes, 5.3%; and lymphocytes, 30%. In innate immunity it is mainly the neutrophils and monocytes that destroy invading bacteria, viruses, and other toxins. The neutrophils are the mature cells that attack and destroy bacteria and viruses in the circulating blood. The monocytes are immature cells that initially have very little ability to fight pathogens in the blood. When they enter tissues near areas of injury, however, they increase their size fivefold (to 80 microns, so they can actually be seen with the naked eye): as these newly enlarged cells called *macrophages*, they have a greatly increased capacity for combatting pathogens.

Acquired or *adaptive immunity* is the ability of the body to develop very powerful and *specific defenses* against particular types of lethal bacteria, viruses, and toxins. Acquired immunity does not develop until after the first invasion of a foreign substance. Any such substance (bacteria, toxins, etc.) capable of stimulating the immune system into action is called an *antigen*. Acquired immunity develops out of the process of recognizing antigens and creating two broad classes of defense against them: humoral and cellular immunity. Both types of immunity originate in the bone marrow, which produces *stem cells*.

Humoral immunity consists of stem cells from the bone marrow that mature into a type of white blood cell called *B-cell lymphocytes*. These are distributed throughout the lymph system of the body by the blood, as illustrated in Figure 6. The blood is continually filtered through these lymph systems (lymph nodes, spleen and Peyer's patches, etc.). If antigens

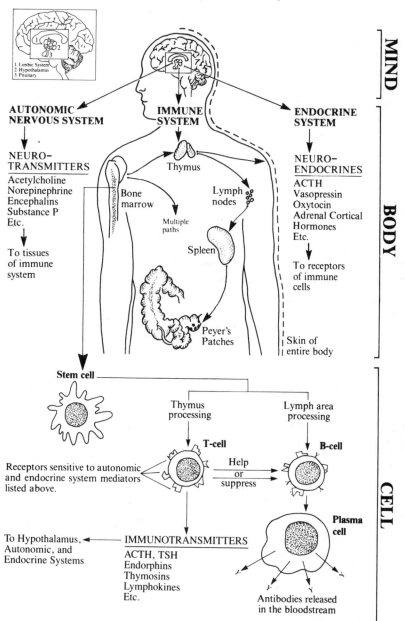

FIGURE 6 Mind modulation of the immune system: some of neurotransmitters of the autonomic nervous system and hormones of the endocrine system that communicate with the immune system, and the immunotransmitters that "talk back."

are present in the blood, they stimulate the B-lymphocytes to evolve into plasma cells which can synthesize *antibodies* (large globulin molecules called *immunoglobulins*) with the specific ability to destroy that antigen. This detection system provides major defenses against viral and bacterial infections and is involved in the allergic reactions. There are five major classes of antibodies which have been named: IgA, IgD, IgE, IgG, and IgM. The *Ig* means immunoglobulin, while the other letters identify the class types. The role of the IgE antibody in producing allergic reactions will be discussed later.

Cellular immunity is developed when stem cells from bone marrow travel to the thymus gland, which matures them into T-cell lymphoctyes (sensitized white blood cells) that destroy the invading antigens directly. Some of these T-cell lymphocytes then travel to the skin via the blood; there the epidermis generates hormones that further facilitate T-cell maturation (Edelson & Fink, 1985). The skin over the entire surface of the body is thus an intrinsic part of the immune system. There are many forms of T-cells that can help or suppress other components of humoral and cellular immunity (Hokama & Nakamura, 1982; Waksman, 1985). Many of these immune components are open to psychosocial influences (Ader, 1983; Ghanta et al., 1985). Acquired immunity thus has a specific developmental history in each individual; its functions are therefore particularly subject to the influence of state-bound information acquired in early life experience.

EVIDENCE FOR THE MIND MODULATION OF THE IMMUNE SYSTEM

To understand how mind can influence the immune system, we need to view one more special aspect of how the T- and B-lymphocytes operate: They have receptors on their cell surfaces that can turn on, direct, and modify their immune functions. These receptors are the molecular basis of the influence of mind on the lymphocytes. Receptors, as mentioned previously, are like locks that can be opened to turn on the activities of each cell. As also discussed, the keys that open these locks are the messenger molecules of the mind-body: the *neurotransmitters* of the autonomic nervous system, the *hormones* of the endocrine system, and the *immunotransmitters* of the immune system. The form and structure of these messenger and receptor molecules, which must fit each other to turn on cellular activity, give us a profound insight into the essentially architectural nature of life and mind.

As we have seen in the previous chapters, mind regulates both the endocrine and autonomic systems in three stages. Figure 6 illustrates a similar path for the mind modulation of the immune system; however, there are additional complications, since the autonomic, endocrine, and immune systems can also modulate each other's activity. The thrust of the most recent thinking of immunologists is that the immune system can communicate back to the hypothalamus and the autonomic and endocrine systems via immunotransmitters. Nicholas Hall and his colleagues (Hall, McGillis, Spangelo, & Goldstein, 1985) have outlined this conception as follows (p. 806s):

> An increasing amount of data supports the hypothesis that there are bidirectional circuits between the central nervous system (CNS) and the immune system. Soluble products that appear to transmit information from the immune compartment to the CNS include thymosins, lymphokines, and certain proteins. Opioid peptides, adrenocorticotropic hormone (ACTH), and thyroid-stimulating hormone (TSH) are additional products of lymphocytes that may function in immunomodulatory neuroendocrinal circuits. It is proposed that the term "immunotransmitter" be used to describe molecules that are produced predominantly by cells that comprise the immune system but that transmit specific signals and information to neurons and other types of cells. . . . Certain thymosin peptides can serve as immunotransmitters by modulating the hypothalamic-pituitary-adrenal and gonadal axes. Considerable evidence . . . supports the hypothesis that the nervous system is capable of altering the course of immunity via autonomic and neuroendocrine pathways.

Figure 6 also lists some of the neurotransmitter and neuroendocrinal mechanisms by which other structures of the brain (e.g., sensory ganglia and pineal gland) may modulate immune function. Ader (1983) has summarized six types of experimental data that document mind-modulating influences on the immune system. I have updated his list with a few basic references as follows:

1) Neuronanatomic and neurochemical evidence for the innervation of lymphoid tissue (bone marrow, thymus, spleen, tonsils, Peyer's patches, lymph nodes, etc.) by the central nervous system (Bulloch, 1985). This means that mind (via the central nervous system) has direct neural access for modulating all these organs of the immune system.
2) The observations that inhibiting or stimulating the hypothalamus results in changes in immunologic reactivity, and, conversely, that activation of an immune response in the body results in measurable

changes within the hypothalamus (Roszman, Cross, Brooks, & Markes-bery, 1985; Stein, Schleifer, & Keller, 1981). Since the hypothalamus is regulated by higher brain centers (via connections with the limbic cortex), these intercommunications between the immune system and hypothalamus may be open to mind modulation.

3) The finding that lymphocytes bear receptors for hormones of the endocrine system and neurotransmitters of the autonomic nervous system (Cohn, 1985; Wybran, 1985). This means that all the mind-modulating effects of the autonomic and endocrine systems may be communicated to the immune system as well. This conclusion is supported by the next point as well.

4) Evidence that alterations of hormone and neurotransmitter function modify immunologic reactivity and, conversely, that elicitation of an immune response is accompanied by changes in hormonal and neu-rotransmitter levels (Besedovsky, del Rey, & Sorkin, 1985; Hall & Goldstein, 1985).

5) Data documenting the effect of behavioral interventions, including conditioning, on various parameters of immune function (Ader, 1985; Gorczynski, Macrae, & Kennedy 1982).

6) Experimental and clinical studies in which psychological factors such as stress (Palmblad, 1985; Stein et al., 1985) and depression (Stein et al., 1985) have been found to influence the onset of disease pro-cesses.

Maclean and Reichlin (1981) also noted many indirect ways in which mind can modulate the immune response through changes in behavior. These include altered diet, circadian rhythms, sleep-wake cycles, body temperature, blood volume, and local vascular reactions.

The ultimate task of the hypnotherapist is to learn how to access and utilize all these mind-body mechanisms. How far we are from actually doing this! Yet the well-documented research cited by Ader (1983) and Locke et al. (1984) concerning the influence of psychosocial factors, mood, and belief systems on illness, disease, and healing clearly indicates that the mind is continually modulating the immune system. What success hypnosis currently achieves in modulating immune function is via the nonspecific approaches that work to a certain degree (even spectacularly well in some cases), even though we usually do not know what the thera-peutic mechanisms of action are. We can drive a car quite well without knowing how the engine operates, but when there is a breakdown, the more detailed our knowledge of engine mechanisms, the better we will be able to fix it. The present state of our hypnotherapeutic knowledge of these mind-body mechanisms is somewhat akin to the average driver who knows there is an engine somewhere that does something when we turn on a key and push the gas pedal. However, currently there are a number of innovative research programs studying how mind modulation and hypnosis can influence specific features of the immune system. In the following sections we will review some of these programs to learn what they can tell us about developing new hypnotherapeutic approaches to facilitating immunological functioning.

MIND MODULATION OF INNATE IMMUNITY

It is currently being demonstrated that the immune system can be influenced by mind methods with appropriate education and training. It will be recalled that neutrophils comprise almost two-thirds of the body's innate immunity of white blood cell defenses. Any means of potentiating their function would surely be a significant step in combatting disease. A recent doctoral dissertation study by Barbara Peavey (1982) investigated the effect of a training program designed to enhance relaxation by biofeedback (using EMG muscle relaxation and temperature biofeedback). She found that while the number of neutrophils remained the same, they were found to function significantly better with successful relaxation training.

An even more fascinating approach to facilitating neutrophil activity has been reported by Schneider, Smith, and Witcher (1984). They combined belief with imagery training to explore the relationship between imagination and the immune system. Students who *believed* they could consciously control their own immune system were first given information about how white blood cells functioned and shown microscopic slides of actual neutrophils, which were to be incorporated into their imagery training. They then listened to an audiotape with suggestions for relaxation and imagery. They practiced imagining and drawing pictures of their imagery, which were later objectively scored. After six sessions of such training, it was found that subjects could greatly increase or decrease the number of circulating neutrophils in their bloodstream.

Neutrophils could be described as the "wandering Samurai warriors" of the bloodstream. As mentioned earlier, neutrophils are an important part of the immune system's response to bacteria, viruses, and other injurious antigens that attempt to invade the body. They can attack foreign antigens even as they circulate in the blood. Neutrophils have a wide range of activities that enhance their abilities to reach and destroy antigens: They can migrate through the bloodstream to the locus of injury, change their shape, and then squeeze through the pores of the blood vessels to reach areas of tissue damage. This process of movement toward an area of injury is called *diapedesis*. Neutrophils may also adhere to the insides of the blood vessel by the process of *margination*. When tissues are invaded or damaged, they respond by creating an inflammation that tends to physically entrap the injurious agents so that they do not spread any further throughout the body. The inflamed area also diffuses chemical agents through the tissues that attract the neutrophils, thus causing them to stick to the sides of the capillary cell walls (margination) and then squeeze through the walls (diapedesis) to the source of inflammation.

In their analysis of four initial experimental studies, Schneider, Smith, and Witcher (1983, 1984) surmised that their imagery training exercises were influencing the process of margination in neutrophils. That is, the exercises were not increasing or decreasing the number of neutrophils per se in the body but, rather, were changing their movement and the potential loci of their immune system activity. As we shall see later in our discussion of asthma, this finding could have profound implications for using imagery and hypnosis to ameliorate hyperactive responses of the immune system in allergic reactions.

MIND MODULATION OF ACQUIRED IMMUNITY

Smith and McDaniel (1983) began their studies of the mind modulation of the immune response by successfully repeating Black's (1963) initial finding that hypnotized subjects could suppress the so-called Mantoux reaction (a mild skin test for tuberculosis that is produced by an antigen-antibody reaction of the acquired immune system). Rather than hypnotizing their subjects, however, Smith and McDaniel used a behavioral conditioning paradigm to demonstrate the role of expectation in modulating this particular immune response: The Mantoux reaction took place on the arm of the subjects where it was expected but not on the other arm where subjects did not expect it. This proved that there was nothing intrinsic about hypnosis in the modulation of the immune system; hypnosis was simply a convenient way of focusing the mind's inner resources to activate or inhibit a physiological response.

Smith, McKenzie, Marmer, & Steele (1985) then sought to establish whether the mind modulation of the Mantoux reaction could be replicated using a different type of antigen-antibody response (the body's response to *varicella zoster* viral antigen) and a different form of mind modulation (meditation rather than hypnosis or conditioning). An advantage of using the *varicella zoster* antigen was that the body's immune response to it could be objectively measured in two ways: (1) in vivo, by measuring the size of the skin test reaction on the subject's arm (just as with the Mantoux reaction), and (2) in vitro, by measuring the degree of lymphocyte stimulation in a blood sample from the subject. Smith and his colleagues (1985) described their elegant, single-case study experimental design, their subject's Eastern meditation method, and the statistically valid results as follows (p. 2110):

> In light of the above findings, we hypothesized that a highly selected subject could use meditation or self-hypnosis to modulate her immune response. The paradigm was a simple, single-case design in which the subject was her own control. She was given a skin test weekly for nine weeks. During the first three weeks (phase 1) she was told to react normally. The second three weeks (phase 2) she was asked to try to inhibit her reaction using any psychologic practice or technique she chose. Finally, for the final three weeks (phase 3) she was again asked to react normally. We hypothesized that the immune response during the second phase would be decreased compared with the first and third phases.
>
> The subject is a 39-year-old woman who has followed an Eastern religious practice for the last nine years. During most of this time, as part of her religious practice, she would usually meditate once or twice daily for about 30 minutes. For the last three years, she has followed a specific tantric generation meditation practice whereby "higher energies" are visualized and she seeks to transform herself into those energies.
>
> During the phase 2 periods of the original and repeat experiment, she would usually reserve about five minutes of her daily meditation for attention to the study. First she would dedicate her intention concerning the study for universal good instead of self-advancement. She would also tell her body not to violate its wisdom concerning her defense against infection. Finally she would visualize the area of erythema and induration getting smaller and smaller. Soon after each phase 2 injection, she would pass her hand over her arm, sending "healing energy" to the injection site. . . .
>
> The data confirmed the hypothesis that this subject could voluntarily modulate her immune responses by a psychic mechanism. Both a clinical measure, delayed hypersensitivity, and an in vitro measure, lymphocyte stimulation of immune response, were affect-

ed. In other words, it appears that the subject, acting with intentions, was able to affect not only her skin test response but also the response of her lymphocytes studied in the laboratory.

Smith et al. concluded their report by noting that their work establishes the "intentional direct psychological modulation of the human immune system." Their emphasis on the intentional and voluntary aspect of the psychological situation is of great importance. Previous work on the mind modulation of the immune system via hypnosis, placebos, and behavioral conditioning demonstrated that mind-body healing processes could be activated by outside influences. The work of Smith and his colleagues, however, implies that humans can train themselves to facilitate their own inner mind-body healing processes. The researchers concluded their paper with a note of cautious optimism as follows (1985, p. 2111):

> The results from this study certainly cannot be generalized to all humans; however, perhaps other people have the ability to modulate their immune response or to develop the capacity to do so. Certainly, these data, along with the previously cited results, should allow for many new carefully designed studies to be undertaken.
> If it proves to be the case that humans can significantly modulate their immune response, then two important outcomes may occur. The mechanism of infectious or neoplastic disease onset associated with various psychological processes such as hopelessness or depression can possibly be better understood. Perhaps, also, intentional modulation can be used therapeutically to increase or decrease immune response, depending on the particular disease state.

Let us now turn to an overview of how the voluntary modulation of immune system responses could facilitate healing in a variety of illnesses such as cancer, asthma, allergies, and rheumatoid arthritis.

Mind Modulation of Immune System Dysfunctions

Bowers and Kelly (1979) have outlined three major ways in which the immune system can become dysfunctional in psychosomatic illness. It can become *underactive, hyperactive,* or *misguided* in its efforts to defend the body. These three errors of the immune system are exemplified by cancer, bronchial asthma, and rheumatoid arthritis, respectively. While this classification is an oversimplification of the facts, it is useful in providing a set of models for organizing our thinking about these issues. In what follows, I will amplify and update Bowers and Kelly's presentation of how the new approaches to therapeutic hypnosis that emphasize patient skills could facilitate healing of these three types of immune dysfunction.

The Underactive Immune System in Cancer

This section will outline how some of the basic elements of the immune system communicate and interact with each other in dealing with the phenomenon of cancer. It is important to understand that the body develops cancer cells as an apparently natural process throughout the entire lifespan without the growth of clinically recognizable cancer tumors. This is illustrated by the fact that one form of cancer cell (neuroblastoma) is much higher even in babies than in the clinical incidence of the disease. On the other end of the scale, postmortem autopsies on practically all males 50 or over show evidence of prostatic cancer cells, yet actual clinical cancer is not evident in most of them.

Since most people do not develop cancer even though cancer cells are continually produced, the body must have a natural immunological surveillance system that seeks out and destroys the single cancer cells before they grow into clinically evident tumors. In general it is found that stress-induced release of adrenocorticosteroids causes a suppression of this natural immunological surveillance system. Amkraut and Solomon (1975), Shavit et al. (1985), and Stein, Keller, and Schleifer (1985) have pointed out that only a slight depression of this system is needed to greatly increase the person's susceptibility to pathogens, particularly those that are constantly present and challenging the body's integrity, such as the spontaneously formed cancer cells.

There are a variety of immune system processes that protect against such tumor formations. These include the previously mentioned macrophages, T-lymphocytes, and B-lymphocytes (Amkraut & Solomon, 1975; Solomon & Amkraut, 1981), as well as K (killer) cells, NK (natural killer) cells, and cytotoxic T cells (see Hokama & Nakamura, 1982, for details). The K cells are of uncertain immunological lineage but are dependent on antibodies for their activity and are therefore also called *antibody-dependent cytotoxic cells*. The NK cells are also of uncertain origin but it is known that their activity against cancer cells is increased by *interferon*. Interferon is a immunological factor that is released by T-cells and macrophages. Recent studies in man indicate that NK cells play a significant role against a variety of viral infections, including those due to herpes and viral oncogenesis (viral-produced cancers). The major theory of oncogenesis is that tumor formation takes place when those components of the immune surveillance system are depressed or underactive (Stein et al. 1985).

Let us now examine a variety of approaches researchers and clinicians are currently developing to fight cancer by enhancing those aspects of the immune system that are depressed. As we found with the autonomic and endocrine systems, it will be necessary to trace the source of the potentially mind-modulating effects on the immune system right down to the genetic and molecular levels.

The Genetic and Molecular Level of Immune System Communication in Cancer. This section will present an overview of current thinking about the genesis of cancer and the lines of natural and acquired defense against it. The cancer story is very much involved with our developing understanding of genes and the messenger molecules that regulate normal cell growth. As we have seen in the two previous chapters, normal cells all have genes that receive messenger molecules from the mind-modulating central control processes in the limbic-hypothalamic system via the autonomic and endocrine systems. Many researchers now believe that cancer begins when these normal growth-regulating genes are damaged and turned into cancer-producing oncogenes. Oncogenes speed up or change the structure of proteins that the cell manufactures so that growth becomes wildly uncontrolled in the form of useless tissues and tumors that eventually take over the entire body and kill it. The normal genes that are turned into oncogenes occupy loci on the chromosomes that are vulnerable to damage. Because of this they are called "proto-oncogenes." They are converted into oncogenes by what have become known as "carcinogens."

Radiation from X-rays, radioactivity, and excess sunlight, *toxins* such as smoke and chemicals foreign to the body, and a variety of *viruses* are among the most well-known carcinogens. Such carcinogens operate by entering the cell nucleus during a vulnerable stage of cell division and transforming a proto-oncogene into an oncogene by (1) causing a genetic mutation (a change in the blueprint for the structure of growth proteins), or (2) breaking the normal arrangement in which genes are recombined into chromosomes.

Natural and Acquired Defenses Against Cancer. There are a number of well-known ways of defeating the growth and spread of cancer cells once they are formed. This section will review three of the body's natural defenses, and a number of ways by which researchers are enhancing them.

Interferon is a messenger molecule protein that facilitates a process of innate immunity or natural defense against infection. It was originally discovered in 1957 by Alick Isaacs and Jean Lindenmann of the National Institute of Medical Research in England. Whenever a virus attacks a cell, the cell produces interferons (alpha and beta are two well-known forms of it) to interfere with the virus's toxic activity. In addition, the interferons can directly attack and kill fully formed cancer cells by (1) interfering with their metabolism or giving T- and B-cells and macrophages messages to destroy cancer cells (Marrack & Kappler, 1986). Early clinical trials with interferon were disappointing because it was only available in small amounts. Researchers have recently learned how to mass-produce interferon in the laboratory, however. When large amounts have been injected into the body, interferon has been successful in enhancing the cancer-fighting potential of T- and B-cells and macrophages against a variety of cancers. In actual practice, it is currently being combined with other forms of anti-cancer processes, such as the following.

Interleukins are also naturally present protein messenger molecules that facilitate immune system communication and defense against pathogens in the body. They operate as hormone or messenger molecules between T- and B-cells and macrophages to facilitate their defense against toxins and even fully formed cancers. A research team lead by Steven Rosenberg (Rosenberg et al., 1985) of the National Cancer Institute has recently suc-ceeded in mass-producing interleukin-2 and using it to activate the body's T-cells to produce cytotoxic T-cells that can directly attack cancer tissues. It has been found to be dramatically effective in shrinking tumors by 50 percent or more (including complete cancer remission) in the human trials recently conducted.

Tumor necrosis factor (TNF) is another natural form of innate immunity against pathogens, originally discovered in 1975 by Lloyd Old at the Sloan-Kettering Cancer Center in New York. It has been found that when bacteria infect the body, macrophages increase in number and secrete the protein TNF, which can directly attack cancer cells and tissues as well. Through the processes of genetic engineering in the laboratory, TNF now can be cloned and mass-produced. When injected into the body, it actually at-tacks and causes cancer cells to blacken and die by some as yet unknown mechanism; when it is used in combination with interferon and other cancer-killing drugs, it is even more effective. In the laboratory, it either destroys or hampers the growth of two-thirds of the cancer cells against which it has been tested. TNF is currently being tested in humans in a variety of major medical centers.

Monoclonals are another feat of genetic engineering that hold promise for destroying a wide variety of cancers in a number of different ways.

Monoclonals are produced by first removing a sample of cancer cells from the body and injecting them into a mouse. The mouse's immune system then produces B-cells that have antibodies designed to attack that particular cancer; that is, an acquired immunity is produced. These B-cells with the cancer antibody are then removed from the mouse and fused with another fast-dividing line of cancer cells in the test tube to produce the so-called "hybridomas"—a kind of hearty hybrid cell that now mass-produces the monoclonal with the specific antibodies for the patient's cancer. These cancer-attacking antibodies are then harvested and purified. Usually their potency is enhanced even further when other anticancer drugs are attached to them. When these mixtures are injected into the original patient, they act as "smart bombs" by attacking only the cancer cells of the body. This occurs because their antibody portion functions as a key that can only turn the receptor locks on the cancer cell walls. Monoclonals are thus deadly messenger molecules designed for a specific cancer-fighting mission.

The National Cancer Institute has estimated that about 50 percent of the cure rate against cancer by the year 2000 will come from these newly evolving cancer therapies. The other 50 percent will come from cancer prevention programs. The point of interest to our material is the fact that, in one way or another, all the current cancer therapies are facilitated by messenger molecules that potentiate the immune system's potency. Our understanding of how mind methods can support these processes at the messenger molecule level is still in an embryonic stage, but as we will see now, evidence is accumulating for the potential application of therapeutic hypnosis in this area.

Psychobiological Models for Facilitating Cancer Therapy. A major line of evidence for a mind-body connection in the genesis of cancer is what has come to be known as the *life change stress* studies (Dohrenwend & Dohrenwend, 1974). Any form of stress resulting in a significant life change (e.g., the death of a family member, job change, family relocation) can activate the cortical-hypothalamic-pituitary-adrenal axis described earlier to produce the corticosteroids that suppress the immune surveillance system. Anxiety, depression, and low ego strength are all associated with underactivity of the immune system. The major thrust of current research in this area is that *coping ability* is the significant factor in determining whether stress will have a depressant effect on immunocompetence. Locke et al. (1984), for example, found that experiencing the symptoms of anxiety and depression in response to a stressful life change indicated poor coping ability and resulted in a decrease in the activity of natural killer cells; on the other hand, good coping ability (few symptoms in the face of considerable life change stress) was associated with higher natural killer cell activity.

Well-controlled experimental evidence that hypnosis can effect changes in the immunological surveillance system is gradually accumulating. Hall (1982–1983) has found that highly hypnotizable young subjects can significantly increase their cellular immunity (both T- and B-lymphocyte activity). Frankel (1985) and his colleagues are exploring the use of hypnotic suggestion to either enhance or depress cellular immunity in response to injections of antigens.

A review of the newer approaches to therapeutic hypnosis that have been found effective in enhancing immunocompetence with cancer patients revealed at least five basic applications: relaxation, imagery, reframing, meditation, and reinforcing coping skills. Since stress depresses the immune system by the production of adrenocorticoid hormones, it was an important breakthrough to find that hypnotherapeutic methods emphasizing simple relaxation could lower the plasma level of these hormones (Sachar, 1969).

The popular visualization/relaxation procedure developed by the Simontons (Simonton, Simonton, & Creighton, 1978) contains an interesting *cognitive reframing approach*. While most people who are afraid of cancer typically view it as a powerfully destructive disease, the Simontons reframe this erroneous view: The cancer cells are described as "weak" and "confused" while the immune system's white blood cells are "strong" and "powerful," like sharks attacking meat. Because their cancer program also includes group therapy for resolving underlying problems and developing coping skills, the Simontons have not been able to differentiate which factor of their approach is most effective. Hall's (1982) work using their imagery and reframing, however, does clarify that this approach can enhance cellular immunity.

A seemingly opposite hypnotherapeutic approach has been developed by Ainslie Meares (1982–83) in what he calls "mental ataraxis." He describes this as a form of intensive meditation that evokes an "inner stillness" that is "central in origin." His approach is the opposite of the Simontons' and of all those who seek to increase the patient's comfort, relaxation, or coping skills, because it requires no act of will. As Meares describes it, "An essential feature of this form of meditation is the absence of striving, of trying, and of using one's willpower." He claims his approach leads to a nonverbal understanding of the self and the universe that can effectively lead to a regression of very serious forms of cancer. Meares has had personal, deep experiences in his form of intensive meditation. He believes that this is communicated to patients nonverbally on an unconscious level, thus providing further positive reinforcement of the possibilities awaiting their experiences with "mental ataraxis."

Most current practitioners use a "garden variety" of all the above approaches (Margolis, 1982–83; Newton, 1982–83). The work of Finkelstein and Greenleaf (1982–83) is typical: For a prospective three-year study of cancer, they have prepared a ten-minute audiotape containing suggestions that seemingly cover the entire range of hypnotherapeutic methods we have discussed. The advantage of these broadly general methods is that they follow the Ericksonian principle of allowing the patient's own unconscious to select which suggestions are needed to facilitate therapeutic activity (Erickson & Rossi, 1979). This lack of specificity, however, means that we cannot determine scientifically just which therapeutic mechanisms are involved.

Most therapists are in agreement that some sort of special condition, state, or utilization of mind can enhance immunological functioning. From the perspective developed in this chapter, it could be said that human functioning is so complex that there appears to be an almost infinite variety of state-dependent learning and memory mind-body systems utilizable for healing purposes. Because each individual has a unique history of learnings and life experiences, every case is essentially a new therapeutic study in which specific and nonspecific hypnotherapeutic approaches can be explored for their effectiveness.

An overall *psychobiological model for facilitating cancer regression* is presented in Box 14, which is an update and expansion of a similar psychophysiological model presented by Achterberg (1984). The most general and easily accessible route to mind-body healing is through the naturalistic ultradian healing response that can be recognized and utilized every 90 minutes (as described in the previous two chapters). Individuals can learn how to optimize their natural ultradian healing responses by accessing the positive state-dependent psychobiological resources associated with life experiences involving effective coping and feelings of efficacy and hopefulness. For some individuals this approach will be sufficient. Others will do better by using the ultradian healing response to optimize their more active efforts in using the Simonton and Achterberg attack imagery on the weak and hopeless cancer cells. Yet other individuals will engage in the deeper, personal psychodynamic processes of active imagination by psychoanalytic therapists (Hillman, 1983; Jung, 1929/1984; Mindell, 1982, 1985a, b; Woodman, 1984), or the more spiritually oriented approaches of Meares (1982–83). The art and science of these forms of mind-body healing involve essentially a creative and constructive process that individuals must ex-

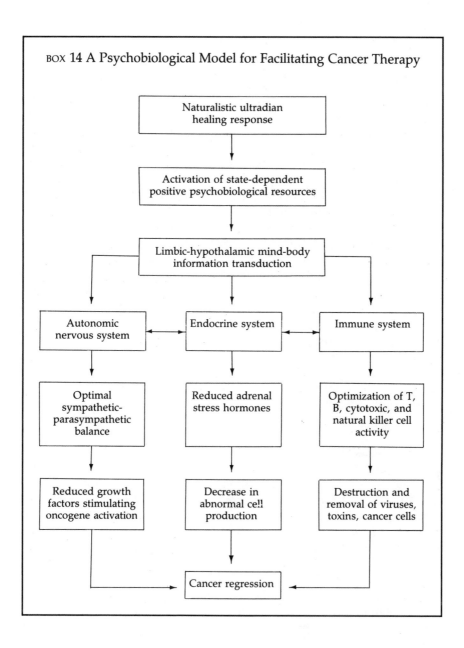

BOX 14 A Psychobiological Model for Facilitating Cancer Therapy

Naturalistic ultradian
healing response

Activation of state-dependent
positive psychobiological resources

Limbic-hypothalamic mind-body
information transduction

| Autonomic nervous system | Endocrine system | Immune system |

| Optimal sympathetic-parasympathetic balance | Reduced adrenal stress hormones | Optimization of T, B, cytotoxic, and natural killer cell activity |

| Reduced growth factors stimulating oncogene activation | Decrease in abnormal cell production | Destruction and removal of viruses, toxins, cancer cells |

Cancer regression

plore in their own way as they learn to maximize their psychobiological potentials.

The Hyperactive Immune System in Asthma and Allergies

Asthma is currently being recognized as a problem characterized by a hyperactive immune response. From the immunological point of view (Hokama & Nakamura, 1982), asthma usually involves a hyperirritability of the bronchial mucosa in the lungs with eosinophils (which, as we have seen, comprise two to three percent of the white blood cell count). Asthma can occur at any age and is recognizable by a wheezing and shortness of breath, which can range from mild discomfort to a life-threatening crisis of respiratory failure. There are two broad classes of asthma: *extrinsic* and *intrinsic* (Hokama & Nakamura, 1982).

Extrinsic (also called by the terms *allergic, immunological,* or *atopic*) asthma is mediated by IgE and can be associated with allergic rhinitis (inflammation of the nasal passages) and urticaria (*hives,* a disease characterized by severe itching and slightly elevated white patches of the skin that rarely lasts more than two days). Skin tests are positive to specific antigens and the IgE levels are usually elevated. This is the form of asthma that is common in early infancy, childhood, and about half of the adult population. It tends to be seasonal on exposure to plant allergins, and so forth.

Intrinsic (also called *nonallergic, nonatopic,* or *idiopathic*) asthma occurs primarily in adults, usually after the occurrence of an infectious respiratory illness (which apparently activates the immune system). It tends to be more chronic, with bronchial obstructions occurring unrelated to seasonal exposure to allergins. In addition, the IgE level is generally normal. In spite of these immunological differences, the clinical manifestations of extrinsic and intrinsic asthma are so similar that their psychophysiological mechanisms are believed to follow the same or similar route. The hypothalamus has been demonstrated experimentally to stimulate or attenuate allergic reactions (Frick, 1976; Stein, Schiavi, & Camerino, 1976) in animals. The sympathetic branch of the autonomic nervous system stimulates the allergic reaction by releasing histamine from the tissues, while the parasympathetic (relaxation) branch inhibits it.

Circadian and Ultradian Rhythms in Asthma. The chronobiological influences of circadian rhythms on the occurrence of asthmatic attacks has been investigated (Reinberg, Gervais, & Ghata, 1977). The peak of dyspenic reactions (shortness of breath) has been shown to coincide in timing with the peak of skin reactions to histamine and allergins over the 24-hour daily cycle, so that most attacks occur between midnight and 3:00 a.m. These daily variations in susceptibility and illness have been traced to circadian rhythms that are apparently initiated in the hypothalamus, which mediates its effects (in association with the pineal gland's responsiveness to the daily light and dark cycle) through the endocrine system. It has been found that circadian rhythms in blood eosinophils depend in part upon the daily rhythms in the release of ACTH from the pituitary and its stimulation of hormones from the adrenal cortex. This is the same hypothalamic-pituitary-adrenal axis described by Selye as the major response to stress in the "Diseases of Adaptation."

There are a number of easily understandable mind-body routes by which the nonspecific hypnotherapeutic approaches (such as Benson's "relaxation response") can ameliorate allergic responses in a variety of psychosomatic illnesses. In my own clinical work, I have found that the form of self-hypnosis described earlier as the ultradian relaxation response is particularly effective when done in combination with symptom scaling so that the patient gradually attains voluntary control over allergic and asthmatic responses. A heightened sensitivity to the minimal cues that signal the beginning of an asthmatic response enable the patient to convert the asthmatic symptom into a signal for facilitating self-healing. Lankton (1987) is currently developing a related Ericksonian approach that combines symptom scaling and metaphor.

In working with asthmatics, as well as with any other symptom reaction that might have a life-threatening potential (e.g., *status asthmaticus* wherein the patient literally cannot get his breath), it is always wise to have qualified medical personnel available on the premises. When using the symptom scaling approach in such cases, one never asks the patient to experience anything more than 25 percent, or at most 30 percent, of the worst previous reaction. The symptom scaling should never get above 50 percent of the type of severe response that could cause a medical emergency. Symptom responses scaled in lower and lower ranges are actually the goal, because we are usually attempting to heighten the patient's awareness of only the most minimal cues that are needed to convert the symptom into a signal for healing.

Studies of the effectiveness of hypnotherapy with asthma and its related clinical manifestations have been reviewed by several researchers (Bowers & Kelly, 1979; DePiano & Salzberg, 1979; Wadden & Anderton, 1982). The great variety of methods described as "hypnotic" makes it difficult to assess these studies, which usually are a mixture of what we described earlier as the specific and nonspecific approaches. It seems likely that satisfactory resolution of these issues will be achieved only by isolating and studying the effects of hypnosis on specifically known and easily measurable allergic responses. Pioneering work in this area has been initiated by Ikemi and Nakagawa (1962) for allergic dermatitis and allergic responses to food, and by Kaneko and Takahashi (1963) for chronic urticaria. The largest body of research in the hypnotic alteration of acquired immunological allergic responses (such as the tuberculin skin test by Black, 1969, and Mason, 1963) is ripe for replication in light of the greater knowledge we now have about the mind-body connections involved. One cannot help but wonder, for example, if the movement of neutrophils facilitated by mental imagery discussed earlier (Schneider et al., 1984) could not be adapted to shift the locus of the closely related eosinophils from the bronchial tracts to ameliorate the hyperactive immune response in asthma and its related allergic dysfunctions.

The Misguided Immune System in Autoimmune Dysfunctions and Rheumatoid Arthritis

An autoimmune dysfunction is one in which the immune system, in a perilous error of identity, attacks the tissues of the self as well as those of foreign invaders. A fundamental issue in immunology is the means by which the body distinguishes between antigens (or foreign substances) and what is natural: This is the distinction between nonself and self that breaks down during an autoimmune dysfunction. Currently it is believed that this "learning" process takes place during fetal development as a result of the direct contact between the body's own substances and the receptor sites on the surface of the white blood cells. The immune system learns to recognize self by disarming the antigen-antibody reaction in relation to all the natural substances (autoantigens) of the body.

As life goes on, however, there are many pathways for the breakdown of the central mechanisms underlying self-recognition. Usually the breakdown involves a disruption of the normal pathways of interaction between the T- and B-cells with autoantigens. Autoimmune disorders are usually associated with malignancies, immune deficiency syndromes, injuries, and aging. In this section we will review recent research on rheumatoid arthritis as an example of how new hypnotherapeutic approaches to autoimmune dysfunctions could be developed.

Rheumatoid arthritis (RA) is a generalized systemic illness that usually has a slow onset manifested by symptoms of fatigue, muscle stiffness, and parasthesias (unusual sensations of burning, prickling, numbness). As the disease progresses, the major joints of the body (shoulders, elbows, wrists, fingers, hips, knees, ankles, and toes) are experienced as swollen and stiff.

Acute and chronic joint pain develops while moving and even at rest, and there is growing restriction in joint movement. The severity of the problem fluctuates over time with periods of remission occurring; sometimes an apparently complete "spontaneous" recovery takes place.

The physiology of the joint problems in RA is still the subject of research, and the autoimmune aspects of the disease are not yet entirely clear. It is thought, however, that the immediate problem is due to the excess growth of the cells in the synovial membrane, which normally covers the interior of the joint in a thin layer and secretes a lubricating fluid. One hypothesis of the mechanism for this process is that the Epstein-Barr virus* alters the synovial tissues (or the cartilage or joint tissues themselves) so that the immune system mistakenly marshals an attack that causes the synovial tissues to proliferate excessively (Silberner, 1985). The excess tissue spreads into the joint, causing the swelling that ultimately destroys the cartilage and, in advanced cases, rendering the joint immobile. It is believed that both cellular (T-cell lymphocytes) and humoral (B-cell lymphocytes) immunopathology are involved in the mistaken identity attack that now takes place. Macrophage activity is then greatly increased to remove the debris. Excess enzymes in turn cause more cartilage damage. It is believed that negative emotions increase muscle tension and the resulting excess activation of the sympathetic branch of the autonomic nervous system can further exacerbate this deteriorating condition (Achterberg & Lawlis, 1980; Weiner, 1977).

The mind-body connection in RA is believed to be mediated via our now familiar *limbic-hypothalamic-pituitary* route. Achterberg and Lawlis (1980) have outlined the possible dynamics of the process, summarized as follows.

1) In the RA patient, the stresses of life that are usually filtered through mind-cortical processes are blunted; the person frequently appears to be devoid of affect, emotionally flat or colorless, and "without soul." This lack of emotion has been described as *alexithymia*—literally, a condition in which one is "without words for feelings." Nemiah, Freyberger, and Sifneos (1976) have proposed that psychosomatic patients have a defective pattern of associative connections between their cortex and their limbic system.
2) Neural activity that is usually associated with emotions is not experienced in the higher cortical pathways of mind but is instead short-circuited through the hypothalamus and its direct associations with

---

* Epstein-Barr virus is a versatile herpes virus which infects many people throughout the world but does not always produce symptoms.

the autonomic, endocrine, and immune systems. RA (and perhaps psychosomatic symptoms in general) is thus a form of body language that substitutes for the lack of verbal (left hemisphere) and imagistic-emotional (right hemisphere) language. This condition has also been described as *pensée opératoire*, or the inability to fantasize.

3) The use of body language instead of cognition, fantasy, and emotion may involve an increase in muscle tension in the RA patient which, in turn, increases joint pain and actually accelerates destruction within the joints by increasing intra-articular temperatures (that stimulate lysomal enzymatic activity).

4) There may be an accelerating cycle of interaction between the immune system and the hypothalamus that is characterized by *positive* biofeedback, which worsens the RA condition instead of correcting it (as would be the case with the normal *negative* biofeedback processes).

The concept of alexithymia as a structural or genetic defect in the mind-cortical and limbic-hypothalamic areas is still a highly speculative theory regarding the genesis of RA in particular, and psychosomatic disorders in general. A more conventional psychodynamic explanation by Erickson and Rossi (1979) was based on the denial, suppression, and/or repression of right-hemispheric experience so that the left hemisphere lacked the information needed to express the problem in words. While further research will be needed to differentiate between the relative merits of these two views, they are in agreement that *state-bound information* is of essence in psychosomatic dysfunctions. The normal accessing and flow of information in the mind-body system are either blocked, short-circuited, or misguided so that the body is left to process information that would be better dealt with at the level of mind in a symptomatic manner.

Erickson's approaches to patients who exhibited varying degrees of chronic pain, hopelessness, apathy, or blunted affect involved his usual exploration of their ability to use the classical mechanisms of hypnotic dissociation, displacement, time distortion, and so forth, in combination with his often unusual approach of *emotional provocation* (see Volume 4 of Erickson, 1980). A great deal of the controversy surrounding Erickson's work has centered on his unconventional use of shock, surprise, and embarrassment (Rossi, 1973/1980) to provoke what we now recognize as heightened states of autonomic system arousal. For example, he frequently used bold measures to provoke patients with a variety of organic brain dysfunctions to higher levels of rehabilitative effort (Erickson, 1963/1980, 1980a).

As I mentally review my observation of Erickson's work with a variety of patients during the last eight years of his life, I now realize that this factor of emotional arousal and provocation was almost always present. Even when he appeared to be acting in a benign and gentle manner, I frequently would catch a gleam of mischievousness in his eye as he used a seemingly innocent word or phrase with hidden levels of meaning that were designed to arouse the patient's emotional dynamics in unexpected ways. More often than not, however, I would miss these multiple levels of communication that could break through the patterns of state-bound information in the patient's total mind-body system until Erickson patiently explained them to me (Erickson & Rossi, 1979, 1981; Erickson, Rossi, & Rossi, 1976). He always seemed to be having a lot of fun as he engaged patients on these multiple levels, and a positive therapeutic bond would exist even when negative emotions had been aroused. In each case Erickson was careful to access and utilize patients' own unique repertory of life experiences to help them create new mental frameworks and identities that engaged their aroused emotions and personality structures. In this regard Erickson used an integration of both nonspecific (emotional arousal and the alarm response) and specific approaches (the patient's unique life experiences) to facilitate the hypnotherapeutic process. Most of these approaches have never been replicated because they were considered to be manifestations of Erickson's idiosyncratic personality and his flair for the dramatic (Hilgard, 1984) rather than of legitimate therapy. As we have seen in our earlier discussions about the mind modulation of the endocrine and autonomic nervous systems, however, the use of the dramatic to arouse state-bound memories and emotions has a sound psychobiological basis. The blocked or dysfunctional memory, emotion, and fantasy processes of patients with rheumatoid arthritis would seem to be an ideal test category for exploring and extending Erickson's pioneering hypnotherapeutic approaches to the arousal and utilization of each patient's unique mind-body repertory of response abilities.

A case illustration of how state-bound aspects of one's total personality can be encoded in the form of rheumatoid arthritis and released by an accessing process of *active imagination* is provided by a Jungian analyst, Albert Kreinheder. He describes his personal encounter with this disease and his self-healing, as follows (pp. 60–61):

> Two years ago my life seemed to be flowing along beautifully. I had gained some respect in my profession, my health was excellent, and all in all I thought I was doing quite well. At this seemingly high point in my life's achievements I was afflicted with rheumatoid arthritis. I became, by necessity, an anti-hero. I had severe pain in

every joint of my body, including even my jaw bones. After being awake for two or three hours and doing my normal sedentary activities, I would be exhausted and need to go back to bed. My shoulders and elbows were so stiff that unassisted, I couldn't put on my jacket nor without help could I rise from a prone position.

I tried everything, including physicians, chiropractors, nutritionists, masseuses, and tarot cards, but nothing seemed to work. Not knowing what else to do, I decided to talk to my pain. Here is a sample of the dialogues that materialized:

> ME: You hold me tight in your grip, and you do not let me go. If you crave my undivided attention, you have received it. Whatever I attend to, I must also attend to you. Even when I write, I feel you in my hand, and always in all parts of my body. I am terribly frightened by you. I have no control over you, no access to you, no power to influence you. You need only go a little further, and then I am utterly helpless. Will you ever stop? Why are you here?
>
> PAIN: I am here to get your attention. I make known my presence. I show you my power. I have a power beyond your power. My will surpasses yours. You cannot prevail over me, but I can easily prevail over you.
>
> ME: But why must you destroy me with your power?
>
> PAIN: I do so because I will no longer let you disregard me. You will bow down before me and humble yourself, for I am He of whom there is no other. I am the first of all things, and all things spring from me, and without me there is nothing. I want to be with you closely in your thoughts at all times. That is why I press you in the grip of my power and make you think only of me. Now, with my presence in you, you can no longer live the same way and do the same things.

These dialogues gave meaning to my disability. Before, my pain was only a curse to be eliminated. Now it is revealed to be "He-of-whom-there-is-no-other." And this great-one desired intimacy with me. Now I knew what before were only words to me: Our wound is the place where the Self finds entry into us. The calamity that strikes may be the election, the call to individuation.

I became aware that my life had to change. When people are in the twenties, thirties, and perhaps through the forties, it is amazing to discover how totally ego-centered people can be and still prosper. But sooner or later, the larger personality asserts itself. "The time is coming," my pain said to me, "when I will put a stop to all those things that come before your love for me." And he said further: "It is so pressing and important that you love me and stay with me that you will be crippled and paralyzed by anything that threatens to be more important than I. Love me first. To ignore me brings death, disease, and destruction."

When a neurosis or a sickness comes to one, it does not mean that he is an inferior person with a defective character. In a way, it is a positive sign showing potentials for growth, as if within there is a greater personality pressing to the surface. When arthritis came to me, I went back into analysis. I did so, I suppose, because I had arthritis. But the intention of the unconscious was probably the other way around. Arthritis came so that I would go back into analysis. We are never fully analyzed. As conditions change, there are new psychic contents to integrate. Once a window is opened to the archetypal world, there is no way to close it again. Either we grow with the individuation urge, or it grows against us.

A recent seven-year follow-up (personal communication) has indicated that Dr. Kreinheder is still symptom-free. This profound view of the deeper possible meaning of illness has been expressed by shamans and healers of all cultures and times. Dr. Kreinheder's experience with arthritis demonstrates how illness can be a call to stop one's habitual activities to seek out the deeper meanings that are evolving in one's existence. This is the basis of the ultradian healing process I call "converting a symptom into a signal."

Converting a Symptom into a Signal

Tuning into a symptom with an attitude of respectful inquiry rather than the usual patient stance of avoidance, resistance, and rejection is the first step to accessing the state-dependent memories and associations that may be signals from those parts of the personality that are in need of expressive development (individuation). I usually introduce the concept of converting a symptom into a signal of the need for a broader creative development in the patient's inner life somewhat as follows (Rossi, 1986b, p. 20):

> You can use a natural form of self-hypnosis by simply letting yourself really enjoy taking a break whenever you need to throughout the day. You simply close your eyes and tune into the parts of your body that are most comfortable. When you locate the comfort you can simply enjoy it and allow it to deepen and spread through-

out your body all by itself. Comfort is more than just a word or a lazy state. Really going deeply into comfort means you have turned on your parasympathetic system—your natural relaxation response. This is the easiest way to maximize the healing benefits of the rest phase of your body's natural ultradian rhythms.

As you explore your inner comfort you can *wonder* how your creative unconscious is going to deal with whatever symptom, problem or issue that you want it to deal with. Your unconscious is the inner regulator of all your biological and mental processes. If you have problems it is probably because some unfortunate programming from the past has interfered with the natural processes of regulation within your unconscious. By accepting and letting yourself enjoy the normal periods of ultradian rest as they occur throughout the day, you are allowing your body/mind's natural self-regulation to heal and resolve your problems.

Your attitude toward your symptom and yourself is very important during this form of healing hypnosis. *Your symptom or problem is actually your friend! Your symptom is a signal that a creative change is needed in your life.* During your periods of comfort in ultradian self-hypnosis, you will often receive quiet insights about your life, what you really want, and how to get it. A new thoughtfulness, joy, greater awareness, and maturity can result from the regular practice of ultradian self-hypnosis.

THE IMMUNE SYSTEM, INFORMATION, AND CONSCIOUSNESS

Stephen Black is an English researcher who pioneered the use of hypnosis in the mind modulation of acquired immunological reactions that previously were thought to be purely biological processes. His research on the use of hypnosis to modulate the immune response of human subjects to the tubercular bacillus (the Mantoux reaction) (Black, Humphrey, & Niven, 1963) and allergic reactions of the skin (Black, 1963; Black & Friedman, 1965) was the inspiration of many researchers described in this chapter (Smith, McKenzie, Marmer, & Steele, 1985; Smith & McDaniel, 1983). Black was guided in his investigation by an ardent philosophical interest in establishing the conceptual unity of mind, body, and life itself. His hypnotic investigations of acquired immunity were for him an empirical means of solving the mind-body problem—the separation of mind and body into two separate conceptual realms since the time of Descartes. Since this is essentially the same mind-body issue we are dealing with in this

---

BOX 15 Converting a Symptom into a Signal

1. *Scaling to convert symptoms into signals*
   On a scale of one to 100 where 100 is the worst, what number expresses the degree to which you are experiencing that symptom right now?
   Recognize how that symptom intensity is actually a signal of just how strong another, deeper part of you needs to be recognized and understood right now.

2. *Accessing and inquiry into symptom meaning*
   When your inner mind (creative unconscious, etc.) is ready to help you access the deeper meanings of your symptoms, you'll find yourself getting quiet and comfortable with your eyes eventually closing. [Pause]
   You can review the original sources of that symptom [pause], you can ask your symptom what it is saying to you [pause], you can discuss with your symptom what changes are needed in your life.

3. *Ratifying the significance and value of new meaning*
   How will you now use your symptom as an important signal? [The significance of whatever new meanings come up usually can be recognized intuitively by the subject. New meaning is invariably accompanied by affects (tears, enthusiasm, thankfulness). A rescaling of symptom intensity at this time will usually ratify the value of this form of inner work.]

---

book, we will review Black's ideas and explore their implications for current thinking.

Black used the newly developing *information theory* of the 1960s as a conceptual base for proposing a common definition of biological life and mind. To understand the significance of his definition it is important to have a basic comprehension of information theory, which we touched upon in Chapter 2. While information theory was originally formulated as a mathematical model (Shannon & Weaver, 1949; Wiener, 1948) for emerging communication technologies, it rapidly was found useful for conceptualizing all processes of change and transformation. In Chapter 2, for example, we summarized the view that all biological and psychological processes could be understood as different forms of information transduction. One way of resolving the mind-body problem is to say that mind and body participate in similar processes of information transduction. We reviewed the work of many theorists and experimental psychologists who used information theory as the conceptual basis for understanding how hypnosis could mediate the mind modulation of the body's physiology (Bowers, 1977).

While information theory is usually formulated in mathematical language, it will be sufficient for our purposes to state its basic idea as follows: *The more improbable an idea or event is, the higher its informational value.* In commonsense terms: Whatever is routine, ordinary, and expected in our lives usually does not contribute any new information to us. What is new, mysterious, and interesting, however, does contribute. Thus whatever is *new* for a person has high informational value.

Chapter 2 described how the ascending reticular activating system (ARAS) and the *locus coeruleus* are the parts of the brain stem that activate consciousness when new and novel stimuli are presented. The *new* can come from the outer environment or be generated within during creative states of thinking and dreaming. Repetitive and routine life situations and habitual patterns of ideation, on the other hand, tend to lower one's level of consciousness and put the mind to sleep. This leads us to the basic insight that consciousness (and mind in general) thrives on information. *Mind is nature's supreme design for receiving, generating, and transducing information.*

In this informational conception of mind, the word *design* has important implications. Design implies form and structure. Information is usually manifest to us as changes in design, form, and structure. The significance of this structural view of information for understanding how the phenomenal aspects of mind and the material aspects of brain and body can be embraced within the same conceptual framework is well described by Karl Pribram (1986, in press):

> Maurice Merleau-Ponty, an existentialist philosopher, has authored a book entitled *The Structure of Behavior* (1963), which in both spirit and content shows remarkable resemblances to our own *Plans and the Structure of Behavior* (Miller, Galanter, & Pribram, 1960; see also Pribram, 1965), which tackles the issues from a behavioral and information-processing vantage. I do not mean to convey here that there is no distinction between a behavioristic and an existential-phenomenalistic approach to mind. Elsewhere I detail this distinction in terms of a search for causes by behaviorists and a search for

informational structure reasonably (meaningfully) composed by phenomenologists (Pribram, 1979). What I do want to emphasize here is that both approaches lead to conceptualizations that cannot be classified readily as either mental or material. Behaviorists in their search for causes, rely on drives, incentives, reinforcers, and other 'force'-like concepts that deliberately have a Newtonian ring. Existentialists in their quest for understanding mental experience come up with structure much as do anthropologists and linguists when they are tackling other complex organizations. And structural concepts are akin to those of modern physics where particles arise from the interactions and relationships among processes.

Understanding how computer programs are composed helps to tease apart some of the issues involved in the "identity" approach in dealing with the mind/brain relationship: Because our introspections provide no apparent connection to the functions of the neural tissues that comprise the brain, it has not been easy to understand what theorists are talking about when they claim that mental and brain processes are identical. Now, because of the computer/program analogy, we can suggest that what is common to mental operations and the brain "wetware" in which the operation is realized, is some order which remains invariant across transformations. The terms "information" (in the brain and cognitive sciences) and "structure" (in linguistics and in music) are the most commonly used to describe such identities across transformations.

Order invariance across transformations is not limited to computers and computer programming. In music we recognize a Beethoven sonata or a Berlioz symphony irrespective of whether it is presented to us as a score on sheets of paper, in a live concert, over our high fidelity music system, and even in our automobiles when distorted and muffled by noise and poor reproduction. The information (form within), the structure (arrangement) is recognizable in many realizations. The materials which make the realizations possible differ considerably from each other, but these differences are not part of the essential property of the musical form. In this sense, the identity approach to the mind/brain relationship, despite the realism of its embodiments, partakes of Platonic universals, i.e., ideal orderings which are liable to becoming flawed in their realization.

In the construction of computer languages (by humans) we gain insight into how information or structure is realized in a machine. The essence of biological as well as of computational hierarchies is that higher levels of organization take control over, as well as being controlled by, lower levels. Such reciprocal causation is ubiquitous in living systems: thus the level of tissue carbon dioxide not only controls the neural respiratory mechanism but is controlled by it. Discovered originally as a regulatory principle which maintains a constant environment, reciprocal causation is termed "homeostais." Research over the past few decades has established that such *feedback* mechanisms are ubiquitous, involving sensory, motor, and all sorts of central processes. When feedback organizations are hooked up into parallel arrays, they become feedforward control mechanisms which operate much as do the words (of bit and byte length) in computer languages (Miller et al., 1960; Pribram, 1971).

Pribram's use of this structural concept of information enables him to unite mental and physiological relationships in a single framework of reciprocal causation or homeostasis that is characteristic of all our illustrations of mind-body communication (Figures 1-7). With this background of understanding, we can now return to Black's use of information theory to conceptualize how the immune system provides a model of mind-body communication and healing. In the following quotations, Black makes use of the concept of information as structures that are new (improbable) to define life and mind (1969):

> It is then the basis of my argument that since the Aristotelian form of *all* matter "contains information" in some degree and since "information in the form of form" is apparently essential to living matter, *it is according to the improbability of the form of matter—as distinct from its energetic substance—that life should be defined.*
>
> I therefore put forward the definition: *that life is a quality of matter which arises from the informational content inherent in the improbability of form.* (p. 46)
>
> I therefore put forward a second hypothesis: *that mind is the informational system derived from the sum improbability of form inherent in the material substance of living things.* (p. 56)
>
> Information, of course, can be transmitted in all sorts of ways—from the modulations in a wireless wave, to the black and white patterns on the pages of this book. And to workers in biology at the molecular level, the concept of both transmitting and recording information "in the form of form" is certainly nothing new.
>
> But the facts here are not generally looked at in this kind of way. Although the difference may even seem trivial—and by some damned as "metaphysical"—it is nevertheless important to my theme. For

I hope to show from the clinical and experimental evidence of psychosomatic medicine, that whatever the stability of the genetic substance, much of the information recorded by the body in the form of form can in the course of life make its own contribution both to sickness and to health. (p. 47)

Black's view of *form* as the in*form*ational essence of life and mind sounds very abstract until we remember that it is true at the molecular level. It is, in fact, the form and structure of messenger molecules and their receptors that turn on and modulate the activity of life within all the cells of the body. Black's pioneering research was a step in demonstrating how this is true for mind-body communication via the immune system, as illustrated in Figure 6. As indicated in previous chapters, we now know it is also true for the autonomic (Fig. 4, p. 106) and endocrine (Fig. 5, p. 126) systems. In the next chapter we will learn how it is valid for the neuropeptide system as well.

It was probably because Black was so concerned with the essentially unconscious nature of mind-body information transduction in psychosomatic problems that he did not give any corresponding definitions of consciousness. I believe that the definition of consciousness as "a process of self-reflective information transduction," which I proposed in Chapter 2, fits admirably well with Black's views, however. Some of the major modalities or forms of information transduction that make up the content of consciousness were presented in Box 6 (p. 85). While these mental modalities (emotions, imagery, cognition, etc.) are at a different level of description than body and molecule, they are all united by *our currently emerging view of life, biology, and mind* as being essentially in*form*ational trans*form*ations of each other.

The practical application of this unitary conception of form in psychobiological phenomena is evident in many of the schools of psychotherapy that developed out of the classical depth psychologies of Freud and Jung. One immediately thinks, for example, of gestalt therapy and all its derivatives. Jung, himself, gave a central place to the significance of form in his basic concept of the archetype as a "psychoid" or psychobiological structure that formed the essence of ideas, symbols, and processes of trans*form*ation. He described his views as follows (Jung, 1960, p. 33):

There is not a single important idea or view that does not possess historical antecedents. Ultimately they are all founded on primordial archetypal forms whose concreteness dates from a time when consciousness did not *think*, but only *perceived*. "Thoughts" were objects of inner perception, not thought at all, but sensed as external phenomena—seen or heard, so to speak. Thought was essentially revelation, not invented but forced upon us or bringing conviction through its immediacy and actuality. Thinking of this kind precedes the primitive ego-consciousness, and the latter is more its object than its subject. But we ourselves have not yet climbed the last peak of consciousness, so we also have a pre-existent thinking, of which we are not aware so long as we are supported by traditional symbols— or, to put it in the language of dreams, so long as the father or the king is not dead.

There are many important associations here. I believe that Black's conception of life and mind as "the informational content inherent in the improbability of form" is the fundamental axiom for an *information theory of image, archetype, symbol, and the mythopoetic dimension of right-hemispheric consciousness in general and mind-body healing in particular.* The profound reach of information theory into our current conceptions of psychotherapy is usually not immediately obvious. When I first formulated the following hypothesis about the significance of original dream experience for the development of identity and consciousness, for example, I had no idea that it was actually a phenomenological expression of an informational theory of mind (Rossi, 1972/1985, p. 25):

HYPOTHESIS 1. *That which is unique, odd, strange or intensely idiosyncratic in a dream is an essence of individuality. It is an expression of original psychological experience and, as such, it is the raw material out of which new patterns of awareness may develop.*

What is "unique, odd, strange or intensely idiosyncratic" is, of course, a subjective experience of what information theory describes as the high informational value of an improbable event. As noted earlier in Chapter 2, we can now better appreciate why the mind-body gives greatest attention to "novel stimuli": Simply put, they have a higher informational value. When we focus patients' attention with what they experience as new or novel, we are maximizing the probability of facilitating therapeutic processes involving information transduction of high value. This can become the basis of many therapeutically stimulating approaches to mind-body healing.

This is probably the reason why patients who have not found help by conventional medicine intuitively turn to the unusual and often seemingly bizarre approaches of other cultures and "holistic medicine." This is how mystery and the *numinosum* (Jung, 1960) of religious practices and strange cults can cure: They all help patients break out of the learned limitations of their familiar thinking and lifestyle that are encoding the adaptive value of their sickness or problem. The unusual practices of the mystery religions and foreign healers break through the constricting and deadening effect of the familiar to access and activate the high informational value of the new within the body-mind of the patient.

This excursion into the byways of an informational theory of psycho-biology and mind-body healing has taken us far from the research of Black on the hypnotic modulation of the immune system and the major concerns of this chapter with mind-body healing. However, this integration of pre-viously separate studies in fields as diverse as philosophy, religion, cul-tural anthropology, psychology, biology, neurology, and molecular genetics is precisely what is most valuable in our developing information theory of mind-body healing. In the next and final chapter, we will witness an even more profound integration of all these areas of inquiry for the crea-tion of consciousness and healing.

10

Mind Modulation of the Neuropeptide System

THE VANGUARD OF neurobiological research today suggests that an entirely new understanding of mind-body communication integrating the autonomic, endocrine, and immune systems is being conceptualized in the *neuropeptide system*. Working in the Brain Biochemistry Division of the National Institute of Mental Health, Pert and her colleagues have proposed that neuropeptides and their receptors function as a previously unrecognized psychosomatic network. They summarized their views as follows (Pert, Ruff, Weber, & Herkenham, 1985, p. 820s):

> A major conceptual shift in neuroscience has been wrought by the realization that brain function is modulated by numerous chemicals in addition to classical neurotransmitters. Many of these informational substances are neuropeptides, originally studied in other contexts as hormones, "gut peptides," or growth factors. Their number presently exceeds 50 and most, if not all, alter behavior and mood states, although only endogenous analogs of psychoactive drugs like morphine, Valium, and phencyclidine have been well appreciated in this context. We now realize that their signal specificity resides in receptors (distinct classes of recognition molecules), rather than the close juxtaposition occurring at classical synapses. Rather precise brain distribution patterns for many neuropeptide receptors have been determined. A number of brain loci, many within emotion-mediating brain areas, are enriched with many types of neuropeptide receptors suggesting a convergence of information at these "nodes." Additionally, neuropeptide receptors occur on mobile cells of the immune systems; monocytes can chemotax to numerous neuropeptides via processes shown by structure-activity analysis to be mediated by

distinct receptors indistinguishable from those found in brain. *Neuro-peptides and their receptors thus join the brain, glands, and immune system in a network of communication between brain and body, probably represent-ing the biochemical substrate of emotion.* (Italics added)

Pert's use of the term "informational substance" to describe the essential messenger function of the neuropeptide system is a new way of integrat-ing the data and behavior from the previously separated fields of knowl-edge in psychology, neurology, anatomy, biochemistry, and molecular biology. There is much research suggesting that the central and autonomic nervous systems, and the endocrine and immune systems are all channels, carriers, or vehicles for the messenger molecules of the neuropeptide sys-tem (Besedovsky, del Rey, & Sorkin, 1985; Blalock, Harbour-McMenamin, & Smith, 1985; Bloom, 1985; Felton et al., 1985). An overview of the neuro-peptide system as far as it is currently understood is illustrated in Figure 7. As can be seen, the neuropeptide system adds to, overlaps with, and integrates all the previously discussed systems of mind-body communica-tion (Figures 1-6). For clarity, we will outline six focal areas of the neuro-peptide system that are the subject of intense research at this time.

1) *The Limbic-Hypothalamic Locus of Neuropeptide Activity.* Our view of the fundamental role of the limbic-hypothalamic system "filter" in mind-body communication that was illustrated in Fig. 1 (p. 26) is confirmed by re-cent conceptualizations of the neuropeptide system, as follows (Pert et al., 1985, p. 821s):

A fundamental feature shared by all neuropeptide receptors whose brain distribution has been well studied is profound enrichment at a number of the same brain areas. Many of these neuropeptide receptor-rich areas can be found within an intercommunicating con-glomerate of brain structures classically termed "the limbic system," which is considered to mediate emotional behavior; in unanesthetized humans undergoing brain stimulation as a prelude to surgery for ep-ilepsy, far-ranging emotional expression can be elicited by stimula-tion of cortex near the amygdala, the core of the limbic system. The amygdala, as well as the hypothalamus and other limbic system-associated structures, were found initially to be enriched in opiate receptors in monkey and human brains. Later maps of numerous other neuropeptide receptors in brain [including substance P, bomb-esin, cholecystokinin, neurotensin, insulin, and transferrin] have

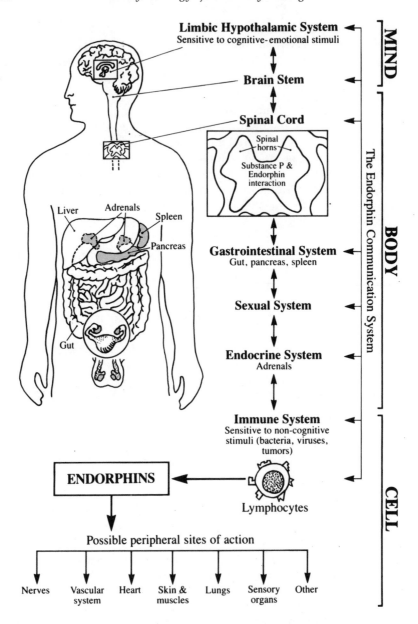

FIGURE 7 The nodal or focal areas of the neuropeptide communication system. The central role of the endorphin neuropeptides in mind/body regulation is emphasized.

continued to implicate the amygdala and other limbic system-associated structures (e.g., the cingulate cortex) as a source of receptor-rich sites where mood presumably is biochemically modified.

Evidence for the central role of the limbic-hypothalamic system and the opiate neuropeptides (the endorphins and enkephalins) in a variety of emotional processes and mood disorders is by now overwhelming. The networks of neurons that mediate these mind-body patterns of communication extend outside the limbic system to other brain areas (olfactory bulb, habenula, interpeduncular nucleus), and to the lower brain stem reticular activating system, to which we will now turn our attention.

2) *The Brain Stem and Spinal Cord Locus of Neuropeptide Activity.* The new methods of neuropeptide research suggest an extension of limbic system boundaries to include the modulation of sensory information, as follows (Pert et al., 1985, p. 821s):

> . . . The dorsal horn of mammalian spinal cord where neurons transmitting information from glands, skin, and other peripheral organs make their first synaptic contact with the central nervous system, is enriched with virtually all neuropeptide receptors. Although it has not previously been considered part of the limbic system, neuropeptide receptors here, as postulated for other sensory way-stations, may filter and prioritize incoming sensory information so that the whole organism's perception is most compatible with survival.

The mind modulation of sensory-perceptual processes is a classical characteristic of hypnotic phenomena (Orne, 1972). The localization of neuropeptide receptors at the major sensory way-stations in the central nervous system strongly suggests that they play an important role in the psychobiological mechanisms of hypnotically generated illusions and hallucinations, as well as in hypnotically induced analgesia and anesthesia.

The periaqueductal grey region of the brain stem and the dorsal horn of the spinal cord are important relay stations for pain transmission; they are rich in their balanced use of the endorphins and the neuropeptide called "substance P." Substance P *facilitates* the transmission of pain; the endorphins *block* pain transmission by inhibiting the release of substance P. There has been a great deal of controversy regarding the possible role of these neuropeptides in mediating hypnotically-induced analgesia. Some early workers (Barber & Meyer, 1977; Goldstein & Hilgard, 1975; Olness, Wain, & Ng, 1980; Spruiell et al., 1983) were unable to demonstrate any effect of hypnosis on their measures of the endorphin neuropeptides, while others (Domangue, Margolis, Lieberman, & Kaji, 1985) continue to find suggestive experimental evidence for it. The many subtle and not easily measurable and controllable variables that influence both hypnosis and neuropeptide activity make these experimental studies doubly difficult to assess.

It is probably significant that the one experimental study that found hypnotic anesthesia to be mediated by endorphins was with a subject who was in a deep somnambulistic trance (Stephenson, 1978). All the other experimental studies in this area used many hypnotic subjects, but they were not carefully assessed in a clinical manner to determine if they had achieved a somnambulistic state. Indeed, many experimentalists (Barber, 1972; Sarbin & Coe, 1972) purporting to use hypnosis do not even believe it is an altered state. Erickson (1967/1980) and Weitzenhoffer (1982) have noted separately how this sad lack of understanding of the classical historical criteria for the somnambulistic state has given rise to many of the ambiguous and negative findings of supposedly controlled experimental studies of hypnosis.

What is clear from these studies, however, is that there are at least two, and probably many, mechanisms of anesthesia. In fact, recent experimental research (Shavit et al., 1985) has confirmed that there are at least two forms of analgesia: One is mediated by the endorphins while the other is not. The immune system suppression effects of stress are associated with the endorphin-mediated form of analgesia. This process will be touched upon in the next section.

3 & 4) *The Immune and Endocrine System Integration by Neuropeptides.* The immune and endocrine systems that are the third and forth loci of neuropeptide action are so closely interrelated that we will discuss them together. Most of the hormones, hypothalamic controls, and neuroendocrinal messenger molecules mentioned in this section are neuropeptides. Blalock, Harbour-McMenamin, and Smith (1985) have described this interrelationship between the immune and endocrine systems as follows (p. 858s):

> While numerous studies have demonstrated that the neuroendocrine system can control immune functions, it is only now becoming apparent that the control is reciprocal in that the immune system can control neuroendocrine functions. In this paper, recent studies which seem to provide a molecular basis for this bidirectional communication are reviewed. These studies suggest that the immune and neur-

oendocrine systems represent a totally integrated circuit by virtue of sharing a common set of hormones, such as corticotropin, thyrotropin, and endorphins, and the receptors. Possible hypothalamic and immunologic controls of this circuitry are discussed.

In a closely related paper, Smith, Harbour-McMenamin and Blalock (1985) have described the overall significance of this interaction between the immune and neuroendocrine systems for mind-body communication in health and disease, as follows (p. 779s):

Numerous indirect and anecdotal examples suggest that there is a link between an individual's mental state and his or her susceptibility to or recovery from disease. Although a direct connection has not been proven, it is logical for this to involve an interaction between the brain and immune system. A growing body of evidence has shown that hormones, in particular glucocorticoids [a group of hormones produced by the adrenal cortex] released during stress, can modulate immune system functions. More recent evidence suggests that neuroendocrine polypeptide hormones are also immunomodulatory. This then is fairly good evidence for a mechanism by which the central nervous system might influence the course of a disease. Conversely, the question of how diseases seem to alter mental states and cause apparently unrelated physiologic or homeostatic changes in the host is only beginning to be answered. A possible explanation for this feature of disease is a recent finding in our laboratory that stimulated leukocytes produce molecules apparently identical to pituitary hormones that are capable of signaling the neuroendocrine system. . . . The immune and neuroendocrine systems appear able to communicate with each other by virtue of signal molecules (hormones) and receptors common to both systems.

The lower portion of Figure 7 (the cellular level) is an adaptation of Smith, Harbour-McMenamin and Blalock's (1985) model. Their work (published in that paper and in Blalock, Harbour-McMenamin, & Smith, 1985) implies that the immune system can function as a sensory "organ," signaling the central nervous system about noncognitive stimuli such as bacteria, tumors, viruses, and other toxins within the body. As can be seen in Figure 7, the endorphin neuropeptides play a central role in the mind-body regulation of all the major systems of the body. If hypnotically induced comfort could be demonstrated to facilitate the activity of any one of these systems, it would be an important link in the growing lines of

evidence supporting the therapeutic use of hypnosis as a means of mind-
body communication and healing.

5) *Enteric Nervous System: The Gastrointestinal Locus of Neuropeptide Activity*. The enteric nervous system regulates the gastrointestinal organs in
semi-independent manner (Bulloch, 1985). This system is estimated to be
of comparable complexity with the neural system of the spinal cord (Gerson,
Payette, & Rothman, 1985), and it has been used as a model to study the
ontogenetic development of the central nervous system. Various hormonal
neuropeptides of the enteric-gastrointestinal system are also independently active in the central nervous system: The endorphins, substance P, and
somatostatin are among the most prominent (see Table 5, pp. 199–201).
The same somatostatin molecule that is used as a messenger substance
in neurons of the cerebral cortex, hippocampus, and hypothalamus,
for example, is used as a hormone messenger when it is produced in the
pancreatic islets to regulate insulin and glucagon secretion.

The use of hypnosis for amelioration of gastrointestinal distress has a
long history (Crasilneck & Hall, 1959; Gorton, 1957; Weiner, 1977). The
current challenge is to illuminate the actual mind-body communication
processes involved in the therapeutic effects. A reassessment of neuropeptide activity in the gastrointestinal areas during hypnosis would seem to
be a good approach to this issue (Weiner, 1977).

When our emotional state is optimal, we are hardly ever aware of the
enteric system's automatic activity. When we are emotionally upset, however, the entire gastrointestinal tract can express our discomfort. The sensitivity of the gastrointestinal tract to mental stress is one of the most
widely recognized manifestations of psychosomatic problems (Alexander,
1950; Weiner, 1977). The way in which the early psychoanalysts such as
C.G. Jung described this connection between mind and stomach is typical
(1976, p. 88):

> There is hardly a case of neurosis where the entrails are not dis-
> turbed. For instance, after a certain dream a diarrhoea happens, or
> there are spasms in the abdomen. . . . I know of a number of cases
> of people who did not know what they ought to do, people who got
> lazy when they should have organized their lives on a somewhat
> larger scale, who omitted their duty and tried to live like chickens,
> and they then got frightful spasms in the abdomen.

In another source Jung wrote (1929/1984, pp. 130–131):

> Instinctive powers are released, partly psychological, partly physi-
> ological, and through that release the whole disposition of the body
> can be changed. People in such a state of mind are in a condition
> for infections and physical disturbances. You know how close the
> connection is between the stomach and mental states. If a bad psy-
> chic state is habitual, you spoil your stomach. . . .

If we update Jung's terminology from "instinctive powers" to "mind-
body communication systems," we could hardly have a better description
of the far-reaching effects of state-dependent enteric-gastrointestinal distress. It could be speculated that the widespread early practices of "reading" the entrails of sacrificed animals for purposes of divination and healing may have come about because of the easily recognized association
between mental and intestinal states. Peoples from many early cultures
felt that their thinking actually came from their abdominal area (Jung,
1950). That modern man can learn how to utilize the enteric-gastrointestinal system as a creative feeling function is illustrated by the interesting
case of the "third voice of the mind-body" presented below.

A lawyer in his mid-thirties had been accidentally shot in the abdomen
a number of years earlier. The bullet had damaged his pancreas and a
portion of his small intestine, which had to be removed surgically. The
emotionally traumatic aspects of the event, as well as the remaining physical sensitivity in the wounded area, left him with a problem. For many
years he had experienced fears, repetitive traumatic dreams, gastrointestinal discomfort, and a haunting lack of self-confidence—even though
he had graduated with honors from one of the leading Ivy League universities, had clerked for a well-known senator in Washington, and was
acknowledged as a future leader in his special field of international law.

Although he was unaware of the periodic ultradian rhythms of gastrointestinal activity (see Rossi, 1986a), he had learned from his own personal
experience that even after recovering from his wound he could no longer
subject himself to the abuse of skipping meals and working for extended
periods with no rest breaks. In spite of this awareness, he recently had
been subjected to a variety of stresses during a critical career shift, which
precipitated a severe bout of diverticulitis. This led him to seek psychobiological counseling.

In therapy he was able to learn self-hypnosis well enough to control the
pain of his diverticulitis. He also felt reassured to learn that the ultradian
rhythms of enteric-gastrointestinal activity were normal, though he recognized that his old bullet wound had awakened him to a special sensitivity

to these rhythms. He had always regarded this sensitivity as a "problem" until I inquired about the details of how he experienced it. He reported that his "guts" would make loud noises that could be heard by others in the room when he was involved in administrative meetings and discussions with his clients. We soon came to regard this problem as a "third voice" that was present particularly when he was in a tight and "sensitive" professional situation in which he needed "extra wisdom." I suggested that, rather than try to suppress this symptom, he let himself become even more sensitive to it so that he could hear what it had to say when it whispered, rather than putting it off until it had to shout so loud everyone in the room could hear it! In this manner I was helping him convert his symptom into a signal (as discussed in the last chapter).

At this point he experienced a medical emergency which his internist described as a life-threatening attack of diverticulitis. He then had the following dream. (See Rossi, 1972/1985, for a general discussion of healing dreams.)

> I dreamed my wife and I were going to the doctor's because I had a cut on my stomach. *I was upset about leaving work for this.* I was also looking at other rehabilitation programs in Philadelphia on the way to the doctor's. I ran into a volunteer nurse from the hospital where I worked. She asked me suspiciously if *I was looking for other work at these hospitals. I told her no—we have visited the hospitals, but did not talk to any administrators about work possibilities.* I felt guilty. Then we went outside this other hospital which we were visiting. *I pulled on a swollen part of my stomach and a huge pustular sac came out from my intestine.* The inside of my intestines started to bleed. *I felt good, relieved that I had gotten the infected part out,* but was afraid of the bleeding. I immediately called my internist.

It would be easy to miss the healing processes constellated in this dream by glibly interpreting the events as depicting conflict and mere wish fulfillment. For a professional workaholic, it was naturally upsetting to leave work and all too tempting to seek more work at a hospital. Instead, his dream ego turns away from using the hospital as a work opportunity and facilitates his own healing process by pulling out the infected pustular sac from his intestine. This suggests that he is now rechanneling his excessive and stressful work activity into inner healing in cooperation with his internist. This dream signaled the significant turning point of transforming his problem into a creative function. Indeed, my client gradually succeeded in reframing his problem as he became more and more aware of what the third voice of his mind-body was saying to him. The outside world's voice might threaten him, his own voice might tremble in response, but the third voice within his gut would let him know in no uncertain terms just where and when he had to draw the line. When his conscious voice vascillated in indecision, the third voice of the mind-body would counsel him as follows:

> Be firm, you have to take care of yourself, don't let the world eat you up! Don't let them take up your lunch hour with yet another meeting.
> Don't let anyone step on your guts, be responsible to yourself when no one else is.
> Accepting human limitations is the better part of wisdom. The ego is a madman that has led many excellent men to their destruction.
> It doesn't matter what others think; it's my comfort that gives me life.

The third voice that would no longer permit him to abuse himself physically or emotionally eventually became a creative function that counseled him on many "touchy" international situations in which he had to negotiate with a special sensitivity that only his gut could provide. After many years he eventually recognized that his was essentially the way of the shaman: he was learning to use his former illness to sensitize himself to the hidden ills and ways of healing the societies in collision around him.

This case illustrates the fundamental difference between our psychobiological approach of conceptualizing symptoms as maladaptive forms of information transduction that can become important signals for creative personal development, and the more typical stance of behavioral medicine and classical conditioning therapy which regard symptoms as problems that have to be extinguished (Gentry, 1984). As illustrated in Box 16, our approach is also very different from the traditional psychoanalytic goal of using analysis as a method of resolving problems. The behaviorist and psychoanalytic approaches both throw away valuable information by placing themselves in opposition to the problem network. Our psychobiological approach uses these data by accessing the state-dependent memory, learning, and behavior systems that encode problems and reframing them into creative functions. *Many types of chronic pain and recurrent symptoms and problems are actually information transducers that amplify the minimal stress signals of the mind-body.*

The process of reframing and rechanneling stress signals into appropriate patterns of personal development and meaning resembles the tradi-

---

BOX 16 Transforming a Problem into a Creative Function

1. *Accessing and amplifying a problem-encoded resource*
   Access the circumstances during which a chronic problem becomes manifest.
   Gradually amplify your sensitivity to milder instances of the problem before it causes your usual discomfort.
   Wonder how your new sensitivity can become a resource for problem-solving.

2. *Transducing a problem into a creative function*
   Use your heightened sensitivity as a radar to scan the minimal cues in the situations that are evoking your "problem."
   See, hear, feel, intuit the meanings of your mind-body responses. Record, draw, and meditate on dreams and fantasies about the problem.
   Recognize what personal developmental changes are needed for a wiser adaptation to life stressors.

3. *Ratifying your new creative function*
   Review and contrast your old, painful and maladaptive way of being with your new understanding.
   Reframe your previous life problems in the light of your new relationship to the world and self-identity that you are actively creating each day.

---

tional approaches of many forms of cultural and spiritual healing. In these frameworks, sickness is frequently conceptualized as a visitation from God to guide us in our uncertain path through the shadows of life. However, many of these ancient healing practices eventually become limited and dogmatic in their perspective, rather than continually experimental and innovative as life is itself. Let us hope that our psychobiological perspective can integrate the best of the old and new approaches to mind-body healing by using nature's own messages as our constant inspiration and guide.

6) *The Sexual System and Neuropeptide Activity*. In a recent assessment of neuropeptides and their receptors as a psychosomatic network, Pert et al. (1985) noted that human testes are "as rich a source of messenger RNA

for the opiate peptide proopiomelanocortin as the pituitary gland.'' Proopiomelanocortin is the celebrated "mother molecule" that generates ACTH and endorphin, which, as we have seen, are perhaps the most ubiquitous messengers of the entire neuropeptide system. A rich research literature is developing around the mind-body connections between the limbic-hypothalamic system, the process of dreaming, and sexual activation (Rossi, 1972/1985). This literature emphasizes the ACTH-endorphin pattern of neuropeptide regulation. Indeed, the relationship between sex, stress, and aggression that has been emphasized in the psychoanalytic literature may find its psychobiological basis in this ACTH-endorphin system. Stewart has touched upon recent thinking in this area as follows (1981, p. 774):

> Although there has been considerable speculation about the role of this brain ACTH-End system, only now is it possible to advance a reasoned hypothesis as to what that role may be. We propose that this set of neurons is a major regulator of central nervous system activity, principally through its influence on the midbrain monoamine systems. In certain circumstances it appears that this system can cause the higher cortical centers to be turned off or else disconnected, so that the organism functions under the control of the evolutionarily ancient midbrain centers mediating primarily instinctive behavior. This "turning off" appears to occur during acute stress, and the "disconnection" during paradoxical sleep (PS).

Stewart continues (1981, p. 778):

> Massive peripheral ACTH release occurs in acute stress, and central events can be presumed to mirror this situation. Acute stress, and particularly asphyxiation, which is considered to be a potent "humoral" stress, cause erection and orgasm, the well-known "agonal orgasm." Some persons can evidently achieve orgasm only under such stress, a fact which leads to accidental deaths from choking and perhaps also to much of the interpersonal violence of our times. Stress-induced orgasm is depicted in such works of literature as Samuel Beckett's *Waiting for Godot*, John Hershey's *The War Lover*, and the works of de Sade.
>
> The diurnal rhythm of ACTH release also contributes confirmatory evidence to the hypothesis. ACTH is secreted principally in bursts during episodes of paradoxical sleep (rapid eye-movement sleep). PS is characterized by sexual stimulation. . . .

Since therapeutic hypnosis has been used to access and modulate this same complex of stress, dreams, aggression, and sexual functioning (Araoz, 1982, 1985), one cannot help but wonder, once again, if neuropeptides are the common denominator.

One of Erickson's most celebrated cases of psychosexual rehabilitation, which took place with a patient who had organic spinal cord damage, dealt with this entire complex of stress and emotions and can serve as a clinical illustration of what is possible in this area. A highly condensed version of this case is excerpted from Erickson and Rossi (1979) as follows (pp. 428–439):

> Some years ago a young woman in a wheelchair approached the senior author and declared that she was profoundly distressed—in fact, suicidally depressed. Her reason was that an accidental injury in her early twenties had left her with a transverse myelitis: she was lacking in all sensations from the waist down, and she was incontinent of bladder and bowel. Her purpose in seeing the senior author was that she wanted to secure a philosophy of life by which to live; the incontinence of bladder and bowel and confinement to a wheelchair were more than she felt she could endure. She had heard the senior author lecture on hypnosis and had reached the conclusion that perhaps by hypnosis some miraculous change in her personal attitudes could be affected. She explained further that as a small child she had been extremely interested in cooking, baking, sewing, playing with dolls, and fantasizing about the home, husband, and children she would have when she grew up. At the age of twenty she had fallen in love and made plans to marry upon completion of college. She had set to work filling a hope chest with hand-sewn linens and designing her own wedding dress. All she had ever wanted was a husband, a home, children, and grandchildren. Her love for her own grandmothers was a strong factor in her life, and she shared much emotional identification with them.
>
> The unfortunate accident resulting in the transverse myelitis put an end to all her dreams and expectations. After some ten years of stormy difficulties and complications, she became able to use a wheelchair and to return to her university studies. Even with this improvement in her situation she saw no future for herself in the academic world, and became progressively depressed with increasing suicidal ideation. She had finally reached a point at which she felt some definite decision had to be made. Therefore she wished the author to induce a "very deep hypnotic trance and discuss possibilities and potentialities for me. . . ."

Her request was abided by and, probably because of her deep motivation, a very deep somnambulistic trance state was elicited. She was tested with great care for her ability to manifest the phenomena of deep hypnosis. Depersonalization, dissociation, time distortion, and hypermnesia of the happy past were either avoided or the suggestions were worded so carefully that there could not be even a seeming attempt to change her views and attitudes. . . .

One suggestion of a therapeutic character that did come to mind was a well-known song of the old variety, which she was asked to hallucinate, visually and auditorily, with an orchestra and singer. The song was the one about the toebone being connected with the footbone, the footbone with the heelbone, the heelbone with the anklebone, and so on. . . . [Erickson continues:]

"I noticed that you were left-thumbed, left-eyed, and left-eared last week, and I made up my mind that you should have free access to what your conscious mind knows about your body but does not know that it knows, and what your body knows freely but that neither your conscious nor your unconscious mind openly knows. *You might as well use well all knowledge that you have, body or mind knowledge, and use all of it well.* What does your body know and know full well, which you know and know full well consciously and unconsciously? Just this little thing! You think that erectile tissue is in the genitals, *just the genitals*. But what does your body know? Just take your finger and thumb and snap your soft nipple and watch it stand right out in protest. It knows that it has erectile tissue. You have had that knowledge without knowing it for a long time. And where else do you have erectile tissue? In New York State you stepped out of doors in thirty degrees below zero and felt your nose harden. Naturally! It has erectile tissue! Why else would it harden? And watch that hot baby slobbering for a kiss from the man she loves and see her upper lip get thick and warm? Erectile tissue in the upper lip!. . . .

The external genitals are connected to the internal genitals, and the internal genitals are connected to the ovaries, and the ovaries are connected with adrenals, and the adrenals are connected with the chromaffin system, and the chromaffin system is connected with the mammaries, and the mammaries are connected with the parathyroids, and the thyroid is connected with the caratid body, and the carotid body is connected with the pituitary body, and the system of all these endocrine glands is connected with all sexual feelings, and all your sexual feelings are connected with all your other feelings, and if you don't believe it, let some man you like touch your bare breasts and you feel the hot, embarrassed feeling in your face and your sexual feelings. Then you'll know that every word I've said is true, and if you don't so believe, try it out, but the deep red flush on your face right now says you know it's so.

"So continue sleeping deeply, review carefully every word I have said to you, try to dispute it, to argue against it. Try your level best to disagree, but the harder you try the more you will realize that I am right.

"Now put a look of starry-eyed expectation on your face, clothe yourself in an air of happy confidence. Romance for you is just around the corner [a crucial statement], I don't know which corner [a statement that leaves the question undecidable and hence requiring further consideration], *but it's just around the corner!* Don't ever forget there's a Rachel for every Reuben and a Reuben for every Rachel, and every Jean has her Jock and every Jock has his Jean, *and around the corner is your "John Anderson, my Jo."*

"One doubt you will have, but naturally you are wrong! Your body knows, so does your conscious mind, so does your unconscious mind. Only you, the person, don't know.

"Is there anything more ecstatic than the maiden's first sweet kiss of true love? Could there be a better orgasm? Or the first grasping of the little lips of the baby on your nipple! Or the cupping of your bare breasts by the hand of your love? Have you ever felt the chills run up and down your spine when kissed on the back of your neck?

"Man has but one place to have an orgasm—a woman has many.

"Continue your trance, evaluate these ideas, make no error about their validity."

A Ten-Year Follow-up

Within two years she was married. Her husband was a dedicated research man, and his field of interest was the biology and chemistry of the human colon. They have been married happily for over ten years, and there are now four children, all by caesarian operations.

Ten years after the marriage the author happened to be lecturing in the state of her residence. She noted a news story on the author and called him on the telephone, asking him to lunch with her the next day. Before meeting her, three duplicate sets of questions were typed out. The answers were filled in on one set, which was sealed in an envelope. The other two sets were placed in separate envelopes.

The purpose of the duplicate sets of questions was to obtain an objective report from her regarding her sexual experiences and compare them with what Erickson thought they would be. Her responses indicated that she was experiencing sexual orgasms three or four times a week with her husband. She had learned to shift her genital orgasmic response to her breasts, neck, and lips. Erickson quoted her descriptions of her sexual experiences as follows (Haley, 1985, Vol. 1, p. 26):

> I have excellent orgasms. I have plenty of orgasms in my breast, I have a separate one in each nipple. I get a very warm, rosy feeling of engorgement in my thyroid, and my lips swell up quite a bit when I have an orgasm, the lobes of my ears. I have the most peculiar feeling between my shoulder blades. I rock involuntarily, uncontrollably, I get so excited.

Erickson liked to use this case as an illustration of the psychoneurophysiological alterations that were possible with therapeutic hypnosis. There is much to suggest that the neuropeptide system is the psychoneurophysiological basis of this type of hypnotherapeutic response. This hypothesis is based on the mind-body communication system illustrated in Figure 7 and the outline in Table 5, which both suggest how neuropeptide messenger molecules, channeled through the autonomic, endocrine, and immune systems, could mediate the all-encompassing scope of Erickson's seemingly nonsensical hypnotic rhyme about "the footbone connected to the heel bone. . . . the external genitals connected to the . . . ovaries . . . adrenals . . . chromaffin system . . . mammaries . . . parathyroids . . . thyroid . . . cartoid body . . . pituitary body . . [and the] endocrine glands connected with all sexual feelings." It will require the ingenuity of unique teams of psychobiological researchers and hypnotherapists to explore the actual mind-molecule communication systems that mediate such healing responses.

The wide distribution of the neuropeptide system, as well as its seemingly unlimited ability for information transduction between all the channels of mind-body communication, can act as a springboard for a number of new approaches to therapeutic hypnosis based on Erickson's work described above. This is particularly the case when a life problem is accompanied by feelings of hopelessness and depression, as in the case above. I have previously described how depression can be a signal of the need to break out of an outmoded pattern of adaptation into the actualization of a new identity that is already developing spontaneously within the person on an unconscious level (Rossi, 1972/1985). I frequently describe the process as "transforming a problem into a creative function."

THE NEUROPEPTIDE SYSTEM AS MEDIATOR
OF THERAPEUTIC HYPNOSIS

The characteristics of mind-body communication via the neuropeptide system, particularly in contrast to communication via central and peripheral nervous systems, suggest that neuropeptides may be a significant factor in the neuropsychophysiological basis of our state-dependent memory and learning theory of therapeutic hypnosis. Since this is an entirely new idea about hypnotherapeutic healing that could not have been conceived of before the recent conceptualization of the neuropeptide system, I will summarize a few lines of evidence that now need further experimental validation to support this view. These lines of evidence touch upon factors, such as the *distribution, timing, archaic quality, conscious-unconscious relations, and flexibility*, which the neuropeptide system seems to share in common with the phenomena of hypnosis.

The wide *distribution* of the neuropeptide messenger molecules and their receptors could account for the idiosyncratic patterns of hypnotic experience that follow the "mind's body image" rather than the classical pathways of the CNS.

Since the neuropeptides are transmitted through virtually all the body fluids (blood, lymph, cerebrospinal fluid, etc.), as well as between neurons, the neuropeptide system is not confined to the traditional neuronal circuits of the central nervous system. The puzzlement that hypnotherapists have had for centuries over the fact that psychosomatic or hypnotically induced anesthesias do not follow the classical CNS pathways innervating specific dermatones (segmental cutaneous areas) of the body, for example, could now be explained: Perhaps the neuropeptide system is mediating hypnotic responses by the "mind's body image" via the limbic-hypothalamic system. Indeed, many mind-body effects that have been disparagingly described as caused by mere imagination and therefore being "unreal" may now have a recognizable biological basis.

As can be seen in Table 5, virtually any cell or pattern of cells in the body can receive information from the neuropeptide system if it has the appropriate *receptors*. The columns of Table 5 fit the classical three-stage paradigm of information theory: sender-channel-receiver. A major area of research is needed to investigate how receptors operate as a highly variable system that can change its patterns of response as a function of life experience encoded as state-dependent memory, learning, sensation, per-

TABLE 5 Information transduction in mind-body communication. Some of the major messenger molecules of the autonomic, endocrine, immune, and neuropeptide systems are listed in the channel column.

SENDER	CHANNEL	RECEIVER	REFERENCES
AUTONOMIC Limbic-hypothalamic brain stem system; spinal nerves	**VIA NEURON CHANNEL** *NEUROTRANSMITTERS* *Amino Acids:* Aspartic Glutamic, etc. *Monoamines:* Acetylcholinie Catecholamines Dopamine Norepinephrine Serotonin *Neuropeptides* Endorphins Somatostatin Substance P, etc.	**Receptors** On neurons to all target organs in ANS, heart, GI tract, lungs, pupils, etc.	**Hypnotic Literature** Barber, 1984; Black, 1969; Braun, 1983a, b; Crasilneck & Hall, 1985; Dunbar, 1954; Erickson, 1943a, b, 1977; Hudgins, 1933; Lewis & Sarbin, 1943; Olness & Conroy, 1985; Sternbach, 1982
ENDOCRINE Hypothalamus	**VIA BLOOD CHANNEL** *HORMONES* Thyrotropin-Releasing Hormone (TRH) Gonadotropin-Releasing Hormone (GnRH) Somatostatin Corticotropin-Releasing Factor (CRF) Growth Hormone-Releasing Hormone (GHRH)	**Receptors** Pituitary	**Hypnotic Literature** Crasilneck & Hall, 1985; Delhounge & Hansen, 1927; Dunbar, 1954; Erickson, 1943a, b, c; Gorton, 1958; Kroger & Fezler, 1976; Wolberg, 1947

(continued)

TABLE 5 *Continued*

SENDER	CHANNEL	RECEIVER	REFERENCES
ENDOCRINE Anterior Pituitary	**VIA BLOOD CHANNEL** Adrenocorticotropic Hormone (ACTH) β-Endorphin Melanocyte-Stimulating Hormone Prolactin Growth Hormone (GH) Luteinizing Hormone (LH)	**Receptors** Glands in endocrine system: adrenals, pancreas, testes, ovaries, thyroid, etc.	**Psychobiological Literature** Besedovsky et al., 1985; Bulloch, 1985; Domangue et al., 1985; Pert et al., 1985; Rosenblatt, 1983; Stewart, 1981; Weiner, 1977
Posterior Pituitary	Vasopressin Oxytocin Neurophysins		
Enteric-Gastrointestinal	Vasoactive Intestinal Polypeptide (VIP) Cholecystokinin (CCK) Enkephalins Endorphins Substance P Neurotensin Bombesin Secretin Glucagon Insulin Gastrin		

IMMUNE
Organs such as bone marrow, lymph, thymus, spleen, tonsils, etc.; lymphocytes, B & T cells, macrophages, natural killer cells, neutrophils, etc.

VIA BLOOD AND LYMPH CHANNELS
ACTH, TSH
Endorphins
Thymosins
Lymphokines
Interleukins
Interferon

Receptors
On neurons in the hypothalamus and other brain areas; leukocytes in blood, spleen, thymus, lymph, skin, GI tract; blood vessels; endocrine glands

Hypnotic Literature
Achterberg, 1985; Black, 1969; Hall, 1982–83; Ikemi & Nakagawa, 1962; Mason, 1963; Schneider et al., 1983

NEUROPEPTIDE
DNA→RNA→Peptide in limbic-hypothalamic system; GI tract and other nodal centers

VIA NEURONE, BLOOD, LYMPH CHANNEL
PEPTIDES
Hypothalamic Releasing Hormones
  e.g., Somatostatin (growth)
Pituitary Peptides
  e.g., ACTH (stress)
  β-endorphin (emotions)
  Vasopressin (memory)
Gut-Brain Peptides
  e.g., Substance P (pain)
Others
  e.g., Bradykinin (shock)
  Angiotensin II (blood pressure)

Receptors
Nodal centers in limbic-hypothalamic, dorsal horn of spine, periacque-duct grey, testes, ovaries, gastrointestinal, immune and endocrine systems

Hypnosis and Placebo Literature
Achterberg, 1985; Barber & Meyer, 1977; Domanque et al., 1985; Goldstein & Hilgard, 1975; Hilgard, 1977; Hilgard & Hilgard, 1975; Olness, Wain, & Ng, 1980; Rosenblatt, 1983; Spruiell et al., 1983

ception, mood, and mental activity (Bloom, Lazerson, & Hofstadter, 1985; Cordes, 1985).

Time relationships are another aspect of the hypnotic experience that may be elucidated by the different *modus operandi* of the CNS and the neuropeptide system: The CNS responds very quickly, in fractions of a second for most behaviors, while the neuropeptide system usually takes several minutes or even hours for some of its responses (Rosenblatt, 1983). The same is true for the full experience of most hypnotic phenomena. Erickson (1952/1980) has described how sufficient time (usually 10 to 20 minutes, but sometimes hours) is necessary to effect the ''psycho-neuro-physiological'' changes characteristic of a genuine hypnotic response, versus the simulation of hypnotic effects that can take place instantly with the help of conscious role-playing.

Many experienced clinicians have commented on the regressive, archaic, or atavistic quality of hypnotic responsiveness (Gill & Brenman, 1959; Meares, 1982-83; Shor, 1959). In tracing the evolutionary origins of the neuropeptide system, Roth and his colleagues (Roth et al., 1985) presented evidence that it is older than the central, autonomic, and endocrine systems; it is the method of communication in one-cell organisms, plants, and lower orders of animal life. Since nature tends to conserve her systems (Bockman & Kirby, 1985), we can now understand how the neuropeptides form a deeper and more pervasive system of mind-body information transduction than does the CNS.

Thus the slower-acting but more pervasive, flexible, and unconscious functioning of neuropeptide activity of mind-body communication more adequately fits the facts of hypnotic experience than the faster-acting, highly specific, and consciously generated processes of the central and peripheral nervous systems. If we were to use a computer analogy, we could say that the peripheral nerves of the CNS are ''hard wired'' in a preset, fixed pattern of stimulus and response, just as is the hardware of a computer. The neuropeptide system, however, is like the ''software'' of a computer that contains the flexible, easily changed patterns of information. The receptors and highly individualized responses of the neuropeptide system are easily changed as a function of life experience, memory, and learning.

Neuropeptides, then, are a previously unrecognized form of information transduction between mind and body that may be the basis of many hypnotherapeutic, psychosocial, and placebo responses. From a broader perspective, the neuropeptide system also may be the psychobiological basis of the folk, shamanistic, and spiritual forms of healing (that share many of the characteristics of hypnotic healing) currently returning to vogue under the banner of ''holistic medicine.''

Summary and Overview

THE SURVEY of the psychobiology of mind-body healing presented in this book has led to a series of ever surprising insights into the changing structure of our understanding of the human condition. Let us summarize some of these insights.

1) *Information theory* is capable of unifying psychological, biological, and physical phenomena into a single conceptual framework that can account for mind-body healing, personality development, the evolution of human consciousness, and a fascinating panorama of cultural practices.

2) *Information transduction* is emerging as the key concept in our psychobiological theory of mind-body communication and healing. The basic laws of biology, psychology, and cultural anthropology are all essentially descriptions of different levels of information transduction.

3) *State-dependent memory, learning, and behavior* form the most general class of psychobiological phenomena that can be used to account for the dynamics of information transduction in humans. Classical Pavlovian and Skinnerian conditioning, as well as the psychodynamics of psychoanalysis, can be economically conceptualized as special cases of state-dependent memory, learning, and behavior.

4) There is no mysterious gap between mind and body. State-dependent memory, learning, and behavior processes encoded in the *limbic-hypothalamic and closely related systems* are the major information transducers that bridge the Cartesian dichotomy between mind and body.

5) Traditional *psychosomatic symptoms* and, perhaps, most mind-body problems are acquired by a process of experiential learning—specifically, the state-dependent learning of response patterns of Selye's General Adaptation Syndrome. Enduring mind-body problems are manifestations of these state-bound patterns of learning that are encoded within a limbic-hypothalamic system "filter" which modulates mind-body communication.

6) This limbic-hypothalamic system filter coordinates all the major chan-

nels of mind-body regulation via the autonomic, endocrine, immune, and neuropeptide systems. *Messenger molecules* (neurotransmitters, hormones, immunotransmitters, etc.) flowing through these channels are the structural in*form*ational mediators of mind-body communication and trans*form*ation.

7) Ongoing research is clarifying the precise pathways by which these messenger molecules are mediating the *mind-gene connection* that is the ultimate basis of most processes of mind-body healing via therapeutic hypnosis, the placebo response, and the traditional practices of mythopoetic and holistic medicine.

8) The new approaches to mind-body healing and therapeutic hypnosis may be conceptualized as processes of *accessing* and *utilizing* state-dependent memory, learning, and behavior systems that encode symptoms and problems and then *reframing* them for more integrated levels of adaptation and development.

9) The *ultradian healing response* is a newly developed approach to mind-body healing that is easy to learn, as people are encouraged to become more sensitive to their natural 90-minute psychobiological rhythms.

10) The *new concepts of therapeutic hypnosis* emphasize natural psychobiological processes of information transduction and state-dependent memory, learning, and behavior to access and facilitate the utilization of patients' own inner resources for problem-solving. This is in sharp contrast to previous methods of authoritarian suggestion, influence communication, covert conditioning, and programming in hypnosis.

The psychology of mind-body communication and healing as presented in this book thus introduces a broadly based information paradigm that is capable of integrating and expanding the scope of all previous views of illness and therapy. Much of this material is still so new that it could only be outlined in a manner that may seem intuitive and visionary; it is, however, scientifically well-documented. The art and science of reframing symptoms into signals and problems into creative functions are only beginning. It will require the dedicated efforts of all of us to gradually sift out what is of value in this work as a guide for future research, theory, and clinical practice.

References

Achterberg, J. (1985). *Imagery and healing.* Boston: Shambala.

Achterberg, J., & Lawlis, G. (1980). *Bridges of the mind/body.* Champaign, Illinois: Institute for Personality & Ability Testing.

Achterberg, J., & Lawlis, G. (1984). *Imagery and disease.* Champaign, Illinois: Institute for Personality & Ability Testing.

Ader, R. (Ed.) (1981). *Psychoneuroimmunology.* New York: Academic Press.

Ader, R. (1983). Behavioral conditioning and the immune system. In L. Temoshok, C. Van Dyke, & L. Zegans (Eds.), *Emotions in health and illness.* New York: Grune & Stratton.

Ader, R. (1985). Behaviorally conditioned modulation of immunity. In R. Guillemin, M. Cohn, & T. Melnechuk (Eds.), *Neural modulation of immunity.* New York: Raven Press, pp. 55–69.

Alexander, F. (1939/1984). Psychological aspects of medicine. Originally published by *Psychosomatic Medicine. 1*(1). Reprinted in 1984 by *Advances, 1*(2), 53–60.

Alexander, F. (1950). *Psychosomatic medicine.* New York: Norton.

Alexander, F., & French, T. (1948). *Studies in psychosomatic medicine: An approach to the cause and treatment of vegetative disturbances.* New York: Ronald Press.

Amkraut, A., & Solomon, G. (1975). From the symbolic stimulus to the pathophysiologic response: Immune mechanisms. *International Journal of Psychiatry in Medicine, 5,* 541–563.

Anokhin, P. (1949). Problems in higher nervous activity. *Izd. Akad. Med. Nauk SSSR,* Moscow.

Anokhin, P. (1955). New data on the afferent apparatus of the conditioned reflex. *Vop. Psikhol.,* No. 6.

Araoz, D. (1982). *Hypnosis and sex therapy.* New York: Brunner/Mazel.

Araoz, D. (1985). *The new hypnosis.* New York: Brunner/Mazel.

Arya, U. (1979). *Meditation and the art of dying.* Honesdale, PA: Himalayan International Institute.

Bakan, P. (1969). Hypnotizability, laterality of eye movements, and functional brain asymmetry. *Perceptual & Motor Skills, 28,* 927–932.

Bakan, P. (1980). Imagery, raw and cooked: A hemispheric recipe. In J. Shorr, G. Sobel, P. Robin, and J. Connella (Eds.), *Imagery.* New York: Plenum, pp. 35–53.

Bandura, A. (1985). Catecholamine secretion as a function of perceived coping self-efficacy. *Journal of Counseling and Clinical Psychology, 58*(3), 406–414.

Banks, W. (1985). Hypnotic suggestion for the control of bleeding in the angiography suite. *Ericksonian Monographs, 1,* 76–88.

Barabasz, A., & McGeorge, C. (1978). Biofeedback, mediated biofeedback and hypnosis in peripheral vasodilation training. *The American Journal of Clinical Hypnosis, 21*(1), 28–37.

Barber, T. X. (1972). Suggested ("hypnotic") behavior: The trance paradigm versus an alternate paradigm. In E. Fromm & R. Shor (Eds.), *Hypnosis: Research development and perspectives.* New York: Aldine-Atherton.

Barber, T. X. (1978). Hypnosis, suggestions, and psychosomatic phenomena: A new look from the standpoint of recent experimental studies. *American Journal of Clinical Hypnosis,* *21*(1), 13–27.

Barber, T. X. (1984). Changing unchangeable bodily processes by (hypnotic) suggestions: A new look at hypnosis, cognitions, imagining, and the mind-body problem. *Advances,* *1*(2), 7–40.

Barber, T. X., & Meyer, D. (1977). Evaluation of the efficacy and neuronal mechanism of a hypnotic analgesia procedure in experimental and clinical dental pain. *Pain, 4,* 41–48.

Barnett, E. (1984). The role of prenatal trauma in the development of the negative birth experience. Paper presented at the American Society of Clinical Hypnosis Annual Meeting, San Francisco.

Beecher, H. (1959). *Measurement of subjective responses: Quantitative effect of drugs.* New York: Oxford University Press.

Bennett, H. (1985). Behavioral anesthesia. *Advances, 2*(4), 11–21.

Benson, H. (1975). *The relaxation response.* New York: Avon.

Benson, H. (1983a). The relaxation response and norepinephrine: A new study illuminates mechanisms. *Integrative Psychiatry, 1,* 15–18.

Benson, H. (1983b). The relaxation response: Its subjective and objective historical precedents and physiology. *Trends in Neuroscience,* July, 281–284.

Bernheim, H. (1886/1957). *Suggestive therapeutics: A treatise on the nature and uses of hypnotism.* Westport, Conn.: Associated Booksellers. Originally published by Putnam.

Besedovsky, H., del Rey, A., & Sorkin, E. (1985). Immunological-Neuroendocrine feedback circuits. In R. Guillemin, M. Cohn, & T. Melnechuk (Eds.), *Neural modulation of immunity.* New York: Raven Press, pp. 165–177.

Black, S. (1963). Inhibition of immediate-type hypersentivity response by direct suggestion under hypnosis. *British Medical Journal,* April 6, 925–929.

Black, S. (1969). *Mind and body.* London: William Kimber.

Black, S., Edholm, R., Fox, R., & Kidd, D. (1963). The effect of suggestions under hypnosis on the peripheral circulation in man. *Clinical Science, 25,* 223–230.

Black, S., & Friedman, M. (1965). Adrenal function and the inhibition of allergic responses under hypnosis. *British Medical Journal, 1,* 562–567.

Black, S., Humphrey, J., & Niven, J. (1963). Inhibition of Mantoux reaction by direct suggestion under hypnosis. *British Medical Journal,* June 22, 1649–1652.

Blalock, E., Harbour-McMenamin, D., & Smith, E. (1985). Peptide hormones shaped by the neuroendocrine and immunologic systems. *The Journal of Immunology, 135*(2), 858s–861s.

Blankstein, J., Reyes, F., Winter, J., & Faiman, C. (1981). Endorphins and the regulation of the human menstrual cycle. *Clinical Endocrinology, 14*(3), 287–294.

Bloom, F. (1985). Neuropeptides and other mediators in the central nervous system. *The Journal of Immunology, 135*(2), 743s–745s.

Bloom, F., Lazerson, A., & Hofstadter, L. (1985). *Brain, mind, and behavior.* New York: W. H. Freeman.

Blum, G. (1967). Experimental observations on the contextual nature of hypnosis. *International Journal of Clinical & Experimental Hypnosis, 15*(4), 160–171.

Blum, G. (1972). Hypnotic programming techniques in psychological experiments. In E. Fromm, & R. Shor (Eds.), *Hypnosis: Research developments & perspectives.* Chicago: Aldine-Atherton, pp. 359–385.

Bockman, D., & Kirby, M. (1985). Neural crest interactions in the development of the immune system. *The Journal of Immunology, 135*(2), 766s–768s.

Bower, G. (1981). Mood and memory. *American Psychologist, 36*(2), 129–148.

Bowers, K. (1977). Hypnosis: An informational approach. *Annuals of the New York Academy of Sciences, 296,* 222–237.

Bowers, K., & Kelly, P. (1979). Stress, disease, psychotherapy, and hypnosis. *Journal of Abnormal Psychology, 88*(5), 490–505.

Braid, J. (1855). *The physiology of fascination of the critics criticized.* Manchester, England: Grant & Company.

Brassfield, P. (1980). A discriminative study of the dissociative states of a multiple personality. Doctoral Dissertation, United States International University.

Brassfield, P. (1983). Unfolding patterns of the multiple personality through hypnosis. *The American Journal of Clinical Hypnosis, 26*(2), 146–152.

Braun, B. (1983a). Neurophysiologic changes in multiple personality due to integration: A preliminary report. *The American Journal of Clinical Hypnosis, 26*(2), 84–92.

Braun, B. (1983b). Psychophysiological phenomena in multiple personality. *The American Journal of Clinical Hypnosis, 26*(2), 124–137.

Brown, F., & Graeber, R. (Eds.) (1982). *Rhythmic aspects of behavior.* Hillsdale, New Jersey: Lawrence Erlbaum Associates.

Bulloch, K. (1985). Neuroanatomy of lymphoid tissue: A review. In R. Guillemin, M. Cohn, & T. Melnechuk (Eds.), *Neural modulation of immunity.* New York: Raven Press, pp. 111–141.

Cannon, W. (1932). *The wisdom of the body.* New York: W. W. Norton & Co.

Cannon, W. (1942). Voodoo death. *American Anthropologist, 44*(2), 169–181.

Cannon, W. (1953). *Bodily changes in pain, hunger, fear and rage* (2nd ed.). Boston: Charles T. Branford Co.

Cannon, W. (1957). "Voodoo" death. *Psychosomatic Medicine, 19*(3), 182–190.

Cannon, W. (1963). *The wisdom of the body.* (2nd Ed.) New York: W. W. Norton.

Cheek, D. (1957). Effectiveness of incentive in clinical hypnosis. *Obstetrics & Gynecology, 9*(6), 720–724.

Cheek, D. (1959). Unconscious perception of meaningful sounds during surgical anesthesia as revealed under hypnosis. *The American Journal of Clinical Hypnosis, 1,* 101–113.

Cheek, D. (1960). Removal of subconscious resistance to hypnosis using ideometer questioning techniques. *The American Journal of Clinical Hypnosis, 3*(2), 103–107.

Cheek, D. (1962a). Ideometer questioning for investigation of subconscious pain and target organ vulnerability. *The American Journal of Clinical Hypnosis, 5*(1), 30–41.

Cheek, D. (1962b). Importance of recognizing that surgical patients behave as though hypnotized. *The American Journal of Clinical Hypnosis, 4,* 227–238.

Cheek, D. (1965). Some newer understandings of dreams in relation to threatened abortion and premature labor. *Pacific Medical & Surgical,* Nov–Dec, 379–384.

Cheek, D. (1969). Communication with the critically ill. *The American Journal of Clinical Hypnosis, 12*(2), 75–85.

Cheek, D. (1975). Maladjustment patterns apparently related to imprinting at birth. *The American Journal of Clinical Hypnosis, 18*(2), 75–82.

Cheek, D. (1976). Short-term hypnotherapy for fragility using exploration of early life attitudes. *The American Journal of Clinical Hypnosis, 19*(1), 20–27.

Cheek, D. (1978). Were you originally left-handed? *Swedish Journal of Hypnosis,* 17–25.

Cheek, D. (1981). Awareness of meaningful sounds under general anesthesia: Considerations and a review of the literature, 1959–1979. *Theoretical and Clinical Aspects of Hypnosis.* Symposium Specialists, Miami, Florida.

Cheek, D., & LeCron, L. (1968). *Clinical hypnotherapy.* New York: Grune & Stratton.

Chiba, Y., Chiba, K., Halberg, F., & Cutkomp, L. (1977). Longitudinal evaluation of circadian rhythm characteristics and their circaseptan modulation in an apparently normal couple. In J. McGovern, M. Smolensky, & A. Reinberg (Eds.), *Chronobiology in allergy and immunology.* Springfield, Illinois: Thomas, pp. 17–35.

Cohn, M. (1985). What are the "must" elements of immune responsiveness? In R. Guillemin, M. Cohn, & T. Melnechuk (Eds.), *Neural modulation of immunity.* New York: Raven Press, pp. 3–25.

Conn, L., & Mott, T. (1984). Plethysmographic demonstration of rapid vasodilation by direct suggestion: A case of Raynaud's disease treated by hypnosis. *The American Journal of Clinical Hypnosis, 26*(3), 166–170.

Cordes, C. (1985). Neuropeptides: Chemical cruise steers emotions. *APA Monitor, 16*(9), 18.

Cousins, N. (1979). *Anatomy of an illness as perceived by the patient.* New York: Norton.

Cousins, N. (1983). *The healing heart*. New York: Norton.

Crasilneck, H. (1982). A follow-up study in the use of hypnotherapy in the treatment of psychogenic impotency. *The American Journal of Clinical Hypnosis, 25*(1), 52–61.

Crasilneck, H., & Hall, J. (1959). Physiological changes associated with hypnosis: A review of the literature since 1948. *International Journal of Clinical & Experimental Hypnosis, 7*(1), 9–50.

Crasilneck, H., & Hall, J. (1985). *Clinical hypnosis*. New York: Grune & Stratton.

Dalton, K. (1971). Prospective study into puerperal depression. *British Journal of Psychiatry, 118*, 689–692.

Davis, J. (1984). *Endorphins*. New York: Dial Press.

Day, M. (1964). An eye-movement phenomenon related to attention, thought and anxiety. *Perceptual & Motor Skills, 19*, 443–446.

Delbruck, M. (1970). A physicist's renewed look at biology: Twenty years later. *Science, 168*, 1312–1314.

Delgado, J. (1969). *Physical control of the mind*. New York: Harper & Row.

Delgado, J., Roberts, W., & Miller, N. (1954). Learning motivated by electrical stimulation of the brain. *American Journal of Physiology, 179*, 587.

Delhounge, F., & Hansen, K. (1927). Die suggestive beeinflussbarkeit der Magen- und Pankreassekretion in der hypnose. *Dtsch. Arch. Klin. Med., 157*, 20.

Dement, W. (1965). An essay on dreams: The role of physiology in understanding their nature. In *New directions in psychology II*. New York: Holt, Rinehart & Winston.

Dement, W. (1972). *Some must watch while some must sleep*. San Francisco: Freeman.

Dement, W., & Kleitman, N. (1957). Cyclic variations in EEG readings during sleep and their relation to eye movements, body motility, and dreaming. *Electroencephalography & Clinical Neurophysiology, 9*, 673–690.

DePiano, F., & Salzberg, H. (1979). Clinical applications of hypnosis to three psychosomatic disorders. *Psychological Bulletin, 86*, 1223–1235.

Dohrenwend, B., & Dohrenwend, B. (Eds.) (1974). *Stressful life events: Their nature and effects*. New York: Wiley.

Domangue, B., Margolis, C., Lieberman, D., & Kaji, H. (1985). Biochemical correlates of hypnoanalgesia in arthritic pain patients. *Journal of Clinical Psychiatry, 46*, 235–238.

Dunbar, F. (1954). *Emotions and bodily changes*. New York: Columbia University Press.

Dunlap, D., Henderson, T., & Inch, R. (1952). Survey of 17,301 prescriptions of Form Ec 10. *British Medical Journal, 1*, 292–295.

Edelson, R., & Fink, J. (1985). The immunological function of skin. *Scientific American*, June, 46–53.

Ellenberger, H. (1970). *The discovery of the unconscious*. New York: Basic Books.

Engel, G. (1968). A life setting conducive to illness: The giving-up-given-up complex. *Annals of Internal Medicine, 69*(2), 292–300.

Engel, G. (1971). Sudden and rapid death during psychological stress: Folklore or folkwisdom? *Annals of Internal Medicine, 74*, 771–782.

Erickson, M. (1932/1980). Possible detrimental effects of experimental hypnosis. In E. Rossi (Ed.), *The collected papers of Milton H. Erickson on hypnosis. I. The nature of hypnosis and suggestion*. New York: Irvington, pp. 493–497.

Erickson, M. (1937/1980). Development of apparent unconsciousness during hypnotic reliving of a traumatic experience. In E. Rossi (Ed.), *The collected papers of Milton H. Erickson on hypnosis. III. Hypnotic investigation of psychodynamic process*. New York: Irvington, pp. 45–52.

Erickson, M. (1939/1980). Experimental demonstration of psychopathology of everyday life. In E. Rossi (Ed.), *The collected papers of Milton H. Erickson on hypnosis. III. Hypnotic investigation of psychodynamic processes*. New York: Irvington, pp. 190–202.

Erickson, M. (1943a/1980). Experimentally elicited salivary and related responses to hypnotic visual hallucinations confirmed by personality reactions. In E. Rossi (Ed.), *The collected papers of Milton H. Erickson on hypnosis. II. Hypnotic alteration of sensory, perceptual and psychophysical process*. New York: Irvington, pp. 175–178.

Erickson, M. (1943b/1980). Hypnotic investigation of psychosomatic phenomena: A controlled experimental use of hypnotic regression in the therapy of an acquired food intolerance. In E. Rossi (Ed.), *The collected papers of Milton H. Erickson on hypnosis. II. Hypnotic alteration of sensory, perceptual and psychophysical processes.* New York: Irvington, pp. 169–174.

Erickson, M. (1943c/1980). Hypnotic investigation of psychosomatic phenomena: Psychosomatic interrelationships studied by experimental hypnosis. In E. Rossi (Ed.), *The collected papers of Milton E. Erickson on hypnosis. II. Hypnotic alteration of sensory, perceptual and psychophysical processes.* New York: Irvington, pp. 145–156.

Erickson, M. (1943d/1980). Investigation of psychosomatic phenomena: The development of aphasialike reactions from hypnotically induced amnesia. In E. Rossi (Ed.), *The collected papers of Milton H. Erickson on hypnosis. II. Hypnotic alteration of sensory, perceptual and psychophysical processes.* New York: Irvington, pp. 157–168.

Erickson, M. (1948/1980). Hypnotic psychotherapy. In E. Rossi (Ed.), *The collected papers of Milton H. Erickson on hypnosis. IV. Innovative hypnotherapy.* New York: Irvington, pp. 35–48.

Erickson, M. (1952/1980). Deep hypnosis and its induction. In E. Rossi (Ed.), *The collected papers of Milton H. Erickson on hypnosis. I. The nature of hypnosis and suggestion.* New York: Irvington, pp. 139–167.

Erickson, M. (1954/1980). Pseudo-orientation in time as a hypnotherapeutic procedure. In E. Rossi (Ed.), *The collected papers of Milton H. Erickson on hypnosis. IV. Innovative hypnotherapy.* New York: Irvington, pp. 397–423.

Erickson, M. (1960a/1980). Breast development possibly influenced by hypnosis: Two instances and the psychotherapeutic results. In E. Rossi (Ed.), *The collected papers of Milton H. Erickson on hypnosis. II. Hypnotic investigation of sensory, perceptual and psychophysical processes.* New York: Irvington, pp. 203–206.

Erickson, M. (1960b/1980). Psychogenic alteration of menstrual functioning: Three instances. In E. Rossi (Ed.), *The collected papers of Milton H. Erickson on hypnosis. II. Hypnotic investigation of sensory, perceptual and psychophysical processes.* New York: Irvington, pp. 207–212.

Erickson, M. (1961/1980). Historical note on the hand levitation and other ideomotor techniques. In E. Rossi (Ed.), *The collected papers of Milton H. Erickson on hypnosis. I. The nature of hypnosis and suggestion.* New York: Irvington, pp. 135–138.

Erickson, M. (1963/1980). Hypnotically oriented psychotherapy in organic brain damage. In E. Rossi (Ed.), *The collected papers of Milton H. Erickson on hypnosis. IV. Innovative hypnotherapy.* New York: Irvington, pp. 283–311.

Erickson, M. (1964/1980). The ''surprise'' and ''my-friend-John'' techniques of hypnosis: Minimal cues and natural field experimentation. In E. Rossi (Ed.), *The collected papers of Milton H. Erickson on hypnosis. I. The nature of hypnosis and suggestion.* New York: Irvington, pp. 340–359.

Erickson, M. (1967/1980). Further experimental investigation of hypnosis: Hypnotic and nonhypnotic realities. In E. Rossi (Ed.), *The collected papers of Milton H. Erickson on hypnosis. I. The nature of hypnosis and suggestion.* New York: Irvington, pp. 18–82.

Erickson, M. (1977/1980). Control of physiological functions by hypnosis. In E. Rossi (Ed.), *The collected papers of Milton H. Erickson on hypnosis. II. Hypnotic alteration of sensory, perceptual and psychophysical processes.* New York: Irvington, pp. 179–191.

Erickson, M. (1980a). Provocation as a means of motivating recovery from a cerebrovascular accident. In E. Rossi (Ed.), *The collected papers of Milton H. Erickson on hypnosis. IV. Innovative hypnotherapy.* New York: Irvington, pp. 321–327.

Erickson, M. (1980b). *The collected works of Milton H. Erickson on hypnosis, 4 Volumes.* Edited by Ernest L. Rossi. New York: Irvington

Erickson, M. (1980c). The hypnotic alteration of blood flow: An experiment comparing waking and hypnotic responsiveness. In E. Rossi (Ed.), *The collected papers of Milton H. Erickson on hypnosis. II. Hypnotic alteration of sensory, perceptual and psychophysical processes.* New York: Irvington, pp. 192–195.

Erickson, M. (1985). Memory and hallucination, Part I: The utilization approach to hypnotic suggestion. Edited with commentaries by Ernest Rossi. *Ericksonian Monographs, 1,* 1–21.

Erickson, M., & Rossi, E. (1974/1980). Varieties of hypnotic amnesia. In E. Rossi (Ed.), *The collected papers of Milton H. Erickson on hypnosis. III. Hypnotic investigation of psychodynamic processes.* New York: Irvington, pp. 71–90.

Erickson, M., & Rossi, E. (1976/1980). Two-level communication and the microdynamics of trance and suggestion. In E. Rossi (Ed.), *The collected papers of Milton H. Erickson on hypnosis. I. The nature of hypnosis and suggestion.* New York: Irvington, pp. 430–451.

Erickson, M., & Rossi, E. (1979). *Hypnotherapy: A exploratory casebook.* New York: Irvington.

Erickson, M., & Rossi, E. (1980). The indirect forms of suggestion. In E. Rossi (Ed.), *The collected papers of Milton H. Erickson on hypnosis. I. The nature of hypnosis and suggestion.* New York: Irvington, pp. 452–477.

Erickson, M., & Rossi, E. (1981). *Experiencing hypnosis: Therapeutic approaches to altered states.* New York: Irvington.

Erickson, M., Rossi, E., & Rossi, S. (1976). *Hypnotic realities.* New York: Irvington.

Evans, F. (1977). The placebo control of pain: A paradigm for investigating non-specific effects in psychotherapy. In J. Brady, J. Mendels, W. Reiger, & M. Orne (Eds.), *Psychiatry: Areas of promise and advancement.* New York: Spectrum, pp. 215–228.

Evans, F. (1981). The placebo response in pain control. *Psychopharmacology Bulletin, 17,* 72–76.

Evans, F. (1985). Expectancy, therapeutic instructions, and the placebo response. In L. White, B. Tursky, & G. Schwartz (Eds.), *Placebo: Theory, research, and mechanism.* New York: Guilford Press, pp. 215–228.

Felton, D., Felton, S., Carlson, S., Olschowka, J., & Livnat, S. (1985). Noradrenergic and peptidergic innervation of lymphoid tissue. *The Journal of Immunology, 135*(2), 755s–765s.

Finkelstein, S., & Greenleaf, H. (1982–83). Cancer prevention: A three-year pilot study. *The American Journal of Clinical Hypnosis, 25*(2–3), 177–187.

Fischer, R. (1971a). Arousal-statebound recall of experience. *Diseases of the Nervous System, 32,* 373–382.

Fischer, R. (1971b). The "flashback": Arousal-statebound recall of experience. *Journal of Psychedelic Drugs, 3,* 31–39.

Fischer, R. (1971c). A cartography of ecstatic and meditative states. *Science, 174,* 897–904.

Frankel, F. (1985). Personal communication. (Also reported by P. Bagne in *Omni,* April 1985, p. 122.)

Freud, S. (1956). *Collected papers.* Edited by Ernest Jones. New York: Basic.

Frick, D. (1976). Immediate hypersensitivity. In H. Fudenberg (Ed.), *Basic and clinical immunology.* Los Altos, Calif.: Lange Medical Publications, pp. 204–224.

Friedman, S. (1972). On the presence of a variant form of instinctual regression: Oral drive cycles in obesity-bulimia. *Psychoanalytic Quarterly, 41,* 364–383.

Friedman, S. (1978). A psychophysiological model for the chemotherapy of psychosomatic illness. *The Journal of Nervous & Mental Diseases, 166,* 110–116.

Friedman, S., Kantor, I., Sobel, S., & Miller, R. (1978). On the treatment of neurodermatitis with a monoamine oxidase inhibition. *The Journal of Nervous & Mental Diseases, 166,* 117–125.

Fromm, E., & Shor, R. (Eds.) (1979). *Hypnosis: Research development and perspectives.* (2nd Ed.) Chicago: Aldine-Atherton.

Gage, D. (1983). Mood state-dependent memory and the lateralization of emotion. Doctoral dissertation, Catholic University of America.

Ganong, W. (1985). *Review of medical physiology* (12th Edition). Los Altos, Calif.: Lange Medical Publications.

Gazzaniga, M. (1967). The split brain in man. *Scientific American, 217,* 24–29.

Gazzaniga, M. (1985). *The social brain: Discovering the networks of the mind.* New York: Basic Books.

Gendlin, E. (1978). *Focusing.* New York: Everest House.

Gentry, W. (Ed.) (1984). *Handbook of behavioral medicine.* New York: Guilford Press.

Gershon, M., Payette, R., & Rothman, T. (1985). Microenvironmental factors in phenotypic expression by enteric neurons: Parallels to lymphocytes. In R. Guillemin, M. Cohn, & T. Melnechuk (Eds.), *Neural modulation of immunity.* New York: Raven Press, pp. 221–252.

Ghanta, V., Hiramoto, R., Solvason, H., & Spector, N. (1985). Neural and environmental influences on neoplasia and conditioning of NK activity. *Journal of Immunology, 135*(2), 848s–852s.

Gill, M., & Brenman, M. (1959). *Hypnosis and related states.* New York: International Universities Press.

Gilligan, S., & Bower, G. (1984). Cognitive consequences of emotional arousal. In C. Izard, J. Kagan, & R. Zajonc (Eds.), *Emotions, cognitions, and behavior.* New York: Cambridge Press.

Gold, P. (1984). Memory modulation: Neurobiological contexts. In G. Lynch, J. McGaugh, & N. Weinberger (Eds.), *Neurobiology of learning and memory.* New York: Guilford Press, pp. 374–382.

Goldstein, A., & Hilgard, E. (1975). Lack of influence of the morphine antagonist naloxone on hypnotic analgesia. *Proceedings of the National Academy of Science, U.S.A., 72*, pp. 2041–2043.

Goldstein, L., Stoltzfus, N., & Gardocki, J. (1972). Changes in interhemispheric amplitude relationships in EEG during sleep. *Physiology & Behavior, 8*, 811–815.

Gorczynski, R., Macrae, S., & Kennedy, M. (1982). Conditioned immune response associated with allogenic skin grafts in mice. *Journal of Immunology, 129*, 704–709.

Gordon, H., Frooman, B., & Lavie, P. (1982). Shift in cognitive asymmetries between wakings from REM and NREM sleep. *Neuropsychologica, 20*, 99–103.

Gorton, B. (1957). The physiology of hypnosis, I. *Journal of the American Society of Psychosomatic Dentistry, 4*(3), 86–103.

Gorton, B. (1958). The physiology of hypnosis: Vasomotor activity in hypnosis. *Journal of the American Society of Psychosomatic Dentistry, 5*(1), 20–28.

Graham, K., & Pernicano, K. (1976). *Laterality, hypnosis and the autokinetic effect.* Paper presented at the meeting of the American Psychological Association, Washington D.C.

Greenberg, R. (1973). Anti-expectation techniques in psychotherapy: The power of negative thinking. *Psychotherapy: Theory, Research and Practice, 10*, 145–148.

Groer, M., Shekleton, M., & Kant, K. (1979). *Basic pathophysiology.* St. Louis: C. V. Mosby Company.

Gruen, W. (1972). A successful application of systematic self-relaxation and self-suggestions about postoperative reactions in a case of cardiac surgery. *International Journal of Clinical and Experimental Hypnosis, 20*, 141–151.

Guillemin, R. (1978). Peptides in the brain: The new endocrinology of the neuron. *Science, 202*, 390–402.

Gur, R., & Gur, R. (1974). Handedness, sex, eyedness, and moderating variables in relation to hypnotic susceptibility and functional brain symmetry. *Journal of Abnormal Psychology, 83*, 635–643.

Guyon, A. (1981). *Textbook of medical physiology.* New York: Saunders.

Hahn, R. (1985). A sociocultural model of illness and health. In L. White & B. Tursky (Eds.), *Placebo: Theory, research, and mechanisms.* New York: Guilford Press, pp. 167–195.

Haley, J. (1963). *Strategies of psychotherapy.* New York: Grune & Stratton.

Haley, J. (1985). *Conversations with Milton H. Erickson.* (3 Vols.). New York: Triangle Press.

Hall, H. (1982–83). Hypnosis and the immune system: A review with implications for cancer and the psychology of healing. *The American Journal of Clinical Hypnosis, 25*(2–3), 92–103.

Hall, N., & Goldstein, A. (1985). Neurotransmitters and host defense. In R. Guillemin, M. Cohn, & T. Melnechuk (Eds.), *Neural modulation of immunity.* New York: Raven Press, pp. 143–156.

Hall, N., McGillis, J., Spangelo, B., & Goldstein, A. (1985). Evidence that thymosins and other biologic response modifiers can function as neuroactive immunotransmitters. *The Journal of Immunology, 135*(2), 806s–811s.

Harding, E. (1955). *Woman's mysteries ancient and modern.* New York: Pantheon.

Harris, G. (1948). Neural control of the pituitary gland. *Physiological Review, 28*, 139–179.

Hawkins, R., & Kandel, E. (1984). Steps toward a cell-biological alphabet for elementary forms of learning. In G. Lynch, J. McGaugh, & N. Weinberger (Eds.), *Neurobiology of learning and memory.* New York: Guilford Press, pp. 385–404.

Hebb, D. (1949). *The organization of behavior. A neuropsychological theory.* New York: Wiley.

Hebb, D. (1963). The semi-autonomous process, its nature and nurture. *American Psychologist, 18,* 16–27.

Henry, J. (1982). Circulating opioids: Possible physiological roles in central nervous function. *Neuroscience & Biobehavioral Reviews, 6,* 229–245.

Hilgard, E. (1977). *Divided consciousness: Multiple controls in human thought and action.* New York: Wiley.

Hilgard, E. (1984). Book review of *The collected papers of Milton H. Erickson on hypnosis. The International Journal of Clinical & Experimental Hypnosis, 32*(2), 257–265.

Hilgard, E., & Hilgard, J. (1975). *Hypnosis in the relief of pain.* Los Altos, Calif.: Kaufman.

Hilgard, E., & Marquis, D. (1961). *Conditioning and learning.* New York: Appleton-Century-Crofts.

Hillman, J. (1983). *Healing fiction.* Barrytown, New York: Hill Press.

Hokama, Y., & Nakamura, R. (1982). *Immunology and immunopathology.* Boston: Little, Brown, & Co.

Holroyd, K., & Lazarus, R. (1982). Stress, coping and somatic adaptation. In L. Goldberger & S. Breznitz (Eds.), *Handbook of stress.* New York: Free Press, pp. 21–35.

Hopkins, J., Marcus, M., & Campbell, S. (1984). Postpartum depression: A critical review. *Psychological Bulletin, 95,*(3), 498–515.

Hudgins, C. (1933). Conditioning and voluntary control of pupillary light reflex. *Journal of General Psychology, 8,* 3.

Hull, C. (1933). *Hypnosis and suggestibility: An experimental approach.* New York: Appleton-Century.

Ikemi, Y., & Nakagawa, S. (1962). A psychosomatic study of contagious dermatitis. *Kyushu Journal of Medical Science, 13,* 335–350.

Ingham, S. (1938). Some neurologic aspects of psychiatry. *Journal of the American Medical Association, 111,* 665.

Izquierdo, I. (1984). Endogenous state-dependency: Memory depends on the relation between the neurohumoral and hormonal states present after training at the time of testing. In G. Lynch, J. McGaugh, & N. Weinberg (Eds.), *Neurobiology of learning and memory.* New York: Guilford Press, pp. 65–77.

Jacobson, A., Hackett, T., Surman, O., & Silverberg, E. (1973). Raynaud's phenomenon: Treatment with hypnotic and operant technique. *Journal of the American Medical Association, 225,* 739–740.

Janet, P. (1889). *L'Automatisme psychologique.* Paris: Felix Alcan.

Janet, P. (1907). *The major symptoms of hysteria.* New York: Macmillan.

Johnson, R., & Barber, T. (1978). Hypnosis, suggestion, and warts: An experimental investigation implicating the importance of "believed-in efficacy." *The American Journal of Clinical Hypnosis, 20,* 165–174.

Jouvet, M. (1973). Telencephalic and rhonbencephalic sleep in the cat. In W. Webb (Ed.), *Sleep: An active process.* Glenview, Ill: Scott Foresman & Co, pp. 12–32.

Jouvet, M. (1975). The function of dreaming: A neurophysiologist's point of view. In M. Gazzaniga & C. Blakemore (Eds.), *The handbook of psychobiology.* New York: Academic Press.

Jung, C. (1910). *Jb. Psychoanal. Psychopath. Forschgg. II(1)* p. 363.

Jung, C. (1929/1984). *Dream analysis.* Edited by William McGuire. Bollinger Series XCIX. New Jersey: Princeton University Press.

Jung, C. (1950). *The symbolic life. Vol. XVIII. The collected works of Carl G. Jung.* Translated by R.F.C. Hull. Bolinger Series XX. Princeton, New Jersey: Princeton University Press.

Jung, C. (1960). *The structure and dynamics of the psyche. Vol. III. The collected works of Carl G. Jung.* Translated by R.F.C. Hull. Bolingen Series XX. Princeton, New Jersey: Princeton University Press.

Jung, C. (1976). *The visions seminars.* Book 1, Part 7. Zurich, Switzerland: Spring Publications.

Kandel, E., & Schwartz, G. (1985). *Principles of neural science.* (2nd Ed.) New York: Elsevier Press.

Kaneko, Z., & Takahashi, N. (1963). Psychometric studies on chronic urticaria. *Folia Psychiatrica et Neurologica Japonica, 17,* 16–24.

Kimble, D. (1965). *Learning, remembering and forgetting. Vol. I. The anatomy of learning.* Palo Alto, CA: Science & Behavior Books.

Kissilef, H., Pi-Sunyer, F., *et al.* (1981). C-terminal octapeptide of cholecystokinin decreases food intake in man. *The American Journal of Clinical Nutrition, 34,* 154–160.

Klein, R., & Armitage, R. (1979). Rhythms in human performance: One-and-a-half-hour oscillations in cognitive style. *Science, 204,* 1326–1328.

Kleitman, N. (1963). *Sleep and wakefulness.* (2nd Edition). Chicago: University of Chicago Press.

Klopfer, B. (1957). Psychological variables in human cancer. *Journal of Projective Techniques, 21,* 331–340.

Kreinheder, A. (1979). The call to individuation. *Psychological Perspectives, 10*(1), 58–65.

Kripke, D. (1982). Ultradian rhythms in behavior and physiology. In F. Brown & R. Graeber (Eds.), *Rhythmic aspects of Behavior.* Hillsdale, New Jersey: Erlbaum & Associates, pp. 313–344.

Kroger, W., & Fezler, W. (1976). *Hypnosis and behavior modification: Imagery conditioning.* Philadelphia, Pa.: Lippencott.

LaBerge, S. (1985). *Lucid dreaming.* Los Angeles: Tarcher.

Lachman, S., & Goode, W. (1976). *Hemispheric dominance and variables related to hypnotic susceptibility.* Paper presented at the meeting of the American Psychological Association.

Lankton, S. (1987). The scramble technique. *Ericksonian Monographs, 2,* in press.

Lankton, S., & Lankton, C. (1983). *The answer within: A clinical framework of Ericksonian hypnotherapy.* New York: Brunner/Mazel.

Lazarus, R., & Folkman, S. (1984). Coping and adaptation. In W. Gentry (Ed.), *Handbook of behavioral medicine.* New York: Guilford Press, pp. 282–325.

Leckie, F. (1964). Hypnotherapy in gynecological disorders. *International Journal of Clinical & Experimental Hypnosis, 12,* 121–146.

LeCron, L. (1954). A hypnotic technique for uncovering unconscious material. *Journal of Clinical & Experimental Hypnosis, 2,* 76–79.

Leonard, G. (1981). *The silent pulse.* New York: Bantam Books.

LeShan, L. (1977). *You can fight for your life.* New York: Evans & Co.

Lewis, J., & Sarbin, T. (1943). Studies in psychosomatics. *Psychosomatic Medicine, 5,* 125.

Lewis, T. (1927). *The blood vessels of the human skin and their responses.* London: Shaw & Sons.

Lex, B. (1974). Voodoo death: New thoughts for an old explanation. *American Anthropologist, 76,* 818–823.

Lienhart, J. (1983). Multiple personality and state-dependent learning. Doctoral dissertation, U.S. International University, San Diego, California.

Locke, S., Kraus, L., Leserman, J., Hurst, M., Heisel, S., Williams, R. (1984). Life change stress, psychiatric symptoms, and natural killer-cell activity. *Psychosomatic Medicine, 46,* 441–453.

Ludwig, A. (1983). The psychobiological functions of dissociation. *The American Journal of Clinical Hypnosis, 26*(2), 93–99.

Ludwig, A., Brandsma, J., Wilbur, C., Benfeldt, F., & Jameson, D. (1972). The objective study of a multiple personality. *Archives of General Psychiatry, 26,* 298–310.

Luria, A. (1966). *Higher coritcal functions in man.* Translated by H. Teuber & K. Pribram. New York: Basic Books.

Lynch, G., McGaugh, J., & Weinberger, N. (Eds.) (1984). *Neurobiology of learning and memory.* New York: Guilford Press.

Maclean, D., & Reichlin, S. (1981). Neuroendocrinology and the immune process. In R. Ader (Ed.), *Psychoneuroimmunology.* New York: Academic Press, pp. 475–519.

Margolis, C. (1982–83). Hypnotic imagery with cancer patients. *The American Journal of Clinical Hypnosis, 25*(2–3), 128–134.

Margules, D. (1979). Beta-endorphin and endoloxone: Hormones of the autonomic nervous system for conservation or expenditure of bodily resources and energy for anticipation of famine or feast. *Neuroscience & Biobehavioral Review, 3,* 155–162.

Marini, J., Sheard, M., Bridges, C., & Wagner, E. (1976). An evaluation of the double-blind design in a study comparing lithium carbonate with placebo. *Acta Psychiatrica Scandinavica, 53,* 343–354.

Markowitz, A. (1985). *Change of life: Dreams and the menopause.* Toronto, Canada: Inner City Books.

Marrack, P., & Kappler, J. (1986). The T cell and its receptor. *Scientific American,* Feb., 254(2), 36–45.

Maslow, A. (1962). *Toward a psychology of being.* New York: Van Nostrand.

Mason, A. (1952). A case of congenital ichthyosiform erythrodermia of Brocq treated by hypnosis. *British Medical Journal, 2,* 422–423.

Mason, A. (1955). Ichthyosis and hypnosis. *British Medical Journal, 2,* 57.

Mason, A. (1963). Hypnosis and allergy. *British Medical Journal, 13,* 1675–1676.

Mazziotta, J., Phelps, M., Carson, R., & Kuhl, D. (1982). Tomographic mapping of human cerebral metabolism: Auditory stimulation. *Neurology, 32,* 921–937.

McGaugh, J. (1983). Preserving the presence of the past: Hormonal influences on memory storage. *American Psychologist, 38(2),* 161–173.

McGlashan, T., Evans, F., & Orne, M. (1969). The nature of hypnotic analgesia and placebo response to experimental pain. *Psychosomatic Medicine, 31,* 227–246.

Meares, A. (1982–83). A form of intensive meditation associated with the regression of cancer. *The American Journal of Clinical Hypnosis, 25(2–3),* 114–121.

Melnechuk, T. (1985). Neuroimmunology: Crossroads between behavior and disease. Reports on selected conferences and workshops. *Advances, 2(3),* Summer, 54–58.

Merleau-Ponty, M. (1963). *The structure of behavior.* Translated by A. Fisher. Boston: Beacon Press.

Meyers, R., & Sperry, R. (1953). Interocular transfer of a visual form discrimination habit in cats after section of the optic chiasm and corpus callosum. *Anatomical Record, 115,* 351–352.

Miller, G., Galanter, E., & Pribram, K. (1960). *Plans and the structure of behavior.* New York: Henry Holt.

Mills, J., & Crowley, R. (1986). *Therapeutic metaphors for children and the child within.* New York: Brunner/Mazel.

Mindell, A. (1982). *Dreambody.* Los Angeles: Sigo Press.

Mindell, A. (1985a). *River's way: The process science of the dreambody.* Boston: Routledge & Kegan Paul.

Mindell, A. (1985b). *Working with the dreaming body.* Boston: Routledge & Kegan Paul.

Mishkin, M. (1982). A memory system in the monkey. *Phil. Trans. R. Soc. Lond., B298,* 85–95.

Mishkin, M., Malamut, B., & Bachevalier, J. (1984). Memories and habits: Two neural systems. In G. Lynch, J. McGaugh, & N. Weinberger (Eds.), *Neurobiology of learning and memory.* New York: Guilford Press, pp. 65–77.

Mishkin, M., & Petri, H. (1984). Memories and habits: Some implications for the analysis of learning and retention. In S. Squire & N. Butters (Eds.), *Neuropsychology of memory.* New York: Guilford Press, pp. 287–296.

Moore, L., & Kaplan, J. (1983). Hypnotically accelerated burn wound healing. *The American Journal of Clinical Hypnosis, 26(1),* 16–19.

Morris, J., & Beck, A. (1974). The efficacy of antidepressant drugs: A review of research (1958 to 1972). *Archives of General Psychiatry, 30,* 667–674.

Moruzzi, I., & Magoun, H. (1949). Brain stem reticular formation. *Electroencephalography & Clinical Neurophysiology, 1,* 455–473.

Murry, E., & Mishkin, M. (1985). Amygdalectomy impairs crossmodal association in monkeys. *Science, 228,* 604–606.

Nauta, W. (1964). Some efferent connections of the prefrontal cortex in the monkey. In J. Warren & K. Akert (Eds.), *The frontal granular cortex and behavior.* New York: McGraw-Hill.

Nauta, W. (1972). Neural associations of the frontal cortex. *Acta Neurobiologiae Experimentalis, 32,* 125–140.

Nauta, W., & Domesick, V. (1980). Neural associations of the limbic system. In A. Beckman (Ed.), *Neural substrates of behavior*. New York: Spectrum.

Nauta, W., & Feirtag, M. (1979). The organization of the brain. *Scientific American, 41*, 78–105.

Nemiah, J., Freyberger, H., & Sifneos, P. (1976). Alexithymia: A view of the psychosomatic process. In D. Hill (Ed.), *Modern trends in psychosomatic medicine. Vol. III*. London: Butterworth, pp. 430–439.

Newton, B. (1982–83). Introduction: Hypnosis and cancer. *The American Journal of Clinical Hypnosis, 25*(2–3), 89–91.

Nugent, W., Carden, N., & Montgomery, D. (1984). Utilizing the creative unconscious in the treatment of hypodermic phobias and sleep disturbance. *The American Journal of Clinical Hypnosis, 26*(3), 201–205.

Olds, J. (1977). *Drives and reinforcements: Behavioral studies of hypothalamic functions*. New York: Raven.

Olds, J., & Milner, P. (1954). Positive reinforcement produced by electrical stimulation of septal area and other regions of rat brain. *Journal of Comparative & Physiological Psychology, 47*, 419–427.

Olness, K., & Conroy, M. (1985). A pilot study of voluntary control of transcutaneous PO_2 by children. *International Journal of Clinical & Experimental Hypnosis, 33*(1), 1–5.

Olness, K., Wain, H., & Ng, L. (1980). Pilot study of blood endorphin levels in children using self-hypnosis to control pain. *Developmental & Behavioral Pediatrics, 1*(4), 187–188.

Orne, M. (1962). The social psychology of the psychological experiment: With particular reference to demand characteristics and their implications. *American Psychologist, 17*, 776–783.

Orne, M. (1972). On the stimulating subject as a quasi-control group in hypnosis research: What, why and how? In E. Fromm & R. Shor (Eds.), *Hypnosis: Research development and perspectives*. Chicago: Aldine-Atherton, pp. 399–443.

Orne, M. (1974). Pain suppression by hypnosis and related phenomena. In J. Bonica (Ed.), *Pain*. New York: Raven Press.

Ornstein, R. (1973). *The psychology of consciousness*. New York: Viking.

Ornstein, R., & Thompson, R. (1984). *The amazing brain*. Boston: Houghton Mifflin.

Orr, W., Hoffman, H., & Hegge, F. (1974). Ultradian rhythms in extended performance. *Aerospace Medicine, 45*, 995–1000.

Overton, D. (1968). Dissociated learning in drug states (state-dependent learning). In D. Effron, J. Cole, J. Levine, & R. Wittenborn (Eds.), *Psychopharmacology: A review of progress, 1957–1967*. Public Health Service Publications, 1836. U.S. Government Printing Office, Washington, D.C., pp. 918–930.

Overton, D. (1972). State-dependent learning produced by alcohol and its relevance to alcoholism. In B. Kissen & H. Begleiter (Eds.), *The biology of alcoholism. Vol. II. Physiology and behavior*. New York: Plenum, pp. 193–217.

Overton, D. (1973). State-dependent learning produced by addicting drugs. In S. Fisher & A. Freedman (Eds.), *Opiate addiction: Origins and treatment*. Washington D.C.: Winston, pp. 61–75.

Overton, D. (1978). Major theories of state-dependent learning. In B. Ho, D. Richards, & D. Chute (Eds.), *Drug discrimination and state-dependent learning*. New York: Academic Press, pp. 283–318.

Palmblad, J. (1985). Stress and human immunologic competence. In R. Guillemin, M. Cohn, & T. Melnechuk (Eds.), *Neural modulation of immunity*. New York: Raven Press, pp. 45–53.

Papez, J. (1937). A proposed mechanism of emotion. *Archives of Neurology & Physiology, 38*, 725–744.

Peavey, B. (1982). Biofeedback assisted relaxation: Effects on phagocytic immune function. Doctoral dissertation, North Texas State University, Denton, Texas.

Pert, C. (1986). Emotions in body, not just in brain. *Brain/Mind Bulletin, 11*(4), 1.

Pert, C., Ruff, M., Weber, R., & Herkenham, M. (1985). Neuropeptides and their receptors: A psychosomatic network. *The Journal of Immunology, 135*(2), 820s–826s.

Peters, C. (1978). *Tell me who I am before I die*. New York: Rawson.

Phelps, M., & Mazziotta, J. (1985). Positron emission tomography: Human brain function and biochemistry. *Science, 228,* 799–809.

Poirel, C. (1982). Circadian rhythms in behavior and experimental psychotherapy. In F. Brown & R. Graeber (Eds.), *Rhythmic aspects of behavior.* Hillsdale, New Jersey: Erlbaum & Associates, pp. 363–398.

Pribram, K. (1965). Proposal for a structural pragmatism: Some neuropsychological considerations of problems in philosophy. In B. Wolman & E. Nagle (Eds.), *Scientific psychology: Principles and approaches.* New York: Basic Books, pp. 426–459.

Pribram, K. (1971). *Languages of the brain: Experimental paradoxes and principles in neuropsychology.* (3rd Ed.) New York: Brandon House.

Pribram, K. (1976). Problems concerning the structure of consciousness. In G. Globus, G. Maxwell, & I. Savodnik (Eds.), *Consciousness and the brain: A scientific and philosophical inquiry.* New York: Plenum, pp. 798–809.

Pribram, K. (1979). Behaviorism, phenomenology and holism in psychology: A scientific analysis. *Journal of Social & Biological Structure, 2,* 65–72.

Pribram, K. (1980). Cognition and performance: The relation to neural mechanisms of consequence, confidence, and competence. In A. Routtenberg (Ed.), *Biology of reinforcement: Facets of brain stimulation reward.* New York: Academic Press, pp. 11–36.

Pribram, K. (1986). The cognitive revolution and mind/brain issues. *American Psychologist,* in press.

Pribram, K., Lassonde, M., & Ptito, M. (1981). Classification of receptive field properties in cat visual cortex. *Experimental Brain Research, 43,* 119–130.

Putnam, F. (1982). Traces of Eve's faces. *Psychology Today,* October, p. 88.

Rank, O. (1924/1952). *The trauma of birth.* (Published in German in 1924; published in English in 1952) New York: R. Brunner.

Reinberg, A., Gervais, P., & Ghata, J. (1977). Chronobiologic aspects of asthma. In J. McGovern, M. Smolensky, & A. Reinberg (Eds.), *Chronobiology in allergy and immunology.* Springfield, Illinois: Thomas, pp. 36–63.

Reus, V., Weingartner, H., & Post, R. (1979). Clinical implications of state-dependent learning. *American Journal of Psychiatry, 136*(7), 927–931.

Rigter, H., & Crabbe, J. (1979). Modulation of memory by pituitary hormones. *Vitamins and Hormones, 37.* New York: Academic Press.

Rosenberg, S., *et al.* (1985). Observations on the systemic administration of autologous lymphokine-activated killer cells and recombinant interleukin-2 to patients with metastic cancer. *New England Journal of Medicine, 23*(3B), 1485–1492.

Rosenblatt, M. (1983). Neuropeptides: Future implications for medicine. *Medical Times,* November, 31–37.

Rosenzweig, M., & Bennett, E. (1984). Basic processes and modulatory influences in the stages of memory formation. In G. Lynch, J. McGaugh, & N. Weinberger (Eds.), *Neurobiology of learning and memory.* New York: Guilford Press, pp. 263–288.

Rossi, E. (1972/1985). *Dreams and the growth of personality: Expanding awareness in psychotherapy.* (2nd Edition) New York: Brunner/Mazel.

Rossi, E. (1973/1980). Psychological shocks and creative moments in psychotherapy. In E. Rossi (Ed.), *The collected papers of Milton H. Erickson on hypnosis. IV. Innovative hypnotherapy.* New York: Irvington, pp. 447–463.

Rossi, E. (1977). The cerebral hemispheres in analytical psychology. *Journal of Analytical Psychology, 22,* 32–51.

Rossi, E. (1981). Hypnotist describes natural rhythms of trance readiness. *Brain/Mind Bulletin,* March, p. 1.

Rossi, E. (1982). Hypnosis and ultradian cycles: A new state(s) theory of hypnosis? *The American Journal of Clinical Hypnosis, 25,* 21–32.

Rossi, E. (1985). Unity and diversity in Ericksonian approaches: Now and in the future. In J. Zeig (Ed.), *Ericksonian psychotherapy. Vol. I. Structures.* New York: Brunner/Mazel, pp. 15–30.

Rossi, E. (1986a). Altered states of consciousness in everyday life: The ultradian rhythms.

In B. Wolman & M. Ullman (Eds.), *Handbook of altered states of consciousness*. New York: Van Nostrand, pp. 97–132.

Rossi, E. (1986b). Hypnosis and ultradian rhythms. In B. Zilbergeld, G. Edelstien, & D. Araoz (Eds.), *Hypnosis questions and answers*. New York: W. W. Norton, pp. 17–21.

Rossi, E. (1987). Mind/body connections and the new language of human facilitation. In J. Zeig (Ed.), *The evolution of psychotherapy*. New York: Brunner/Mazel. (In press)

Rossi, E., & Ryan, M. (Eds.) (1986). *Mind-body communication in hypnosis. Vol. III. The seminars, lectures, and workshops of Milton H. Erickson*. New York: Irvington, in press.

Roszman, T., Cross, R., Brooks, W., & Markesbery, W. (1985). Neuroimmodulation: Effects of neural lesions on cellular immunity. In R. Guillemin, M. Cohn, & T. Melnechuk (Eds.), *Neural modulation of immunity*. New York: Raven Press, pp. 95–109.

Roth, J., LeRoith, D., Collier, E., Weaver, N., Watkinson, A., Cleland, C., & Glick, S. (1985). Evolutionary origins of neuropeptides, hormones, and receptors: Possible applications to immunology. *The Journal of Immunology, 135*(2), 816s–819s.

Sachar, E. (1969). Psychological homeostasis and endocrine function. In A. Mandell & M. Mandell (Eds.), *Psychological strategies in man*. New York: Academic Press.

Sagan, C. (1977). *The dragons of Eden: Speculations on the evolution of human intelligence*. New York: Random House.

Salk, J. (1969). Immunological paradoxes: Theoretical considerations in the rejection or retention of grafts, tumors, and normal tissue. *Annals of New York Academy of Science, 164*(2), 365–380.

Saltz, E. (1973). Higher mental processes as the bases for the laws of conditioning. In F. McGuigan & D. Lumsden (Eds.), *Contemporary approaches to conditioning and learning*. New York: Wiley.

Sarbin, T., & Coe, W. (1972). *Hypnosis: A social psychological analysis of influence communication*. New York: Holt, Rinehart, & Winston.

Scharrer, E., & Scharrer, B. (1940). Secretory cells within the hypothalamus. *Research Publications of the Association of Nervous & Mental Diseases*. New York: Hafner.

Schneck, J. (1948). Psychogenic cardiovascular reaction interpreted and successfully treated with hypnosis. *Psychoanalytical Review, 35*, 14–19.

Schneider, J., Smith, W., & Witcher, S. (1983). The relationship of mental imagery to white blood cell (neutrophil) function: Experimental studies of normal subjects. Uncirculated mimeographs. Michigan State University, College of Medicine. East Lansing, Michigan.

Schneider, J., Smith, W., & Witcher, S. (1984). The relationship of mental imagery to white blood cell (neutrophil) function in normal subjects. Paper presented at the 36th Annual Scientific Meeting of the International Society for Clinical & Experimental Hypnosis, San Antonio, Texas, October 25th.

Schreiber, F. (1973). *Sybil*. Chicago: Regnery.

Seltzer, L. (1985). *Paradoxical strategies in psychotherapy*. New York: Wiley & Sons.

Selye, H. (1936). A syndrome produced by diverse noxious agents. Cited in *The stress of life*. (1976). New York: McGraw-Hill.

Selye, H. (1974). *Stress without distress*. New York: Signet.

Selye, H. (1976). *The stress of life*. New York: McGraw-Hill.

Selye, H. (1982). History and present status of the stress concept. In L. Goldberger, & S. Breznitz (Eds.), *Handbook of stress*. New York: MacMillan, pp. 7–20.

Shands, H. (1969). Integration, discipline, and the concept of shape. *Annals of New York Academy of Science, 164*(2), pp. 578–587.

Shannahoff-Khalsa, D. (1983). Personal communication.

Shannon, C., & Weaver, W. (1949). *The mathematical theory of communication*. Urbana: University of Illinois Press.

Shapiro, A. (1971). Placebo effects in medicine, psychotherapy and psychoanalysis. In A. Bergin & S. Garfield (Eds.), *Handbook of psychotherapy and behavior change*. New York: Wiley.

Shavit, Y., Terman, G., Martin, F., Lewis, J., Liebeskind, J., & Gale, R. (1985). Stress, opioid peptides, the immune system, and cancer. *The Journal of Immunology, 135*(2), 834s–837s.

Sheehan, P., & Perry, C. (1976). *Methodologies of hypnosis.* Hillsdale, New Jersey: Lawrence Erlbaum Publishers.

Shor, R. (1959). Hypnosis and the concept of the generalized reality-orientation. *American Journal of Psychotherapy, 13,* 582–602.

Shorr, J., Sobel, G., Robin, P., & Connella, J. (1980). *Imagery: Its many dimensions and applications.* New York: Plenum Press.

Siegman, A., & Feldstein, S. (Eds.) (1985). *Multichannel integrations of nonverbal behavior.* Hillsdale, New Jersey: Lawrence Erlbaum Publishers.

Silberman, E., Putnam, F., Weingartner, H., Braun, B., & Post, R. (1985). Dissociative states in multiple personality disorders: A quantitative study. *Psychiatry Research, 15,* 253–260.

Silberner, J. (1985). A new look at arthritis origins. *Science News, 127*(23), 358–359.

Simonton, O., Simonton, S., & Creighton, J. (1978). *Getting well again.* Los Angeles: Tarcher.

Sizemore, C. (1977). *I'm Eve.* New York: Harcourt Brace Jovanovich.

Smith, E., Harbour-McMenamin, D., & Blalock, J. (1985). Lymphocyte production of endorphins and endorphin-mediated immunoregulatory activity. *The Journal of Immunology, 135*(2), 779s–782s.

Smith, G., & McDaniel, S. (1983). Psychologically mediated effect on the delayed hypersensitivity reaction to tuberculin in humans. *Psychosomatic Medicine, 46,* 65–73.

Smith, G., McKenzie, J., Marmer, D., & Steele, R. (1985). Psychologic modulation of the human immune response to varicella zoster. *Archives of Internal Medicine, 145,* 2110–2112.

Snyder, S. (1980). Brain peptides as neurotransmitters. *Science, 209,* 976–983.

Solomon, G. (1985). The emerging field of psychoneuroimmunology with a special note on AIDS. *Advances, 2*(Winter), 6–19.

Solomon, G., & Amkraut, A. (1981). Psychoneuroendocrinological effects on the immune response. *Annual Review of Microbiology, 35,* 155–184.

Sperry, R. (1964). The great cerebral commissure. *Scientific American, 210,* 42–52.

Spiegel, H., & Spiegel, D. (1978). *Trance and treatment.* New York: Basic Books.

Spruiell, G., Steck, C., Lippencott, C., & King, D. (1983). Failure of naloxone to modify the depth of hypnotic trance. *Experientia, 39*(7–12), 763–764.

Stein, M. (1985). Bereavement, depression, stress, and immunity. In R. Guillemin, M. Cohn, & T. Melnechuk (Eds.), *Neural modulation of immunity.* New York: Raven Press, pp. 29–53.

Stein, M., Keller, S., & Schleifer, S. (1985). Stress and immunomodulation: The role of depression and neuroendocrine function. *The Journal of Immunology, 135*(2), 827s–833s.

Stein, M., Schiavi, R., & Camerino, M. (1976). Influence of brain and behavior on the immune system. *Science, 191,* 435–440.

Stein, M., Schleifer, S., & Keller, S. (1981). Hypothalamic influences on immune responses. In A. Ader (Ed.), *Psychoneuroimmunology.* New York: Academic Press, pp. 429–447.

Stephenson, J. (1978). Reversal of hypnosis-induced analgesia by naloxone. *Lancet,* (28097), 991–992.

Sternbach, R. (1982). On strategies for identifying neurochemical correlates of hypnotic analgesia. *International Journal of Clinical & Experimental Hypnosis, 30*(3), 251–256.

Stewart, J. (1981). Brain ACTH-endorphin neurones as regulators of central nervous system activity. In K. Brunfeldt (Ed.), *Peptides, 1980.* Copenhagen, Denmark: Scriptor, pp. 774–779.

Stewart, J., Krebs, W., & Kaczender, E. (1971). State-dependent learning produced with steroids. *Nature, 216,* 1233–1234.

Teitlebaum, H. (1954). Spontaneous rhythmic ocular movements: Their possible relationship to mental activity. *Neurology, 4,* 350–354.

Thigpen, C., & Cleckley, H. (1957). *The three faces of Eve.* Kingsport, Tenn.: Kingsport Press.

Thompson, R. et al. (1984). Neuronal substrates of learning and memory: A "multiple-trace" view. In G. Lynch, J. McGaugh, & N. Weinberger (Eds.), *Neurobiology of learning and memory.* New York: Guilford Press, pp. 137–164.

Tinterow, M. (1970). *Foundations of hypnosis.* Springfield, Illinois: C. C. Thomas.

Ullman, M. (1959). On the psyche and warts: I. Suggestion and warts: A review and comment. *Psychosomatic Medicine, 21,* 473–488.

Vaihinger, H. (1911). *Philosophy of the as-if.* Translated by C. K. Ogden in 1924. London: Routledge.

Wadden, T., & Anderton, C. (1982). The clinical use of hypnosis. *Psychological Bulletin, 91*(2), 215–243.

Wain, H., Amen, D., & Oetgen, W. (1984). Hypnotic intervention in cardiac arrhythmias. *The American Journal of Clinical Hypnosis, 27*(1), 70–75.

Waksman, B. (1985). Neuroimmunomodulation of homeostasis and host defense. *Journal of Immunology, 135*(2), 862s.

Walford, R. (1983). *Maximum lifespan.* New York: Avon Publishers.

Watkins, J. (1978). *The therapeutic self.* New York: Human Sciences Press.

Watkins, J. (1980). The silent abreaction. *International Journal of Clinical & Experimental Hypnosis, 28,* 101–113.

Watzlawick, P. (Ed.) (1984). *The invented reality.* New York: W. W. Norton.

Weeks, G., & L'Abate, L. (1982). *Paradoxical psychotherapy: Theory and practice with individuals, couples, and families.* New York: Brunner/Mazel.

Wehr, T. (1982). Circadian rhythm disturbances in depression and mania. In F. Brown & R. Graeber (Eds.), *Rhythmic aspects of behavior.* Hillsdale, New Jersey: Lawrence Erlbaum Publishers.

Weinberger, N., Gold, P., & Sternberg, D. (1984). Epinephrine enables Pavlovian fear conditioning under anesthesia. *Science, 223,* February 10, 605–607.

Weiner, H. (1972). Presidential address: Some comments on the transduction of experience by the brain: Implications for our understanding of the relationship of mind to body. *Psychosomatic Medicine, 34*(4), 355–380.

Weiner, H. (1977). *Psychobiology and human disease.* New York: Elsevier.

Weingartner, H. (1986). Memory: The roots of failure. *Psychology Today,* January, pp. 6–7.

Weingartner, H., Miller, H., & Murphy, D. (1977). Mood state-dependent retrieval of verbal associations. *Journal of Abnormal Psychology, 86,* 276–284.

Weingartner, H., & Murphy, D. (1977). Brain states and memory. *Psychopharmacological Bulletin, 13,* 66–67.

Weitzenhoffer, A. (1971). Ocular changes associated with passive hypnotic behavior. *The American Journal of Clinical Hypnosis, 14,* 102–121.

Weitzenhoffer, A. (1982). In search of hypnosis. *International Journal of Clinical & Experimental Hypnosis, 30*(2), 210–211.

Werntz, D. (1981). Cerebral hemispheric activity and autonomic nervous function. Doctoral dissertation, University of California, San Diego.

Werntz, D., Bickford, R., Bloom, F., & Shannahoff-Khalsa, D. (1981). Selective cortical activation by alternating autonomic function. Paper presented at the Western EEG Society Meeting, February 12, Reno, Nevada.

White, L., Tursky, B., & Schwartz, G. (1985). *Placebo: Clinical implications and new insights.* New York: Guilford Press.

Wickramasekera, I. (Ed.) (1976). *Biofeedback, behavior therapy and hypnosis.* Chicago: Nelson-Hall.

Wickramasekera, I. (1985). A conditioned response model of the placebo effect: Predictions from the model. In L. White, B. Tursky, & G. Schwartz (Eds.), *Placebo: Theory, research, and mechanisms.* New York: Guilford Press, pp. 255–287.

Wiener, N. (1948). *Cybernetics, or control and communication in the animal and the machine.* New York: Wiley.

Williams, J. (1974). Stimulation of breast growth by hypnosis. *Journal of Sex Research, 10,* 316–326.

Wolberg, L. (1947). Hypnotic experiments in psychosomatic medicine. *Psychosomatic Medicine, 9,* 337–342.

Woodman, M. Psyche/soma awareness. (1984). *Quadrant, 17*(2), 25–37.

Wurtman, R., & Anton-Tay, F. (1969). The mammalian pineal as a neuroendocrine transducer. *Recent Progress in Hormone Research, 25,* 493–513.

Wybran, J. (1985). Enkephalins, endorphins, substance P, and the immune system. In R.

Guillemin, M. Cohn, & T. Melnechuk (Eds.), *Neural modulation of immunity*. New York: Raven Press, pp. 157–161.

Yanovski, A. (1962). The feasibility of alteration of cardiovascular manifestations in hypnosis. *The American Journal of Clinical Hypnosis, 5*, 8–16.

Zeig, J. (1980a). Symptom prescription and Ericksonian principles of hypnosis and psychotherapy. *The American Journal of Clinical Hypnosis, 23*(1), 16–22.

Zeig, J. (1980b). Symptom prescription techniques: Clinical applications using elements of communication. *The American Journal of Clinical Hypnosis, 23*(1), 23–33.

Zeig, J. (Ed.) (1985). *Ericksonian psychotherapy. Vol. I. Structures*. New York: Brunner/Mazel.

Zornetzer, S. (1978). Neurotransmitter modulation and memory: A new neuropharmacological phrenology? In M. Lipton, A. di Mascio, & K. Killam (Eds.), *Psychopharmacology: A generation of progress*. New York: Raven Press.

Index